The Ex in My Glass

How I Refined My Taste in Men & Alcohol

LISA M. MATTSON

Cheerz!
Lisa M. Matta

THE EXES IN MY GLASS
Copyright © 2018 Lisa M. Mattson
ISBN-ebook: 978-1-508091-94-3
ISBN-13: 978-1-519330-86-4
ISBN-10: 1519330863
2nd Edition Published: March 15, 2018
Publisher: CreateSpace

Cover design by Anna Dorfman. Illustration by Megan Piontkowski.

Find out more about the author at lisamattsonwine.com.
Follow @lisamattsonwine on Instagram and Twitter.

For all the women who want to take that leap
outside their comfort zone

My Dating Palate

A Note from the Author

This book is the result of a decade-long journey through men and alcohol to better understand my fate in this world. Girls with my roots are supposed to grow up and develop a taste for Coors Light and men named Bubba—not spend their weekends cruising through Napa Valley in a convertible. But two laser-sharp focuses have remained constant in my life—dating and drinking—and the heartaches and headaches that followed led me down a remarkably humbling, unexpected road. The irony that my father was an alcoholic and I've spent my entire career peddling adult beverages is still hard to swallow today.

My first sober confession in this exercise: I lost count of my ex-boyfriends around forty. That's enough men to fill three NBA teams, and for years, my approach to dating was as weak as the cheap drinks they bought me at bars. But the healing powers of time—paired with a glass of rosé bubbly—have helped me face down embarrassment and embrace the beauty of all that heavy baggage. With this tipple time capsule of my love life, I can reflect on what I've learned from my mistakes. I can laugh at my insecurity in relationships and my bumbling progression into oenophilia.

I now realize it was my destiny to find happily ever after through trial and error. My ego (and my liver) seem stronger as a result.

This hard time on the dating circuit gave me enough perspective and experiences to write a book about my bewildering transition from lust to love and cheap beer to fine wine. (This is an autobiographical version of my novel, *The Exes in My iPod: A Playlist of the Men Who Rocked Me to Wine Country*, which was discontinued at the debut of my memoir, and this second edition includes more scenes and insights from my restaurant and wine jobs.) These stories are a work of memory, twenty years in the making. Time left some sinkholes in my recollections that had to be filled; names have been changed and identifying facts have been altered to protect personal privacies. Some events were moved and others combined or altered for cohesion and reader enjoyment, making the book about eighty percent true. I recognize that my exes' memories of the events described in this memoir are probably different than my own. I've lost touch with most of them and enjoy keeping up with a few on Facebook. I am forever grateful for our time together—no matter how sad or laughable the fading memories are in hindsight.

Because I didn't want to write a book as long and as horrifying as Stephen King's *IT*, many ex-boyfriends did not make the cut for this book. (My apologies to the Puerto Rican techno dancer, the Harley-riding waiter, the Egyptian poet, the Bolivian saltwater fish salesman, the exotic flower importer, the South Beach hotel manager, the wine collector, the medical marijuana defender and the cougar-chasing construction worker.) And that only includes half the rejects of one decade! This whittling act resulted in a fitting number of exes—thirteen—who left their mark on the most pivotal years of my young life. Revisiting those relationships was an exercise in self-discovery with a poignant reminder: being unlucky in love doesn't have to mean being unlucky in life.

So, grab a chair. Pour yourself a glass of Champagne. Read along. Laugh at my dating mistakes. Distant memories can be unlocked from the corner of your mind too by sipping your way through the memories of your exes.

The wildfires that raged through wine country in October 2017 changed the lives of thousands of Sonoma County residents, including me. Fortunately, I have the means to repair and rebuild, even where insurance fell short, but so many others are not as lucky. Proceeds from this book will be donated to Sonoma Family Meal, created to help families in need of nourishment after the devastating wildfires. If you enjoy my story, please buy copies for your girlfriends, share my book on social media, and leave a review on Amazon, iTunes or GoodReads. #sonomastrong

The Exes in My Glass

How I Refined My Taste in Men & Alcohol

Lisa M. Mattson

"Here's to alcohol, the rose colored glasses of life."

— F. Scott Fitzgerald

Lisa pheasant hunting

Beginnings

"Every woman that finally figured out her worth, has picked up her suitcases of pride and boarded a flight to freedom, which landed in the valley of change."

—Shannon L. Alder

Lisa holding Cooter

CHRIS
The Cheap Beer Days

I mastered the art of being a dating barnacle at an early age, clinging to boys so tightly they'd have to lance me off like a boil. My shell of insecurity only grew firmer in high school, partly due to a hideous Cyndi Lauper haircut and overexposure to Aqua Net. But the moment my reckless attachment to coupledom reached new heights was the summer I dropped out of college and followed a Deadhead to Florida.

Hey, no one can say I didn't like boys who were going places.

But Chris didn't nomad around the country in a Volkswagen van like other Grateful Dead devotees. He was a scuba diver, someone who could disappear. I relished the thought, knowing life would never be the same if I followed him in the wake of my shattered dreams. Fifteen hundred miles? Seemed far enough away from home for me. My road map to marriage had already been wrecked. I had nothing left to lose.

The fact that I'd managed to rebound into a serious relationship with the kind of guy who vacationed on Caribbean islands seemed like an unimaginable feat for a chubby redneck girl from rural Kansas who knew how to shoot guns and gut fish, who started drinking beer in sixth grade. I'd grown up the only daughter of a self-employed carpenter who split his time equally between hunting, fishing, drinking and fixing other people's houses. An escape plan had been hatched before high school graduation: follow my sweetheart to Kansas State University, be the first woman in my family to graduate from college, marry said boyfriend in the same Catholic church as my parents, get a 9-to-5 job and move to the big city—*Kansas City*. Pop out a couple kids, live happily ever after. The end.

Instead, I found myself sardined between sunburned tourists on a dive boat, wondering how to introduce myself without stepping into a Jeff Foxworthy punch line. "Hi, I'm Lisa. An unemployed waitress from the Midwest, a college dropout, a girl who has watched bulls get their balls chopped off. Oh, and I had a pet raccoon named Cooter. Were you a *Dukes of Hazzard* fan, too?"

Chris fiddled with gauges on a cluster of dive tanks at the back of the boat's hull. "Don't forget. Breathe out your mouth." Seriousness swept through his tone, and I appreciated the change from his usual childish demeanor. "Never your nose. Snorting saltwater blows." His long bangs fell over his round, sunburned face, as he dunked snorkel masks into a plastic pail of water. Chris stood just 5-foot-8 with a thick, squatty build like a keg of beer. Slip on a black wet suit, and he looked like a snake that had just eaten a rat.

My blue flippers rapped on the wet floor of the dive boat. *Breathe?* For the first time since my freshman year of college, I felt like I could breathe again. I gazed at the clear, turquoise waters glistening in the fiery sun and inhaled with purpose, savoring the foreign feeling of salty, warm air filling my lungs.

Never again will I live without the ocean. The epiphany kept playing in my head.

The boat's captain, a leathery old man named Bob, stood over the boat's back platform wearing only shorts and a floppy sun hat, shouting instructions to the snorkelers.

Chris stepped into the middle of the swaying boat, hefting fists full of wet masks into the air. A ring of pasty-white blubber peeked out from under his tie-dyed Dancing Bear T-shirt, and a wave of embarrassment swept across his brow.

Deep inside, I cringed for him. Chris was always one doughnut away from a Weight Watchers intervention. "I'm 200 hundred pounds of aquatic fury," he liked to say. The extra weight made him extra cuddly, like the nappy blanket I'd slept with until fourth grade.

Granted, I was no Uma Thurman—a short blonde with permed hair, tree-trunk legs riddled with dimples, mosquito bites for boobs and a face you'd want to play Whac-A-Mole on. Chris had told me I was pretty when other guys would have called me...well, a booty call.

He handed me a dripping-wet mask. "You're up."

My heartbeat shot up like a bottle rocket. *My first dip in the ocean!* Dips had usually involved a jar of Cheez Whiz, a tin of chewing tobacco or swimming in a murky pond. My idea of an adventure was coon hunting with my dad after midnight. I hail from a tiny farm town near the Kansas-Missouri border—the land of soybean fields, decaying manufacturing plants and monster trucks. Our entire population could live inside a hotel on the Las Vegas Strip. Most locals don't travel. My grandma never even learned to drive a car.

Chris's crash course in snorkeling etiquette replayed in my head. *Squirt. Rub. Rinse. Face down. Fins out.* His lifestyle was a conch shell of mysteries I wanted to crawl into and call home. He had money, courage, an overused passport and a carefree spirit—coveted things. His bucket list had a bucket list. I would have followed him into a trashcan and smelled roses.

The beach towel wrapped around my thick legs made me feel like a steaming burrito in the humid air, squelching my excitement. A knot of shame formed in my stomach. *I'd rather swim to Cuba than have strangers see me in a bathing suit.*

I squinted at the blazing sun in a cloudless sky and tried to find the bright side of my insecurities. At age twenty, I was still resting on the surface of life, seeing myself only through young men's eyes, a physical portrait—the scars across my pubic area from a childhood surgery, the sliced up knees from a teen car accident, the forehead gash from playing catch with a metal water nozzle in grade school. Part of me wondered why any boy would want to date such a damaged girl.

Captain Bob extended his weathered hand.

I peeled away my tortilla wrapper of a towel and plopped down on the submerged platform. The back of the boat blended right into the turquoise ocean. Soaking up the moment, I pictured myself from the cloudless sky—a tiny speck of a human, hanging off a boat near the Florida Keys, living out the kind of fantasy many country girls dream about while sipping Slurpees in the Wal-Mart parking lot. It was September of 1994 and as hot as a Crock-Pot everywhere in Miami, except on the water.

Sunshine sparkled across the ocean's tiny waves. My eyes fixed on the crystal-clear surface—a gigantic window into an undiscovered world, a parallel universe I'd have to get used to.

I fumbled my goggles strap over my bushy ponytail. It felt like a Shop-Vac hose was sucking my face. I stuffed the snorkel in my mouth and looked back at Chris, grinning with gratitude. His dreams were taller than the grain elevator that towered over my hometown. He was my first gateway boyfriend, and if you want a colossal life change, you'll need at least one of these angels.

I plunged into the cool water, electrified. It felt like a second baptism, remnants of redneck being washed away instead of my sins.

Chris had touched my emotional plane at just the right time. Two weeks into my first semester at K-State, my high school sweetheart had dumped me for a Kappa Kappa Gamma—a Kappa cow! Talk about Pan-Hellenic devastation. Enter Chris, four months later. It was hard not to notice him, the only person at the frat party sporting a cable-knit sweater, cut-off jean shorts and hiking boots, when six inches of snow had fallen the night before. I'd been wallowing in Kleenex and chocolate for months, letting my "Freshman 15" balloon to twenty-six pounds. But, he'd pumped the keg for me without prompting—the highest form of collegiate chivalry. Chris didn't have a rattail. He didn't drive a pick-up truck or own a shotgun. He loved Pearl Jam and hated Birkenstocks—just like me. His parents were divorced, too. *We could build a real life around this,* I'd thought.

My flippers splashed against the surface. I kicked with conviction, picturing the scissor-legged form from Chris's instructional guide. I peered through my foggy mask, a porthole into his world. Every breath felt like my first, deeper and more controlled than ever before. Lavender sea urchins and green anemones clung to staghorn and brain corals as iridescent rainbows of fish swam by. I hadn't seen that much color since my Rubik's Cube.

I grabbed a disposal Kodak lassoed to my wrist and snapped off more shots than the paparazzi, tickled to think of how far we'd come in just eighteen months.

Within twenty-four hours of our keg meeting, I'd latched on tight to the yin of my yang. We'd spent most nights in his basement bedroom at the frat house, snuggling under a blanket on his stilted platform bed, drinking crappy beer and eating cold pizza in the dark, playing his *American Beauty* CD over and over until it was time for a cigarette break. Puffing the occasional cancer stick helped check off another box on our "things in common" list. The preppy sorority girl had morphed into a poser hippie who knew that *Dick's Picks* were not penis photos.

Chris's eyes never wandered, his attention never waned. I'd loved the secure feeling of knowing he'd never leave me for another girl. Four weeks had passed before Chris took off his bulky shirt in front of me. He was the first college boy who didn't go straight for my zipper, which seemed hopelessly romantic back then.

An unspoken frustration with weight gain had bonded us, and my money issues had pushed us closer together. During my sophomore year, I'd lost all financial aid because Federal Pell Grant policies had changed, extending the timing of when a child became financially independent. In the government's eyes, my mom could afford to put half her annual income toward my college, about $9,000. McDonald's had turned down my job application despite a glowing referral, inflicting long-term damage on my ego. Then the engine had blown out in my 1981 Mazda RX-7—my first ride, my baby. Life felt like an avalanche of bad luck.

Such adversity was met with a hefty helping of good old-fashioned elbow grease in my family. I'd taken on two student loans and three part-time jobs. *Keep your head down. Keep working hard.* Birkin-sized bags had formed under my eyes from juggling school and work through a hellish winter, waddling across campus through muddy snow in duck boots and a parka. I was living on my own dime and drowning in reality.

"Fuck this place. We should move to the Caribbean," Chris had said. He loved tropical fish as much as he loved Jerry Garcia—and had enough chutzpah and money to flee the frozen tundra.

I've always been a big believer in signs, and I could no longer ignore the red flashing lights of fate. Disruptive events happen for a reason. They rip holes in our lives so that we can step outside and find a new road, if we so choose. They are escape hatches. They are wake-up calls, and fear is the snooze button. I didn't have the guts to take such a risk on my own back then. Like every good diver, I needed a buddy. Chris encouraged me to challenge social norms and the low expectations I'd set for my own life—the kind of gambles that were unthinkable for a kid like me from an insular corner of rural America.

So, I took the plunge.

A pack of pastel-painted fish buzzed below, their tiny tails leaving bubbles in their wake. I popped my head out of the water. "Parrotfish! Two Queen, one Spotlight!" The words flew from my salty mouth, remembering the names from Chris's plastic identification card.

Chris stood at the back of the boat clutching a bag of Wonder Bread with his pudgy hands. His round face glowed with content. "Back in Manhattan, everyone's buying books for the fall semester right now." Chris's psychedelic T-shirt hung off his shoulders like a tent.

"Hey, now." My Kansas drawl rang out over the sloshing water. "Let me enjoy my freedom. I'll be back on campus before you know it." Being out of school and out of work felt like missing an arm. I'd started waiting tables right after my fifteenth birthday so I could buy a car and start saving money for college. After high school graduation, I'd taken on a second job working the drive-thru at McDonald's. My life had always had that sharp, yet narrow focus.

"School is the farthest thing from my mind." His sun-kissed cheeks plumped with an air of elation only permanent vacation can provide. "When are you going to buck up and take some real classes?" Chris hefted a black buoyancy compensator (BC) vest in the air. He'd always dreamed of becoming an island-hopping dive instructor, rather than following in his father's footsteps as a successful video game designer.

I spit into my mask and rubbed, employing Chris's trusty defogging trick. "I can see the fish just fine from the surface." I could move half way across the country with a tubby smoker from Shawnee, but I couldn't strap an oxygen tank on my back and go underwater. *That* was too risky.

Chris laughed. "Come on. This reef is our campus." When I'd met Chris, he was a fifth-year senior contemplating number six. The only time he'd attended class was right before midterms and finals—just enough time to score notes from a friend and speed-cram over a carton of Camels. The invisible tractor beams that drew me into relationships with my polar opposites must have been turbo-charged by all the Zima I drank.

"Once I get my residency, I'm going back to school." My responsible side fired the rebuttal as I treaded the sparkling waters. Getting through college as soon as possible—with a GPA of no less than 3.5—had been my focus at K-State. I'd never skipped class. I was the girl in the front row scribbling enough notes in one semester to fill two binders. My parents never went to college and lived paycheck to paycheck.

"Why don't you start acting like a Floridian and relax?" Chris threw his meaty hands to his sides then fished around his back pockets. He raised an unlit Camel Light to his lips.

I rolled my eyes in disgust. "What happened to 'I will never smoke in the state of Florida'?" Chris loved to hide his upper-class roots and brainpower behind concert T-shirts, cigarette butts and the occasional magic mushrooms trip at a Dead show. In college, his dad had paid for his tuition, his Ford Probe GT, his rent, even his beer money. I'd grown up too aware of my financial liability. I'd quit the middle school basketball team during try-outs once I'd found out the price of high-top sneakers and had given up softball in high school to work extra shifts at Chicken Mary's, a restaurant deep in southeast Kansas strip mining country.

He tossed another handful of bread chunks into the air, ignoring me. "Say hello to my little friend!" His tone was more playful than sinister, a pitiful impersonation of Al Pacino in *Scarface*. Chris's personality made up for his weight. Put a couple beers in him, and Chris would streak anywhere on a dare—the frat house lawn, the streets of Aggieville, the football field during a game. I'd loved the fact that he didn't care what other people thought. If you could bottle and sell insecurity, my dad would have made millions.

The bread fell like confetti onto the tepid water surrounding me. I watched the Zebra-striped sergeant majors with puckering lips swarm for their snack. My heart rate jumped.

"Go deeper." Chris leaned over the boat, smiling like a Chum Lord looking over his kingdom. My own Mr. Miyagi, minus the karate.

I took a deep breath and disappeared into the ocean, following the taut, algae-covered rope down to the boat's rusty anchor, to a new life. My legs kicked with fervor, diving into my own shadows, releasing the pain of my past. The sand looked like dust floating off the bottom as yellowtail snappers darted by, sparkling in the underwater rays of sun. I finally felt free. Free of responsibility. Free of rattails. Ready to be surrounded by the kind of natural beauty I could never find back home—or within myself.

Poor kids are best equipped to become rich with a drive to live a better life, and I'm glad I hit the determination Powerball. Leaving Kansas and my family was my first step toward fulfilling a deep desire to do more, to be more. The "what ifs" will always be there—what if I hadn't endured a record-breaking winter without a car, what if my parents would have been happily married, what if my dad would have been the father figure I'd desperately needed. Then again, my mom says I was a fireball of independence from the moment I learned how to walk, just shy of nine months old. She'd decided nothing should get between my ambition and me, so she'd stepped aside and let me spread my wings. I'd sold peanut brittle for four years in high school to finance a week in France with a language study group. There was a little spirit of Amelia Earhart living inside me, and Chris had unleashed it.

I thumbed the camera's plastic wheel and turned to find my next parrotfish. My eyes bugged out as the wide, pointy nose hovered in my face. Adrenaline flooded my veins. The unmistakable hooked dorsal fin crested the surface.

"SHAAAUUKKK!" The scream bubbled from my mouth. I shot to the surface like a guided missile. My heartbeat hammered in my ears. *My bad luck followed me in Florida?!* I'd survived two car accidents and three tornados—only to be eaten by a goddamn shark during my first dip in the ocean. Shark attacks were my grandma's greatest fear when I'd told her I was moving to Miami. Like my mom and dad, she'd lived her entire life in the quaint town of Girard, and she'd watched *Jaws* at least three times.

I flew up the boat's metal ladder faster than a child on a jungle gym. I ripped off my mask and jumped behind Chris, my protective wall. "I...saw...a...shark!" My chest fluttered between words.

"Gross. Get away from me." Chris batted me off like a fly. "You're all wet."

"A shark tried to French kiss me!" My lips snarled with rejection. "I should have had a buddy!" I gripped my wet knees to slow my breathing. Captain Bob chuckled, deep creases forming in his weather-beaten face.

"You're my good luck charm." Chris hopped around like a first grader on a field trip and soft-punched me in the arm. "We rarely see nurse sharks."

My lungs panted. "How big was it?" I grabbed my beach towel and speed-wrapped it around my waist.

"He was a baby!" Chris grinned. "I bet a Chihuahua could have eaten him." He bounced around the boat, leaning deep over the hull. Typically, he didn't get amped up about anything besides diving deep-sea shipwrecks and going to Grateful Dead concerts.

"Really?" I tugged my beach towel tighter and sat down on the bench. "He looked so big."

Chris plucked the snorkel and fins from my hands. A big smile rippled across his face. "Everything looks bigger underwater because our eyes are truly open."

🍷🍸🍷🍸🍷

FALL ARRIVED IN Miami without the telltale signs of the North. Palm trees were still lush with vibrant green leaves, and temperatures continued to hover around a muggy eighty-five degrees. We took showers three times a day and learned that was common practice. I found a waitressing job and started pulling in double the tips. The shine of living and working in a tropical climate couldn't fade on me; my eyes were still opening to our new world.

Late one morning, sun peeked through the drawn vertical blinds on our apartment's sliding glass doors. Grateful Dead's twangy "Box of Rain" filled the room, drowning out the vents blasting frigid air from the ceiling. It was a Tuesday in early October, and Chris and I finally had a day off together. Working in a region where the economy was (and still is) driven by tourism, we got one day off a week and often spent half of it doing laundry.

"It's almost eleven o'clock already," I said with a snip, perched on his tanker-sized leather couch wearing a tank top and shorts. "Let's get out of this ice box." Our thermostat was always parked at sixty-seven degrees, helping us either recover from, or prepare for, the wall of humidity outside. My chattering teeth were beyond ready to explore the gateway to South America, the city Madonna called home (at least half the year), a sprawling metropolis with beaches and causeways and exotic trees that all required my close examination.

Chris sat Indian-style on the floor with his back to me. "I don't wanna drive." His baggy concert T-shirt pooled around him like an oversized curtain as his eyes stayed glued to the plastic jackets of Memorex cassette tapes strung around his bare feet. "It's too hot to be outside anyway." Chris grabbed a pencil and scribbled on the cassette's paper jacket. His only extracurricular activity, besides smoking and diving, was making and trading Grateful Dead mixtapes.

"Well, we decided not to live on the beach, and I'm not walking twenty miles." I yanked the scrunchie from my hair and squeezed it like a stress ball. Our apartment building backed up to a skinny canal filled with green slime and cattails overlooking Miami's largest landfill. The ocean sunsets we'd dreamed of watching from our third-story balcony on Saga Bay were replaced by views of dump trucks and dust clouds, complemented by the stench of decomposing food on a windy day. How did we choose where to live before the Internet? Close review of two maps and a three-pound manila envelope filled with marketing brochures. Our moving van was the turnip truck. United, we fell off...

Chris let out a groan. "We've been through this before."

I glared at the back of his head. *Yes. I know. There are no dive sites near Miami Beach, and Cutler Ridge was a compromise.*

Chris turned toward me. The white living room was almost as dark as his basement bedroom at the frat house. "It's not that bad here." He pushed his hair from his eyes. "I did my best."

I looked at Chris's defeated eyes. Remorse rolled through me. *He's right. Why can't I just be grateful?* Our open-concept apartment was sparkling white from floor to ceiling and four times the size of my college dorm room. My childhood home had a sagging back porch with plastic stapled to the windows to keep in the heat. In Florida, we had central air conditioning, a dishwasher and even a swimming pool—things on my bucket list. Chris had made so many sacrifices for us. He'd dropped out of college midsemester and had taken a freelance job writing computer code to cover all our moving expenses. He didn't even complain when I'd started researching universities and had asked him if we could move to southeast Miami-Dade County instead of the Virgin Islands or the Florida Keys. I wanted to crawl into the pantry and eat a bag of Doritos to feed my guilt.

I scurried over and bear-hugged him from behind, hoping to release the tension. He patted my arm like a schoolteacher and returned to his music project, awakening my emotional rejection.

"I just thought it would be different." I looked away toward our sliding glass doors—doors Chris always wanted to keep closed. Hurricane Andrew, the costliest hurricane in history at the time, had demolished our new hometown exactly two years before. Neighborhood streets were still lined with roofless homes that looked like concrete boxes. The smell of the dump, however, remained strong.

"You've already quit one job." Chris scribbled on another mixtape jacket. "I thought you'd be happier now."

Ouch.

I'd daydreamed about wearing sunscreen as part of my uniform, serving strawberry daiquiris to men in Hawaiian-print shirts at a beachfront bar with sand squishing under my feet, but had ended up waiting tables at a sports bar in a Publix grocery strip mall. The rowdy regulars and my coworkers had the kind of life stories that got revealed on *Maury*.

"Hey. There was a better opportunity." I sunk uncomfortably into the leather cushion. "I'm making more money." Quitting would have been unthinkable back in southeast Kansas, where job openings were scarce, and most family and friends worked at one of three manufacturing plants for decades—if not their entire careers. I'd been offered a server position at The Cheesecake Factory, which was opening its first restaurant in Florida. Chains were the engine of restaurant business back then; chef Norman Van Aken, one of the godfathers of new American cuisine, was still a year away from opening Norman's in swanky Coral Gables.

My new job included a thirty-minute drive north to a waterfront community, Coconut Grove. The Grove was having its moment as Miami's bright star, a hamlet along Biscayne Bay with a three-story, open-air entertainment complex called CocoWalk, a magnet for tourists. Dan Marino had a sports bar there, which was like Dolly Pardon opening Dollywood to people in Tennessee. Cheesecake Factory was CocoWalk's newest tenant, and the local media were lathering on the news coverage. More than thirty flavors of cheesecake alone!

"We don't need more money." Chris sifted through the cassettes littering the floor. "You work too much." The words seethed from his tight jaw.

I let out a sigh. Our monthly rent was $600. No matter how many times Chris told me not to worry about money, I still did. The starting wage for a certified dive instructor was a whopping $6 per hour at the time, Chris couldn't drive past Dairy Queen without a Peanut Buster Parfait pit stop, and the thirty-three mile drive to Key Largo had morphed into an hour-plus commute when "high season" arrived and tourist numbers tripled.

"Well, I'm off today." I folded my arms across my tank top and regrouped my thoughts. "And the beach is only thirty minutes away." My shoulders began to tire from the argument. *Maybe I should just go to work.* I'd been picking up extra shifts every week. Serving Chinese chicken salads in an Oxford and tie on a Mediterranean-style veranda felt like a vacation compared to making potato salad in Chicken Mary's kitchen. I never wanted to leave the restaurant—its energy, the colorful personalities, the foreign languages spoken—every shift seemed like traveling to another country.

Cuba, Trinidad, Haiti, Colombia. I found myself mesmerized by the code-like vocabulary of the kitchen, the bakery, the bar and the food runners—"SOS" for sauce on the side, "on the fly" for urgent orders, "campers" for people who wouldn't leave their tables, etc. The diversity was like a drug. I wanted to be "in the weeds" all day.

"We moved here to get away from the cold." I looked down at my baggy jean shorts and couldn't stop the grin from forming. At Cheesecake, employees got all the free soup and bread they could eat, which kept us from scarfing down dead plates or customer left-overs. After living off cups of soup for a month, I'd dropped ten pounds, and finally felt confident enough to wear a bikini without a towel wrap. "On your day off, you want to stay home, make mixtapes and eat ice cream?"

He penciled on. "What's wrong with that?"

I folded my arms in a huff. Each pound lost seemed to put a mile of distance between us. Every time I drove up Old Cutler to work, a long winding road that snakes through tunnels of banyan trees, it felt like an escape to a more peaceful world, void of argument and responsibility.

"We're not in Kansas anymore, Chris." I pictured myself in my other life in my white uniform, sponging as much culture and attention as possible from my coworkers. I'd never met a gay man, a lesbian, a Cuban, a Brasilian, a Bolivian, an Egyptian or a Pakistani, and definitely not a gay radio jingles singer from Alabama. I'd also never said "hello" with a cheek kiss. Miami's Latin sensuality only amplified the touchiness of the restaurant business.

"Don't be so cliché." Chris glanced up at his stereo speakers.

"Whatever." My eyes rolled. Working in restaurants, the shifts are long and relationships form fast. I was spending far more time and having far more fun with my new friends at work.

"Shhhhh. It's a China-Rider." Jerry Garcia began singing the chorus, and Chris raised both hands in the air like a concert conductor. His deeply tanned arms had a rosy hue from spending eight hours a day on a dive boat. He tugged at his navy T-shirt to cover his girth. Behind closed doors, Chris always seemed uncomfortable clothed or naked. I never realized the irony. He couldn't turn on the lights while naked with the girl he loved, but he could streak the 50-yard-line at a K-State football game in front of 30,000 people.

I grabbed a sweaty can of Keystone Light off the end table and took a long sip, letting the feeling of being a mature adult trickle through me. Drinking cheap beer wasn't just about feeling grown up for me; it helped me feel closer to my dad. My expectations of taste had been set pretty low, sneaking swigs off half-empty cans of Busch he'd left in the living room. The cards were stacked against my palate, growing up in the 1980s in the state with the longest prohibition in our country—a state that still only allows the sale of 3.2 alcohol beer in grocery stores, a state that upheld a ban on Sunday liquor sales until 2005. The only corkscrew in town was our county fair roller coaster. My first and only wine experience in high school had started with a bottle of Boone's Farm Strawberry Hill and ended with me hugging a toilet bowl.

Chris stared at the cassette tape in his hands, whistling along with the music. My eyes fixed on his wide body.

"Why can't we just go somewhere?" I took a musty, metallic sip, unaware of the world of flavors that existed beyond the can. "There's so much of Miami we haven't seen yet." The sweeping waterfront gardens of Vizcaya, the walled fortresses near the mansions of Sylvester Stallone and Madonna, the drive-up beaches on Virginia Key, Everglades National Park—all were at our doorstep. We had moved to Florida so we could be outside all year-round, exploring. Chris was acting like a spoiled brat who belonged in Alaska...in an igloo.

"Whenever you're not working, you're still working," Chris muttered, never looking up. "If you're not studying, you're making lists and planning a vacation day." His voice was cold and sober. "I just want to rest. You should, too."

My mouth fell open.

"Work hard, play hard." My ponytail whipped around my shoulders. "I thought that was the plan." When I'd scored ninety-three points on the final service exam at The Cheesecake Factory, Chris didn't even say, "Good job." I'd spent two weeks enduring nine-hour training sessions to learn every ingredient in a twenty-page menu that was more exotic than an issue of *National Geographic*. I had to work harder than the other servers to memorize all the dishes because I'd never tasted things like artichokes, ahi tuna, calamari and tamarind sauce. My tongue had finally been exposed to a new world of flavors, and my eyes were jealous. I'd earned a day trip and a supportive boyfriend.

"But I'm cooped up inside all day." The words shot from my lips with frustration. My hands anchored on my hips. "I wanna go relax in the sun. Somewhere. Not here." My days were spent racing through an alcoved dining room with fresco ceilings and grandiose stone pillars. If I couldn't be at the restaurant soaking up the energy, I wanted sand on my feet and sun on my shoulders. Sheryl Crow had just released "All I Wanna Do," and I'd made it my personal anthem.

Chris threw back his head. "I don't want any more sun." A sigh of exasperation escaped his clenched jaw. "I get enough at work."

"But I don't." I flung my arms into the air. "Just wear sunscreen." My cheeks plumped. I squeezed my hands like a valet about to park his first Ferrari. "We have money. We can do things." I'd never been able to break $35 in tips back home, and I'd leave every shift at Cheesecake with $100 in my apron. I wanted to celebrate a life where I finally had money—and chimichurri sauce.

Chris groaned with irritation. "It's not about the money." His eyes met mine. I remembered the time I'd proudly fanned out my thick stack of tips in his face like a deck of cards. Chris had rolled his eyes and said, "It's just money." Now, Chris gently stacked three plastic cassette boxes on the floor. "Go to the store if you want to go somewhere." His voice was snippy and colder than our apartment. "We're out of ice cream and pop." Once we lived together, it seemed like all we did was argue about groceries, bills and chores.

"It's called SO-da." My voice snapped with a hiss. We'd been transplanted to another world, and Chris wasn't even trying to blend in with the locals. Pop was called soda. Supper was dinner and dinner was lunch. Thongs were flip-flops. But most importantly, perms and fanny packs were *not* cool.

Chris shoved a clear cassette tape back in its jacket. "Whatever, big city girl."

My shoulders squared. "Don't be mean." I stared at Chris in silence until he looked up at me. "You said we weren't going to eat crap once we moved here." I tugged at the belt loops on my saggy jean shorts. We were living in a place where women with tanned, baby-oiled bodies sauntered down the street in bikini tops and Daisy Dukes, and my body still belonged in a burka. To lose weight, we needed the buddy system—just like scuba divers.

I sighed and clenched my fists. Bits of frustration snapped together in my chest. I looked down at Chris, huddled over his milk crate of Dead tapes like a hen protecting her eggs. Leaving his cubbyhole to party with other Greeks wasn't his preferred way to spend a Saturday night in college, and driving sixty minutes to Miami Beach to get our first glimpse at Ocean

Drive wasn't either. The life of a scuba diver—not as adventurous as once thought.

I marched over to the blinds. "I can't stand it." I tugged the cords. Sunshine poured into the room. "I can't be inside all the time. I need fresh air. I need light." Chris covered his squinting eyes with the back of his forearm. Vampire in a past life? Maybe Count Chocula.

Chris pushed his pile of tapes aside. His prankster grin reemerged. "What you need is a Hot Carl."

"I'm serious. This isn't funny." My hands gripped the hips of my jean shorts. Chris always dropped a toilet humor bomb at the most serious moments. He was a walking urban dictionary.

Chris hopped to his bare feet. "Could you do me a favor?" He pushed his hair from his eyes, exposing his round, tan face. "Pull my finger."

WORKING IN A restaurant with a strict uniform helped me value the importance of dressing for success. The daily routine before each shift felt like serious business: iron long creases into the arms of a white dress shirt, starch my white apron and iron a straight crease between the pockets, polish my white sneakers and tie a Windsor knot with the precision of a CEO. As I scuttled through the dining room in my white uniform, the long apron wrapped around my legs felt like a cloak of civility. Only waitresses at classy restaurants wore button-downs, neckties and aprons as long as a First Communion dress, I thought.

But, at the end of each shift, when the refuge of an air-conditioned dining room was gone, I felt like a sweaty mummy. I'd rush home in my dirty uniform with the air-conditioning blasting in my car, dart upstairs to my apartment and take a cold shower—my third of the day.

One afternoon in late October, I dragged myself up the open-air stairwell to our apartment in my post-shift routine, legs feeling like dive tanks in the sweltering heat.

As the front door swung open, slivers of sunlight peeked through the vertical blinds on our sliding glass doors, lighting the silhouette of Chris's stereo system in the living room. The welcomed wall of chilled air hit me before the faint scent of smoke, sending my stomach into nauseating shock.

I flipped on the light switch.

My jaw dropped.

A crushed Bud Light can rested on a white paper plate in the middle of our dining table, surrounded by dirty, wadded up napkins and two empty bags of chips. My shoulders caved. I'd grown up in a house where crumpled beer cans on the table were commonplace, but this looked like a very different kind of party. Little specks of ash circled the can like a trail of black pepper.

My eyes scanned the room, looking for the ashtray.

I dropped my backpack and apron on the tile floor. The reality soaked into my conscience like the buzz from a stiff drink. *I moved to Florida with a liar and a pig.* For five years, I'd been making money by picking up other people's messes at restaurants. The last thing I wanted to do after a nine-hour shift was come home and clean up Chris's shitty cigarette butts. The glitter of living together had already faded. It had been two weeks since our big fight, and we'd both just kept working on our jobs, not on *us*.

I grabbed the can contraption with both hands and coughed hard from the moldy, herbal stench. My chest began to thump. The memory of our first and only Grateful Dead concert together raced from my head to the pit of my stomach.

Holy shit. It's a bong. Pothead Chris is back!?

I thought we'd left the ghost of his past in a muddy ditch off 1-70 when our moving van had crossed the state line. My fists clenched. I'd never so much as seen a bud of grass before meeting Chris. Drugs were for scuzzballs in my tiny hometown. Medical marijuana was still a few years away from legalization in California, and crystal meth was still just an electronic pop duo. Smoking marijuana had its place in the experimental phase of many lives—just not mine.

My ears got hot. I gritted my teeth. Recent events rolled through my mind like cherries on a slot machine. First, the urgent notice mailed to Chris from World Credit Services. Chris had had a few run-ins with credit collection agencies back in college, which he'd brushed off as "misunderstandings" that had been handled. Then, the past-due letters from Florida Power & Light flashed in my head. We'd also received an overdraft notice from NationsBank. Another promise Chris had broken: handling all our bills and paying them on time. I'd been stuffing $75 to $100 in Chris's sock drawer six days per week for nearly a month.

The bong was *my* boiling point.

I ripped open the sliding glass doors to our patio. My lungs sucked in the fresh, humid air as I stood along the balcony's railing, shaking, staring down at the swamp below. I wanted to attack him like a rabid Spuds MacKenzie.

I collapsed onto the couch. *A deep-sea diver filling his most precious asset with cancerous smoke?* Chris could have been cracking code for the CIA or helping his dad launch another new line of video games. Instead, he wanted to drink cheap beer, smoke weed and play "pull my finger." Not the escape from my past I'd banked on.

A trail of Doritos crumbs dotted the crease between two cushions on the couch. I flicked the tiny orange pieces onto the floor like paper footballs. *Are all guys slobs?* I ripped off my necktie and grabbed our broom.

I swept the medley of chips and sand from the floor. My brain stumbled through the affirmation. I actually believed a man two years older than me—who'd lived in a frat house basement for five years—would have a magical metamorphosis once we'd left college and moved to South Florida. I'd been asking Chris to quit smoking—cigarettes! I'd also asked him to clean the sand off his diving equipment, shorts and shoes in our breezeway before coming into the apartment. Since the moment we'd moved in, sand was sprinkled on our floor like rock salt on a frozen road. And as much as I love sand between my toes, a girl can only take so much.

I looked out the window to the muddy canal below our balcony, twirling my hair. The signs were all there in college—the pot smoking, the class skipping, the binge eating, but I'd ignored them, stifled by my own insecurities and fear of being single again. Taking Chris on the live-in test drive was supposed to determine if we could make it to happily ever after. I didn't want to marry the wrong guy. My parents had broken up and gotten back together more times than Whitney Houston and Bobby Brown. Girls back home got engaged during college and popped out all their kids before age twenty-six. My mom got married at nineteen and gave birth to my brother two months after she turned twenty-one.

And I was living with a guy who asked me to smell his farts.

My chest ached with anger. It was a kind of fiery hurt I'd never felt with a boyfriend—not the usual, ego-crippling pain of being dumped for another girl.

I marched over to the leaning pile of unopened mail littering the kitchen counter and started digging. I grabbed a pen. It felt like a butcher knife in my hand. *How does this whole dumping thing really work?* I'd only abandoned ship on a boyfriend twice in my life.

Writing a great break-up letter is an art form a girl like me should have had mastered. I'd worked for a newspaper writing obituaries the summer before moving to Miami. I specialized in unhappy endings.

Thoughts shifted to my mom. She'd left my father three times, packing up our belongings at night because she'd gotten fed up with his drinking again. Dad had never known there was a problem until he'd arrived home and found our beds and dressers empty, and one of Mom's hand-written letters on the kitchen table, spilling her heart. As a child of instability, I'd lived in relationship quicksand for years, making it easy to sink into the same hole.

I spun around and looked at the bong on our table. My nostrils flared. I stared at the pen in my shaky hand, thinking of all the frustrations I needed to get off my chest. The bills. The food. The cigarettes. The drugs.

I let out a deep sigh and dropped the pen next to the crumpled can.

He'll get the hint.

🍺🍷🍸🍷🍾

TROPICAL STORM GORDON blasted Miami and the northern Keys in mid-November. My side of the bed was still empty the night Gordon made landfall. I'd been couch-surfing through coworkers' apartments, avoiding Chris like back-to-back double shifts. My late nights were spent "closing down" Loggerhead, a beloved local bar, over pitchers of beer with fellow servers from the South and South America. They introduced me to beers like Red Dog, Sam Adams, Amstel and Heineken—about as esoteric as beer got in the nineties. Dark lagers and ales seemed so rich and full to my fledgling palate, and their ice-cold mugs felt like the right place to drown my guilt about leaving Chris without saying a word to his face. My tastes were changing quickly—and luckily, the acceptance of fake IDs was not.

🥃🍺🍷🍸🍾

TEN DAYS LATER, I drove to our apartment around three thirty when I thought Chris would be at work. As I pulled into my parking space, a knot formed in my throat. His white Probe, plastered with Grateful Dead and Greenpeace stickers, was parked in its designated spot. I gripped the steering wheel, feeling the tension build in my neck and shoulders. We shared a lease agreement and a checking account. It was time to face Mr. Hot Carl.

I pushed my legs up the stairs, feeling the beads of sweat under my white work uniform. I stood outside the front door in the thick humidity for five minutes, breathing out of my mouth. My hand trembled as I slid my key into the lock.

My body froze. Chris stood two feet from the door, stacking cassette tapes in a laundry basket on the kitchen table. His green eyes were dark and distant. His ever-rosy cheeks were covered with stubble. Greasy chunks of hair fell around his stout face. My stomach squished. Part of me wanted to crawl under the table and die from shame, part wanted to call his mother.

He glanced back into the basket, before hefting it into his arms. My nerves dangled like the keys hanging from our open front door.

Chris brushed past me in the doorway, laundry basket tucked under his arm. A look of disgust and sadness coated his face. "I can't believe you would do this, Lisa." He paused with the front door to his back. The air around us smelled of sweat. I looked into his watery eyes. My heartbeat banged so hard I felt it in my ears. "You disappeared. You couldn't even tell me why. How could you just throw two years of our lives away?"

My mouth went dry. The weight of frustration and disappointment resting on my back was instantly doubled by a barbell of shame and sympathy. I tried to scrape the remnants of courage from the kitchen counter still littered with unopened bills.

"I...I am...sorry." My voice trembled; my tongue felt paralyzed. My approach to breaking up was about as mature as a Natty Light beer pong game.

"I love you." His voice shook. "I love you more than I've ever loved any girl." His eyes burned through my skull.

I wanted to say, "If you loved me, you wouldn't use drugs. You would stop smoking. You would pay the bills. You wouldn't tell me you want to 'check my oil.' You would stop eating a pint of Ben & Jerry's every day." My lips quivered the silent rebuttal. My anger stayed bottled inside my flat chest, like always. I'd never looked someone in the eye and delivered bad news. Bad news hurts people. I'm from the Care Bears generation. I give too much of a shit.

"Rent is paid through the end of the month..." His voice trailed off as his flip-flops smacked down the stairs. "I'll be back to get *my* furniture then." His emphasis on the word "my" made the sting worse. I'd moved to Miami with nothing but a dream and truckload of stuff he'd bought for our new life. I would be starting over with a papasan chair, a fish tank and four milk crates full of clothes.

My feet tried to step toward the front door, but my knees locked. I wanted to chase him down and block the stairwell. I didn't want to become enemies. The thought of having someone who once loved me hate me still makes me sicker than watching *The Blair Witch Project*.

My watery eyes scanned the eerily quiet apartment. I wiped my cheeks and walked over to a pile of jewel cases in front of his stereo. The milk crates of Grateful Dead tapes were gone, and only my favorites remained: Indigo Girls, Sarah McLachlan, Gin Blossoms and New Order.

When I tapped the fast-forward button, it had new meaning. The strumming six-string guitar from Indigo Girls' "Closer to Fine" danced in the air. I snapped open the vertical blinds and let sunshine bathe the entire room, trying to find the bright side.

I walked into the bedroom and pulled my last stack of white milk crates out of the closet. The Indigo Girls' voices filled my ears. I sang along, pulling K-State T-shirts from the bottom dresser drawer. Tears ran down my cheeks. Chris gave me one of the greatest gifts of my life. If Lance had not dumped me, I would have never met Chris. I would have never left Kansas. I may have never stopped wearing acid-washed jeans or using Aqua Net hairspray. When Chris pumped that keg for me back at Kansas State, he opened the first door to my destiny.

Every person we meet, every relationship we have, every breakup we endure, is for a reason. Age just teaches us how to appreciate the failures. My first attempt at living with a boyfriend now seems as thin and salty as that stale party beer. I'd never had a taste of anything better, so how would my dating palate know?

I couldn't fight the smile from forming. A new course in life had just been chartered. Destination: unknown. I'd sailed my ship of safety all the way to Florida, and had sank it in less than ninety days. It was time to taste all that Miami had to offer, and beer from a can would not be on the menu.

JAMES
The Dark Beer Days

*P*repping for my first hurricane was a bonding experience, especially because duct tape and a hot medical school student were involved.

"I guess we can eighty-six the customers," James said as he ripped a long piece of shiny tape off the roll and smeared it across two window panes.

"I wish we could eighty-six this fuckin' rain." I stood next to him on the large banquette with a twisted face in my bright-white uniform, staring at the empty tables on Cheesecake Factory's veranda. It was the first week of November, and Tropical Storm Gordon was forecast to make landfall in eight hours.

He stuffed the silver doughnut in my face. "Now, your turn."

"Kidnapper tools?" My hands fumbled the duct tape with apprehension. "That's what's gonna to save the restaurant?" When tropical storms brewed in the Atlantic, Miamians who didn't have storm shutters plastered their windows with tape—like a busted taillight on a car. Big hurricanes called for plywood. I found all of this utterly fascinating, considering that the only thing we did in Kansas during a tornado warning was hop in the bathtub and throw a mattress over our heads.

"How should I know?" James laughed as he continued to cover the wall of windows with diagonal silver Xs. "I'm from Atlanta." His feathery bangs bounced along with the southern drawl in his voice. My stomach began making a quilt. We'd gone through server training together and usually worked the same shifts. I'd become acutely aware of the bounce in his step, the way his bangs parted, the way his Levi's fit so snug on his round butt—and the fact that we were among the few straight gringos on staff who didn't smoke.

"Window bondage is not my idea of side work." I ripped my first strip and watched it tangle into a mangled mess. Slow shifts always meant more side work at restaurants, but back home, we scraped gum from the underbelly of tabletops with a butter knife and flushed the lines in the soda fountain.

A gust of wind smacked against the glass. I shrieked and jumped onto the terra-cotta floor, feeling my bushy ponytail flopping like a horse's tail. "Screw this. I'd rather be quadruple sat." I collapsed into a two-top booth across the skinny dining room and stared at the two-foot-tall stack of white linens on the tabletop. I relished the mindless side duty of folding linens after years of working in the kind of restaurants that served food with paper napkins.

"Don't forget the roll-ups." The sound of him ripping tape off the roll filled my ears. "We should double the par. I'd rather roll 'em now than Saturday at midnight." Restaurant lingo sounded like poetry coming from his lips. James's boyish face and thick bangs reminded me of Alex P. Keaton from *Family Ties*. Mad crush.

"It's too late for me. I'm toast." I grabbed a short stack of napkins in a huff and started the methodical triple fold. *Fold left. Rub the crease. Fold right. Rub the crease. Flip. Repeat.* The tension crept deeper into my shoulders. Locals were stockpiling supplies as if Gordon was a Category 5, and I had only two bags of Doritos and a liter of Coke in my pantry.

James sat down in a booth across from me and began folding his own napkin tower. My eyes moved from his blue-striped necktie to mine, which was the same color and style—a telltale sign of our compatibility. He always looked more like an attorney than a waiter, with his crisp, white shirt and perfectly knotted tie.

Wind howled as heavy rain slapped the windows. A wave of anxiety washed over me.

"It's like I'm marchin' into a war zone without a fuckin' gun." My fingers sped through the folds, as the starchy smell of the freshly laundered linens filled the air. The familiar scent didn't calm my nerves. I didn't mention Chris; James had heard plenty about him during pre-shift napkin-folding sessions, which were basically staff gossip sessions.

"Chill...tornadoes are way worse," James said in his carefree tone, folding a napkin three times with the same precision he used to part his bangs. He always carried a black plastic comb in his back pocket, just like my dad.

"I don't git it." My curly ponytail brushed my shoulders. "Why does everyone here think a fuckin' tornado is worse than a hurricane?" I stacked my folded napkins into a leaning tower. Wind whistled against the windowpanes. I said "fuck" a lot in the city to appear more calloused, less Catholic.

"You did it again." James's voice had a sassy tone.

"Did what?"

"You say 'git' not 'get.' You don't pronounce your g's when you say 'fucking' either."

I looked away in a blush. "Your accent is stronger than mine." I could feel my chest getting warm under my white oxford, despite the humming

AC vent above my head. Everyone at work said I talked like a Kentucky girl who'd just had a root canal. They kept baiting me to say words that ended in "ing." I felt like a circus act of gerunds. I'd become increasingly conscious of my speech and began trying to articulate every syllable like a spelling bee finalist.

"Have you ever eaten a prairie oyster?"

My head swung toward him. "They're called mountain oysters, and the answer is 'hell no.'" Coworkers had more questions about Kansas than tourists had about Gloria Estefan and Sly Stallone. I wondered if the redneck trivia would ever end.

The glass doors to the veranda swung open. Micah, the radio jingle singer, bounced in with his head of wavy hair and a trail of confidence. Guys like him were as foreign to me as foie gras, and I felt more worldly and strong-willed simply by being in his presence.

"Oh, good Lord," he said with his thick Alabama accent. "You're already done tying up those windows like sex slaves, and now you're on roll-ups." Micah had spent the eighties in New York, snorting coke at clubs and having sex with strangers. He was HIV-positive and didn't let his diagnosis affect his pep or pride.

"What's your side work?" I asked mid-fold.

"I'm buffing tea pots, of course," he smirked with his nose in the air. "I'm gay. I could polish a turd and make it sparkle." He plucked three kettles from a cabinet below the service station and strutted back to the main dining room as his booming voice carried, "Now get back to work, Dorothy, before I feed Toto a shepherd's pie, and he shits all over your carpet."

I snorted a laugh. "Hey, you forgot my ruby-red slippers." Listening to gay guys get snarky felt like watching a stand-up comedy show. I loved their crass senses of humor, their ability to say anything and be themselves without the fear of judgment. When delivered correctly, a *Wizard of Oz* joke at my expense always made me giggle.

"Here's the deal." James looked up while continuing his folding ritual. "We get days to prepare for a hurricane. You get like five minutes with a tornado warning."

"Okay, fine." I tried not to focus on his Greek God-like arms, his muscular hands gently turning each starched linen. Cue more butterflies. *What should we name our firstborn?*

"We just need to wait it out and see which way the storm turns."

My eyes stared out the blurry windows. "I hate all this waiting." Waiting for a slow-moving cyclone. Waiting to save enough money to get my own apartment. Waiting for James to ask me out. Waiting sucked.

A radio in the main bus station blared weather reports through the empty restaurant. Major flooding was already reported in Goulds, Homestead and the Redlands, not far from my apartment. Visions of my Pontiac Grand Am stalling in four feet of water on Old Cutler Road rushed through my head, but the fear of drowning paled in comparison to confronting Chris. It had only been seven days since Chris had left me a homemade bong as a kitchen table centerpiece. I'd spent days bouncing from one coworker's couch to the next, with milk crates of clothes in the trunk of my car, trying to decide when to deal with the baggage of our breakup.

I slammed my eyes shut.

"I can't go home. Wherever *that* is." The words huffed from my pouty lips like a desperate plea. Our apartment never felt like a home. It was just a place to store things and sleep. Being in the restaurant, feeling productive and feeding off the dining room's energy—that was where I felt most comfortable.

A look of concern crimped his lean face. "You're welcome to crash at our place." His words were as comforting as the sound of opening a beer tab. I kept my eyes locked on the stack of napkins in front of me, hiding my rosy-red face. My mind began to free-fall through the possibilities—the looming end of my first live-in relationship, the storm surging toward the shore, the quest to procure my next boyfriend.

I fluffed my bangs to make sure they hid my forehead scars. My eyes followed the razor-thin crease pressed into the arm of his dress shirt. He even wore his waiter's uniform like a Wall Street businessman. Boys like James had been reduced to mere eye candy once I'd gained twenty-six pounds in college. I'd shed half the extra weight, and it seemed as if every guy but Chris had noticed. James had an undergraduate degree in mechanical engineering and was planning to attend University of Florida's med school next fall. Chris? I hoped he'd enroll in Jenny Craig.

🍷🍷🍷🍷🍷

I PULLED MY raincoat over my head and darted through the parking lot, following James and his fancy, wood-handled umbrella. We slipped through the metal gate of his apartment building into a lush courtyard of traveler's palms and bougainvillea bushes, raindrops bouncing off our jackets.

James raced ahead and ducked under a concrete stairwell that sheltered his doorway. The sight of the simple metal door made my heartbeat surge. I knew crossing that threshold would mean something. My sneakers scuffed against his doormat for longer than necessary. As I pulled off my raincoat, the guilt crept deeper into my chest.

His apartment looked staged for an open house. My eyes skimmed the room, searching for his most prized possession. The kitchen and living room were one big space with white cathedral ceilings and a sparkling chandelier. A spotless, oak dining table separated the kitchen from his min-

imalist living room, dotted with a chocolate leather couch, sleek glass coffee table, a big screen TV and a stereo system tower. *Where is it?*

"What can I get for you?" James asked in his server's voice while loosen-
ing his tie. He kicked off his white Nike sneakers by the hallway closet and
walked over to the kitchen. Heavy rain pelted the rooftop and windows. I
stood in the entryway and loosened my tie, fingers shaking along the way.

"I'll have whatever you're having." I unlaced my sneakers, following his
lead. My strategy for getting boys to like me was simple—be as low mainte-
nance as possible, like what they like and do what they do.

James pulled open the refrigerator door.

My eyes continued scanning, searching. "I trust you. You have good
taste." Two weeks had passed since our dinner with two coworkers at Chart
House, celebrating our ninety-plus scores on The Cheesecake Factory's final service exam. It had counted as a double date to me. James had pe-
rused the wine list skillfully like a gemologist at a jewelry display case. "We
should have the Silverado Sauvignon Blanc," he'd said. "It's from Napa, so
it must be good. We'll need the acidity to complement our conch ceviche."
I didn't even know how to pronounce "conch" or "ceviche," but I knew I
wanted to know more about debonair James. He was nothing like the boys
back home, nothing like my father.

James poked around his fridge. "German. Austrian, Jamaican. Should I
keep going?"

"Surprise me." I stood behind his plush couch in my white work jeans
and oxford, feeling the barrier between us.

He grabbed a bottle opener from the cabinet.

I finally spotted the long neck sticking out from the side of his stereo
tower: his precious acoustic guitar, a Gibson J-45. James was a double
threat. He knew how to sing *and* play the guitar. When single, I could never fight the pull of becoming some musician's new groupie. Both my mom

and brother were guitarists, and I'd dated a shaggy-haired guitar player (another Camel smoking college student) my sophomore year of high school. Even Lance, my heartbreaker, was a choirboy.

James strutted toward me with an Amstel Light and a Red Dog. "Here. I know you like the Dog." His sweet hospitality made me want to beg for more. Every bar in CocoWalk sold Red Dog back then, a new beer from Miller Brewing Company made with two barleys and five hops. All the girls at work had quickly traded up from Miller Lite. The only craft beer back then was Sierra Nevada, but we East Coasters didn't want to drink that California hippie crap.

I plucked the cold, brown bottle from his soft hands in a blush. Our fingers touched, and I looked away. *He drinks imports. Classy, of course.*

"You're getting there, Kermie." He tipped his bottleneck in a toast. "You'll never go back. Cheap American shit is for undergrads. I can't drink that piss anymore." He tilted the bottle to his lips.

Hearing my childhood nickname roll of his tongue made my nerves short circuit. I took a long swig, feeling the hint of alcohol enter my system and begin its soothing work. "See. You can take the girl out of the trailer park, and you *can* take the trailer park out of the girl." I grinned with pride between sips. At our Chart House dinner, my novice taste buds were jolted awake as the citrusy, crisp white wine danced with the juicy, spiciness of the conch. It was my first fine food and wine pairing experience; James had planted a seed in me that would grow into something—I just had no idea what, back then. The fanciest meal of my life had occurred at the Topeka Olive Garden on my birthday, when Chris had given me a gold chain and threatened to fart at the table. When we'd arrived at the Chart House, James had pulled out my chair for me. I was twenty years old and felt like a debutante arriving at my first gala.

"Make yourself at home." His four words seemed to float in the air, buoyed by his sexy accent. *Has he forgotten that I practically live out of my car?* I could have been unpacked in five minutes.

James sipped his beer with refinement, sinking into the bulky couch. "You hungry?"

"Not really." I continued downing the dark lager, feeling it coat my empty stomach. "I went to town on the soup of the day." I'd had three cups of the chicken and artichoke medley during the slow shift, but my stomach was growling, and I wanted to feel skinny in his presence. Really smart move.

He made himself a turkey sandwich on whole wheat like any healthy, respectable boy would.

I watched him eat, acutely aware of the space between us on the couch, wondering if he'd try to kiss me that night, picturing myself making my own sandwich in his kitchen once I'd moved in.

My bottle emptied quickly, so I grabbed two Amstel Lights from the fridge. "Why did you choose Cheesecake? You could have easily gotten hired at a fancy place with bigger tips." I placed his fresh beer on a new coaster, feeling useful and caring.

"Cheesecake is just a job," he said. "The beach is where the money is, and it's easy to get hooked on fast cash. I don't want to get too cozy. I've only got ten months before medical school." Joe's Stone Crab and The Forge on Miami Beach were the main fancy restaurants back then. With all that class, James belonged in fine dining.

We sat down on the couch with ample space between us. I caressed the plush leather cushions, admiring his apartment.

"What about you?" James turned toward me. "You look the part."

"Hardly." I scoffed at his unexpected compliment. "You think I could get hired at a place like that?" Cheesecake Factory beverage training was my introduction to wines that had corks, and didn't have the words like "dog" or "bird" in the name. But, I already viewed my Keystone days and the 3.2 Flu as distant memories from a past life—just like my pet raccoon.

"Yes, don't sell yourself short," he replied between small bites. The man ate as mannerly as an Upper East Side grandmother. "You'd just need to learn more about wine."

I took a dainty sip, trying to look and sound sophisticated. "My customers rarely order wine. I need to get better at upselling." Many Americans believed they had to be celebrating a birthday at a restaurant where the waiters wore tuxedos in order to drink wine. Luckily, change was in the esters. *60 Minutes* had aired its "The French Paradox" segment a few years before; it was only a matter of time before wine became mainstream in America.

James wiped his mouth with a napkin and folded it neatly on the table, concluding his meal. My mind checked another box: Mr. Clean, unlike Chris.

"Did you find an apartment yet?" he asked.

"Not yet." I took a long swig to hide my procrastination. "I need to start looking. I think I might get a roommate. Not sure I'm ready to live alone." The last thing I wanted was to be single again, to feel the absence of coupledom, that dark shadow of loneliness.

"Why isn't your roommate home?" The words flew from my lips without a thought.

"He's staying at his mom's house," he said between dignified sips. "She's scared of storms." A band of wind smacked rain hard against his windows.

I jumped and squeezed my beer for comfort. "I'm scared."

"You shouldn't be." We sat in silence, sipping our beers. I wondered if we were talking about the same thing. My loosened mind began reflecting on life, letting it soak in—living alone two time zones away from everyone I've ever known, adopting a new city and finding my place in it.

I tugged my scrunchie from my hair, and layers of long curls cascaded down my back. Note to my twenty-year-old self: letting your hair down in front of a guy sends a message. Make sure that is the message you want to send.

James floated over to his stereo and clicked some buttons. I chugged the rest of my beer to build up my nerve to ask the big question.

Counting Crows began crooning about rain kings.

"How fitting." James returned to the kitchen, bouncing to the beat.

I smiled into my beer bottle. "Are you going to play something tonight?" My voice had that frisky lift and confident tone that only comes with a good buzz. I tipped my beer to James's Gibson, cradled in a metal stand next to his stereo tower. His mother was a high school music teacher in Georgia. She'd taught him to play guitar and piano before age six. He could listen to any song on the radio then pick up his guitar and start strumming the tune. Talk about turn-on.

He looked down at me on the couch. "Sure, I'm always taking requests."

James grabbed his guitar and sat down next to me. My heart leapt into my throat. I rushed over to my linen backpack by the door and fished my Frente! jewel case from the side pouch.

I shoved the CD in his face. "Will you play song eleven, please?" I plopped down Indian-style on the couch. Ever since our double date at Chart House, I'd been jamming out to "Labour of Love" everyday while ironing my work apron and dress shirt. I'd daydreamed about us performing a duet, even though my tone-deaf vocals would have made Biz Markie cringe.

His fingers bounced over the guitar strings. James crooked his head toward the stereo speaker, studying the playful lift in every note. He effortlessly strummed away as the first chorus began. I grinned like a front-row groupie, shoulders swaying from side to side. My head was filled with a hazy mix of frayed emotions from the open wounds of a breakup. That was always the easiest—and riskiest—time to fall right back into love.

When his pick hit the last string, I clapped with delight.

He smiled and returned his baby to her cradle. "I'm beat. We should go to bed."

My chest tightened with nervousness. *We? That's couple talk.* My buzz had shifted into top gear, unleashing the dark ideas hidden away in my young, love-hungry mind. *Maybe I should sleep with him.* Sex would be my sword, driving a permanent wedge between the Kansas girl and the new me, between my past with Chris and a new relationship with James.

"I'll bring you a few things." James disappeared into a hallway and returned with a stack of blankets, clothes and a fluffy pillow.

He draped a sheet over the couch. I fidgeted with my empty beer as he continued making my temporary bed. The awkwardness between us seemed wider than the Intracoastal Waterway.

James placed a flashlight on the coffee table. "Just in case." His smile, his accent, his caring side—all continued to suck me in. Most guys back home would have belched in my face three times by then. "You'll be okay out here?"

I emptied the last drop of beer into my gut. *Was that an invitation?* I didn't know if I was ready to RSVP. I listened to the howling wind and thought of Chris home alone.

"I'll be okay," I whispered through my beer breath.

He handed me a neatly folded pair of flannel boxers and a Georgia Bull-dogs T-shirt. As my fingers touched his clothes, every nerve in my body felt frazzled, ready to unravel.

I brushed my teeth with my finger in the hallway bathroom and changed into his clothes. I stared into the mirror, trying to see myself through his eyes. With the alcohol on and the extra weight off, my forehead scar, moles and blocky chin didn't seem as noticeable. *Am I pretty enough for James? Why else would he have been so sweet to me?*

I returned to the couch with his T-shirt hanging down to my thighs. James emerged from his bedroom doorway off the living room, shirtless. *Oh, my.* Hormones spread through my hips like wildfire. The waistband of his plaid boxers hung low on his hips. In the dim light, his muscles looked carved from marble. My lower half began to throb with desire.

I tugged at the baggy T-shirt. "It doesn't fit." My body temperature began rising under his clothes. I pushed my long curls off my shoulders, sending him another signal.

James laughed. "I'm glad it doesn't."

I lay down across the three cushions of the couch. James's pecs flexed as he draped a fuzzy blanket over me. "Good night, Kermie," he said with a smile, before disappearing into his bedroom. *Wow. What a gentleman.* A McNugget of my naughty tipsy side wanted him to grab me by the neck and plunge his tongue deep into my mouth. His restraint seemed romantic, yet perplexing in my groggy state of mind.

I looked up at James's cathedral ceiling in the darkness, shaming Chris and his irresponsibility. He deserved to be deserted. He was ruining my good credit! If I'd lived another day with him, I could have been arrested for drug possession. We were beyond done. James was a clean-cut, future doctor with manners that could put a five-star-hotel concierge to shame—everything Chris could never be.

Gusts of wind shook the palm trees outside the window. I pulled the blanket to my chin and stared at James's bedroom door in the dark, picturing my legs dangling off the back of a boat in the ocean of possibility.

A DOOR CREAKED in the middle of the night, startling me. I sat up on the couch in drunken disorientation. A Richter-scale-worthy headache started bagging between my ears. My eyes finally focused on James's silhouette in the doorway to his bedroom. He wore only cotton boxer shorts. My heart began to pound harder than Donkey Kong on a barrel. A streetlight outside the window bathed the room in hues of gray.

"Were you asleep?" he whispered, his southern accent lingering in the air like cologne.

"No," I lied.

James rubbed his biceps. "I can't sleep either. It's freezing out here. Aren't you cold?"

I shrugged and rubbed away the remnants of my goose bumps. I'd never been inside a Miami building that wasn't colder than an icebox. The wind continued howling. I tried to listen to the rain and not my runaway thoughts.

"Come in here and warm up." His voice sounded as caring as my grandma's. My heart hammered against my chest. I gripped the edge of the couch, looking at him in the darkness, speechless. He extended his bare arm. "Don't worry. I won't bite."

My body raised slowly, weighted with conflicting thoughts. *What does he mean? Does he want to cuddle?* I never had the courage to ask myself (or the guys) such important questions before entering a bedroom, and I should have known the answer. Ninety-nine-point-nine times, they want sex. I was at the nascent stage of understanding young men and their true motivations in relationships.

My toes pushed into the plush carpet. His long, soft fingers laced between mine, and I felt like I'd just tried on a new pair of shoes—fancy Steve Madden platforms.

His bedroom doorknob clicked behind us. James was a door into yet another world of new discoveries. Feelings of guilt and nervousness began battling in my chest. *Was my unspoken breakup with Chris official enough, or is this cheating?* I took a deep breath and exhaled, feeling James's T-shirt heavy on my chest.

A parking lot light outside his window gave his bedroom an eerie glow. My eyes moved from the waistline of James's thin boxers to his muscular chest. A gold chain around his neck twinkled. His room had no furniture, only a couple cardboard moving boxes in the corner and a double mattress on the floor—the frat-house special.

Pump the brakes on this train. That's what should have been going through my mind. I looked down at his baggy T-shirt and felt like a sorority girl shacking up.

"No need to buy furniture if I'm not staying long, right?" I could hear the smile in his voice. "It's more comfortable than the couch. I promise." His hand pressed against the small of my back. Tiny currents surged under my skin, blocking my ears from hearing the words "not staying long." James had moved to Miami from Georgia in September and seemed as unsettled as me. He wasn't leaving for Gainesville until next summer, so we had plenty of time to start a serious relationship.

He kneeled in front of the mattress then pulled back a fluffy down comforter. His hand glided me down to the floor. He tucked me under the blanket, and I quickly turned my back to him. The heat of his skin next to mine made my heartbeat do the Roger Rabbit. I couldn't stop the waves of lust thrusting through my tipsy body. He'd invited me over. He'd waited on me hand and foot. He'd covered me in blankets.

He really cares about me. This is the first step to making our relationship legitimate.

James's fingers gripped my shoulder softly, turning my body toward him. His hazel eyes sparkled in the dim light. I lay there like a mummy trying not to touch him, while my hormones did somersaults between my legs.

He pressed his tongue hard into my mouth, locking his lips onto mine. My lower body throbbed like a kick drum under his boxers.

"Should I stop?" James began kissing my ear, softly. I lay immobilized like a patient on a stretcher. My mind ping-ponged between the discomfort with my own body, the thrill of being with someone new, and the shame of leaving Chris without a proper breakup. My moral compass was looping like a hula hoop.

I stared at his dark ceiling, letting my mind reel. "Umm. I guess I'm okay." My voice shook with trepidation. I looked away toward the window. *No turning back now.* Sure, I really liked James, but I didn't want him to think I was a slut. I didn't feel ready to sleep together yet, but I'd crawled into his bed. Before I'd met Chris, whenever a guy would kiss me, sex followed. Making out was a runaway train heading straight to sex central, and I could never stop it. I thought my right to consent ended once I'd walked in his bedroom door.

Our tongues starting darting around our bodies like frogs catching flies. My mind began to justify the situation. *You've spent six days a week with this guy for two months. You're not sleeping with a stranger. He's a server like you. He's going back to college like you. He's got a southern accent!* Once I'd started giving boys what they'd wanted, they'd always stuck around. And I wanted James to stick around. Having sex and feeling love were symbiotically chained in my gullible heart.

James continued kissing my lips in his tender, sweet way before pulling his boxers off me. He unwrapped a conveniently accessible condom. His consideration seemed so romantic. *He wraps it. He really cares.* I glossed over his presumption and wrapped my arms tight around his shoulders, waiting for him to be close to me in the most intimate way—making me feel wanted, filling my heart with love.

🍺 🍷 🍸 🍶 🍾

WORKING AT A restaurant and not expecting to get involved with a coworker is kind of like going to a dog park and not expecting to step in shit. Sixty hours a week, we were rubbing elbows and trading jokes on the floor. The average couple spends about twenty waking hours together weekdays. When we weren't socializing while serving guests, we chose to relish in the same pleasures at bars where the tables were turned. Our post-shift beers were dark, flavorful and mysterious to me. I could feel my taste improving, and James played a pivotal role in my metamorphosis. Getting loaded together after a long shift in the wee hours of the morning was about as close to a date as I could get with James. But, I didn't mind. The server lifestyle of after-hours socializing and imbibing thrilled my inner country bumpkin.

Groping was always on the menu. Blame it on all the Madonna videos we watched. I never thought twice about it. My boobs were so small that only my gay friends grabbed them anyway. Regardless of how touchy we were with coworkers, I kept my relationship with James "all business" at work. Upon arrival at the restaurant, I didn't greet James with a double-cheek kiss like all the Latin American servers did. When he passed me at the bread station, I never pinched his butt. When we folded napkins, I didn't sit in the booth next to him—I'd sit across from him. I delivered his desserts and folded half of his napkins, showing my love as only a working waitress could. I began "closing down" Loggerhead with James, outspoken Alicia (a loud, bushy-haired Colombian girl with a Brooklyn accent) and other coworkers every night, slurping my mug of Red Dog until the bar lights went on, waiting for him to invite me to sleep over. Even when James told guys at work that we'd slept together, I didn't get mad. Guys don't like girls who bitch and nag.

I moved into a bright, airy apartment in an old Spanish-style building in Coconut Grove. It had a charming courtyard filled with coconut palms and banyans that towered above the bay windows of my second-floor bedroom. A little slice of tropical heaven. Alicia became my part-time roommate, paying me $200 per month to keep a futon in the living room. I'd never lived alone before and didn't feel tough enough to start then. Only ten years had passed since the 1980s drug wars; I'd grown up watching way too much *Miami Vice.*

My new place was located on a tree-lined street less than a mile from work and just five blocks from James's apartment—a big factor in my decision. When I wasn't daydreaming about James playing guitar on my couch, I pondered transferring to University of Florida for fall semester, even though our entire romance fit inside a two-week pay period.

&&&&&

A WAVE OF new hires arrived at Cheesecake to relieve us from the endless string of double shifts, and there were enough hot chicks to fill a Pussycat Dolls' roster. James didn't look at the new girls any differently than the other servers, busboys and line cooks. I stared at their curvy butts and full breasts, too. The sexy meter always ran high with female servers in Miami. It was (and still is) a beautiful place filled with beautiful people.

James and I were promoted to junior trainers and asked to shadow two hotties on their floor shifts—a skinny blonde named Ashley with big teeth and bigger boobs and an adorably pencil-thin Latina ballerina named Victoria. When around those girls, my chest felt so flat and my hips so wide, I considered experimenting with bulimia.

After two days of shadow shifts, James stopped showing up at Loggerhead for our usual post-shift pitchers. *He's just tired from work*, I told myself. I doubled down on my *subtle* displays of love. I hugged and kissed him at first sight before each shift. I buzzed through the dining room, clearing the dirty plates on James's tables, running his appetizers, delivering his cappuccinos and cheesecakes and folding his napkins. Boundaries were for border patrol, I thought. If I would have been any farther up his ass, I could have kissed his bellybutton.

"What are you doing for Thanksgiving?" I asked James during pre-shift in the back hallway. It was mid-November, and we'd been sleeping together for three weeks, despite a five-day dry spell. It seemed like an eternity to me.

He shrugged his shoulders and kept his eyes fixed on the napkin stack in his lap.

"It's my first holiday away from my family," I replied, folding napkins on an upside down milk crate—our usual makeshift seating. "I don't have plans yet." I'd been planning—what I'd wear and what I'd say to his parents once he invited me to spend the holidays at their winter home in Coral Gables. We were sexually involved, which meant we were serious, and serious meant time to meet his parents. My dating ignorance was thicker than Everglades swamp air.

"Who wants to share a jambalaya?" James called out, turning his back to me.

THERE ARE ONLY two seasons in South Florida, season and off-season. Season started in late October or early November, when the humidity released its grip over our coastal city and tourists flooded in. Working in a restaurant that had a wait-list all day seven days a week, I didn't notice much of a difference in the annual cycle at first. During season, there were more Canadians. More old people. More piña colada orders.

The daily cycle of a server's lifestyle, however, became much more evident. Eat, work, party, sleep. Do it all over again. Watching the white-clad servers lumber into the restaurant with zombie faces never got old from the perch of my milk crate. Half of the staff played deep in party animal jungle and half stayed on the sidelines. It made for great gossip.

One Sunday morning, James stumbled into the back hallway of CocoWalk before our brunch shift. Dark bags weighed down his sensitive eyes. His wet, tousled hair had lost its perfect part. He wore a wrinkled white apron with coffee stains from the previous shift.

"Look what the cat dragged in," Micah sneered with a stack of napkins in his lap. "You look like Eddie Vedder on a bender."

James dropped his backpack and collapsed onto a spare milk crate—halfway down the hall from me.

I marched to the wall and clocked my time card, watching him zip straight to the soup station for a hangover lube job.

An hour later, while filling water mugs in the main bus stand, I noticed Ashley and her big boobs, wildly stuffing straws in Bloody Marys at the bar. Ashley loved partying until dawn and smoking marijuana. She had dropped out of University of Florida after her freshman year and didn't know what she wanted to do with her life. She liked to talk about Gainesville with James, who was eager to become a Gator. Being a dropout didn't seem like enough common ground for me to buddy up with a lost soul like Ashley. I wanted to be surrounded by focused, responsible people like me—people like James.

Ashley slid the highball glasses onto a cork tray. "That party was off the hook." She was chatting up Krista, a bartender with porcelain skin and black-painted fingernails. Ashley's ponytail was cockeyed, her eyes bloodshot. A crooked, striped tie fell between her big boobs. She continued gabbing about Fat Cat nightclub. "They" didn't leave the club until eight in the morning and "they" had to be at work for the brunch shift by nine thirty.

The blender in my head started churning a recipe for drama. My fists squeezed the full mugs of water in both hands until my knuckles turned white.

"Behind you!" I charged out of the bar area toward my station. My lips forced a smile at every table while "Hey Jealousy" by the Gin Blossoms played over and over in my head; I tried to distract myself with my customers' needs—who didn't have bread, who needed a coffee refill, etc. Ashley and James—the party-all-night duo—were always close enough for me to smell the booze oozing from their pores, punching orders and delivering cheesecakes. Their eyes were as bloodshot as a banshee. Micah said he'd bet me an Alabama Slammer they'd been popping pills. It was my first peek into a dark side that often comes with the unrelenting pace of restaurant life.

But, my obligatory smile remained. Only lame girlfriends whined about the friends their men hung around. I always wanted to be the cool chick that never got jealous; I thought that was a big reason why guys end up falling in love with a girl.

THANKSGIVING WEEK ARRIVED with its balmy, sun-drenched days. I was still wearing shorts and tank tops outside of work. I was also still waiting for James to invite me to meet his parents. Every forty-eight hours, the cycle repeated: go to work, see James, get brushed off, drink, sleep, work, hear about James's partying with the lead pussycat.

"I don't know what went wrong," I whispered, my head hanging over a cup of soup in the back hallway. I looked down at an artichoke heart and sliced it with my spoon. "He's a far better match for me than Chris." I glanced over at Linda, standing across from me in the back hallway behind Cheesecake Factory, wearing her whites and a polka-dot tie. She twirled a straw in her mug of Diet Coke. The word "confrontation" was still as foreign to me as *churros*, so I'd asked her to do some snooping. Linda was the oldest daughter of a police captain in Tampa, who ran their house like a cadet academy. She'd fully embraced the secret investigation project. I pressed my back against the scuffed white wall to take the weight off my aching legs.

Linda rested her mug on the concrete floor then draped a white napkin over a milk crate neatly. "You shot craps, Kermie." She sat down on the makeshift seat. "You slept with a guy who's leaving for med school, and you did it before you'd moved out of the apartment you shared with your boyfriend." She took a precise sip of her soda. "That's borderline cheating, and cheaters never get respect." I looked down the hall to make sure no one was listening. Plates banged, and voices shouted from the kitchen.

I grabbed a milk crate with both hands and flipped it upside down. Her words felt like spears of asparagus pelting my face. Or maybe just rotten eggs. "It was over with Chris." I dropped onto my crate and sank my head in my hands. "James knew that. I'm the right girl for him, not her." James had a shelf life in Miami, and I ignored it. Ten months seemed like plenty of time to fall crazy in love and build a life together before he left for med school. I should have known we'd expire faster than a boat of balsamic vinaigrette.

"His idea of the *right* girl is the one he's fucking *right* now," Linda said. She never pulled any punches. "The guy is twenty-two years old and has eight months of freedom before med school. A serious relationship is the last thing on his mind." I glanced down at my white sneakers, feeling dirty and alone. James had tossed my heart into the trash like a bag of expired lettuce. James, his guitar and his diploma fit neatly into my world—he was the right guy for me, the polar opposite of Chris. My dating pendulum could swing farther than Tiger Woods with a nine iron.

I placed the half-full cup of chicken-artichoke soup in an empty bus tub on the concrete floor. She'd nailed me.

I sighed deeply. "But we slept together five times." I leaned back against the wall and banged my head in frustration. "I woke up with his arms around me. He kissed me in the morning. He invited me back again and again." I couldn't imagine sex being meaningless to someone. Sex wasn't just physical to me. A bond formed. The guy had to feel that emotion, too. When it came to understanding how men were wired, I was still wearing training wheels.

"It was a fling. You gotta move on." She straightened the crease on her apron without raising her eyes to mine. My shoulders caved. Her brutal honesty made me feel like a freshly sliced fillet on a fishmonger's table. She was always insightful and accurate.

I reached for my mug of water, feeling the shame roll down my long face. Sex had jumpstarted almost every long-term relationship I'd ever had. James shouldn't have been any different. I returned to banging my head against the wall.

"You also forgot a golden rule of dating—never start a relationship just before the holidays," she smirked. I'd never heard that before, but I've watched it play out in my life and with my friends for twenty years since Linda's golden nugget. Winter holidays are a ticking time bomb for new relationships. The Holy Grail of serious coupledom. It's like guys think they only have two choices—bring the girl home or dump her. Once she's carved a turkey with Mom, forget it. The ring must come next...

Linda adjusted the headband in her brown, wavy hair. "You're not in Kansas anymore. You need to watch out. Marriage is the farthest thing from these guys' minds. College guys think with their dicks. And dicks are trouble." She raised her soda to her lips. Her hazel eyes stayed fixed on my face. We sat in silence, listening to plates bang in the kitchen. I felt as dirty and used as oil in a deep fryer.

She shoved a finger at my face. "And cut back on the alcohol. It's bad for your legs."

"Huh?" I asked, puzzled. "What does it do to your legs?"

Linda leaned closer to me. "It makes them spread."

The heat of embarrassment flushed my cheeks. I tugged on the straw in my water mug. "Thanks for making me feel like shit." I took a long drink, soaking in her advice. I straightened my blue-flowered tie. Her sharp words were still seeping through my skin. It was my first real dose of dating reality as a Miamian.

"How about you eighty-six the assholes," she said, primping her hair. "Find a nice, stable guy without a moving date."

I wiped away a falling tear. "I'll never fold his napkins again."

Micah's head popped out from around the corner. "Well, that sounds kinky."

Our laughter rippled through the empty hallway. My life wasn't a falling stack of dirty dishes. Maybe I'd lost James, but I'd found some great new friends—a kaleidoscope of personalities who'd all came to Miami in search of a new life and ended up waiting tables together. Linda, Micah, Alicia,

Walter the gay interior design student, Angela the gay biologist graduate student, Rupert the gay gold digger, Diana the Egyptian lesbian who swore she could convince me to switch teams—they were my Miami family. I belonged with them on Thanksgiving.

ROBERT
The Cocktail Days

I crossed over into Robert's world with what seemed like a fearless move: I bought him a drink.

Staring into the murky bottom of my third White Russian, I couldn't think of a more mature way to show my interest in the hot blond across the smoky room, towering over his huddle of friends. For two hours, I'd been perched on my favorite barstool at Dan Marino's in CocoWalk, praying that Robert would come talk to me while my wing-woman Alicia ran the pool table. Sending him a highball of booze? It was my Hail Mary pass—my first and only play of the night. A whole week had passed since the fallout with James. Dating was like breathing for me, and if men were the oxygen of life, the bar was my air tank. As a kid, I'd spent many Sunday afternoons with my dad and his hunting buddies at the American Legion, stocking up on male attention.

Three hours later, Robert tugged me toward the shore along Biscayne Bay, his curly hair glowing under the moonlight. "Trust me. It's worth it." The words flew from his mouth as his smooth hands gripped mine.

The thrill of his touch surged up my arms. *This cannot be happening.* My nerves tangled with the remnants of alcohol in my bloodstream. *He is for real.* I bounced behind him, feeling sand pour into my sandals as dreams of us sprinted through my head. (I'm not saying you should add "picking up a guy in a bar" to your dating bucket list, but it does wonders for the ego until the vodka wears off.)

A few yards ahead, the Key Biscayne lighthouse sprayed a fuzzy beam into the starry sky.

Robert lifted his muscular arm in the air. "You see those tiny red lights? That's Stiltsville." His skin was a deep, golden tan from countless hours spent boating. Golden ringlets bounced around his head as he described the village of abandoned overwater shacks one mile offshore. He looked like he'd just left the set of a Nautica photo shoot in his yellow golf shirt, white dress shorts and boat shoes. His Ivy League look seemed so foreign to a girl who had grown up wearing camouflage.

I looked down at our laced hands and prayed my palm wouldn't get sweaty.

We flipped off our shoes, and wet sand squished under my toes. I rolled up my Gap jeans, watching the full moon reflect a glistening strip of white on the water's dark surface. My thoughts continued to race with my pulse. *I'm standing at the edge of the Atlantic Ocean with a gorgeous guy, wearing a sleeveless top and jeans...in December.* No one had told me that my parka-free paradise would be filled with beautiful beaches *and* hot men.

The lighthouse's rotating beam of light flashed over the calm, endless bay.

"What's that blobby thing?" I pointed to an iridescent bubble floating a few inches from the beach.

"Jellyfish. Portuguese Man O'Wars." Robert clicked his tongue. "Watch out for the tentacles." My eyes danced around Robert's face as his arms demonstrated the length. Robert had grown up in Miami and knew more about the city than any of my coworkers.

"Well, it looks pretty harmless." My head bobbed with confidence. "Try looking a forty pound carp in the eye after midnight. That'll sober you up." My cool voice rippled with the waves. Showing off my night-fishing prowess was required because the matchmaking cards were stacked against me higher than Kid n' Play's flattop. When Robert wasn't waiting tables at Dan Marino's (he'd just gotten off work that night), he modeled on South Beach: men's suits, underwear...the real shit. I couldn't believe such an Adonis had just swooped into my life. You'd expect to find a guy like him on a deserted island, swimming in a blue lagoon with Brooke Shields, not serving burgers and pints in a shopping center.

Dating another coworker seemed out of the question, but dating a fellow server with the same night-owl schedule seemed as genius as the advent of the crimping iron.

Robert's teeth sparkled in the light of the moon. "Glad you know your way around the water. Most girls don't." His hand grabbed mine for the third time. Tiny currents bolted through my chest as he tugged me toward a nearby jetty. I scuttled right behind him like a Chihuahua trying to hump his leg.

A secluded wall of moonlit boulders jetted out from a sandy shoreline. My long curls floated off my shoulders in the gentle sea breeze. I wore a black belly shirt, and my exposed skin tingled from the subtle chill in the night's air. The fashion philosophy in Miami was always less is more—less fabric and more skin—which had motivated me to drop another eight pounds.

I inhaled the salty air, savoring the moment. Years had trickled by since I'd felt pretty enough to woo a boy like Robert. But the busboys and line cooks at work had been lathering me in compliments. Every body part I'd written off as hopeless the Latin guys praised. My confidence was growing faster than Barry Bond's biceps.

Robert pulled his body effortlessly onto the rocks. "You scared?"

"No." I scaled the boulder with his helping hands. "Why should I be?" Skyscrapers splashed shades of lavender and pink onto the bay—back when the only high rises in downtown Miami were banks and a couple Brickell condo towers.

"We just met." Robert glided from rock to rock like Baryshnikov, his toned calf muscles flexing. "And you're still a newbie." He rattled off the names of every lit building and bridge on the mainland.

"I can handle myself." I swaggered behind him, my sea legs enjoying the waterside exercise. MacArthur Causeway's neon pillars looked like lightsabers in the distance.

Robert turned to me from a few rocks ahead. His glittery, green eyes were like tractor beams, and I couldn't fight the pull.

"Come closer." He waved his arms like a *maître'd* ushering me to a table.

I would have followed him to Jonestown and drank his Kool-Aid.

My pulse dashed as I hopped toward him, watching my sandals touch each wet rock. We stared out into the inky bay, listening to the occasional car whiz by on the causeway. A candy-pink glow began to form on the horizon.

"It's way past time for a midnight swim." He grabbed my hand, tugging me back along the rocky ridge toward the shore.

When we reached the beach, my heels dug in the sand. "I don't skinny dip."

Robert pulled off his golf shirt and threw it on the shore. "That's your problem, not mine." *Time to change the subject.*

"I can't believe it's almost winter." I rolled up my jeans above the knees. "And we're about to go for a swim." My mom would be scraping ice off her windshield in a few hours. Robert had studied for two years at Brown, a private university in Rhode Island, but had just moved back home because he'd hated the weather.

"I can't believe you're going to wear those jeans in the water."

"I'll come prepared next time," I smirked.

Robert shook his head in frustration. "You'll want to come back here again and again." Robert unzipped his shorts and dropped them to the sand. Only a pair of cotton boxers remained on his lean, smooth body. *Holy fuck. I have more hair under my fuzzy navel than him.* I gulped a mouthful of salty air. *This is never going to work.*

He raised both arms to the rising sun like a preacher at the altar. "You'll never want to leave Miami. It's not just the weather." He waded in, gliding his hands across the water's surface. "No one will judge you here. You can be yourself. Your spirit is free."

The sky turned pink, and I looked down at my body in the glow of morning sun. His sermon-like speech soaked into my skin. *No one will judge you.*

I followed him in. It only took a few hours for that man to become my captain. At the bar, Robert had twirled the straw in his Tanqueray & Tonic like a majorette leading a band. Another box checked: his taste in alcohol. Any guy who didn't hunch over a beer mug like Norm on *Cheers* aced part one of my dating litmus test.

As the cool water climbed my bare legs, I was oblivious to the reality of what could happen after a girl leaves a bar with a stranger. Have you seen photos of Ted Bundy in suit? He was pretty good-looking, too. When Robert had ordered me his go-to, courting cocktail—Sex on the Beach—I'd shrugged off the trepidation. He had the kind of personality you'd expect would buy such an inappropriate drink: confident and presumptive. The schnapps must have clogged my common sense valve. Then again, nothing says, "I'm an easy target" quite like hitting on a guy in a bar. But there were good signs! We both liked our drinks on the rocks. We shared a passion for all things outdoors and aquatic. We were both servers. We were both on hiatus from college. Little did I know, finding a guy who's at the same place in life is a good thing when you're thirty and gainfully employed—not while you're an underage college dropout.

I fought back a yawn as the salty water splashed against my calves. "What time is it?" Shades of orange and pink flowed across the sky.

Robert shrugged his shoulders. "Who cares? We'll sleep when we're dead."

I stood knee-deep in the water, nodding, letting his words seep into my brain. It was a mantra I'd remember for the rest of my life. The water sloshed against Robert's bare chest. He extended his hands to me like an impatient parent. "Come on. It feels amazing out here."

I stepped slowly toward him, feeling the thighs of my jeans soak up water. Before I could take the next hesitant step, he whipped back around.

His face looked Tang orange in the rising sun. "I'm hungry. Let's go to Denny's." He barreled toward the beach, his wake sloshing me. I cracked a giggle. Robert could switch gears faster than Mario Andretti.

A few hours later, we tiptoed into my apartment.

"We have to shower or we'll itch for days." Robert's whisper had a dire sense of urgency.

I gasped. "I can't shower with you. I hardly know you."

"We just spent the last seven hours together." Robert pulled off his shirt in the darkness of my tiny bathroom. "You know more about me than most people."

I stared at his lean, toned body, as he stripped off his underwear. He turned his firm, hairless butt cheeks to me, and I looked away in a blush.

"Stop being a prude," he whispered, stepping into the shower.

I pulled off my clothes and stepped into the shower backwards, hiding the scars and my gremlin crotch.

"Turn around," he barked, inspecting me. "You're worried about me seeing that? It's hardly noticeable." He rubbed the loofa on my flat stomach. My forehead gashes? The model man didn't even notice. My heart filled with love as he washed sand, salt and my insecurities down the drain. I felt bonded to him with super glue.

He rubbed his hair dry with my towel. "Cool if I crash here?"

I grabbed another towel and wrapped it quickly around my torso. "Well, uh, my roommate is here. I don't know if she'd be cool with it."

He tucked my towel around his waist like a skirt. "She'll never even know I was here." *Yeah, right.*

As the morning sun peeked through my blinds, Robert crawled into my bed. "I won't do anything you don't want me to do." His palm stroked my blank face.

I lay on my bed, frozen and expressionless, like Beavis and Butt-Head watching TV. My ears strained to hear my roommate's sleeping breath through the bi-fold plantation doors that separated us. He didn't know my middle or last name, my birthday or my phone number. It was that uncomfortable situation I found myself in times before: not ready to have sex with a guy but unsure of what to say. I'd let him into the most intimate place, my bedroom, not realizing the levity of expectation that brings.

He reached for my towel.

"Wait," I whispered.

"Shhh," he said, kissing me.

"No," I whispered.

"Shhh."

My lips stopped moving. Giving in was always easier than saying, "no." *Just shut up and let him do what he wants.* I'd learned that self-esteem crushing tactic my sophomore year of college after inviting a frat boy to my apartment for a beer. I'd said "no" and "wait" so many times in my bedroom, but he'd just kept pushing. I didn't consider it rape or sexual assault; I'd felt angry with myself and avoided him at all costs for the rest of my days on campus. That first night with Robert seemed different. Robert had seen my scars and still wanted to sleep with me. My heart was already his.

I needed an elevator pitch. Why didn't I have a game plan for how to talk about having The Talk? I put more effort into prepping for a presentation at school than planning to have a serious conversation about sex *before* sex. Only one of those things could lead to herpes! The Talk deserved to be rehearsed more times than a school play. That remains one of my greatest dating regrets.

🍺 🍷 🍸 🍶 🍸

EVERY NIGHT WITH Robert started and finished just like the first. His only speed? Warp. He'd work a double-shift and want to go dancing until three on South Beach. He could drink beer until eight o'clock in the morning then insist we eat egg-white omelets at his favorite diner. The only meal we ever ate at a restaurant was breakfast *before* bed—how's that for a sign that your relationship is unconventional? Robert didn't have an off button, and he never ran out of batteries. I couldn't help but wonder if he was part-vampire like Corey Haim's hot brother from *The Lost Boys*.

Not since my sophomore year of high school, when a svelte lifeguard who drove a T-top Camero asked me out, had I dated a guy as handsome as Robert. I'd expected a one-night stand even though I'd wanted so much more from someone who seemed so far above my league. I began exerting extra energy into all aspects of life. I Rollerbladed faster and farther. I switched to non-fat milk in my White Russians. I applied my make-up like a patient artist instead of a NASCAR driver taking a time-trial lap.

The early morning shower ritual went south fast—literally—when, despite my wet-lipped pleas, he grabbed a disposable razor and shaved off my gremlin bush. "The sex is way better without all the hair," he said. My crotch looked like a freshly plucked chicken and felt like a fire ant attack. *Welcome to dating a big city boy*, I thought.

The things I did for that man.

When he lit up a cigarette and offered me the half-empty pack of Marlboro Lights, I coolly pulled out a cancer stick and took a couple puffs. When Robert passed me a joint behind Loggerhead, I plucked the doobie from his fingers and took a long drag. Chris would have lost his Doritos! I needed Robert to believe I was 100 percent cool and zero percent country. I bought a Motorola pager—life before cell phones!—so he could reach me 24/7. I felt really important.

When Robert disappeared for a few days, I didn't complain. He worked two jobs and spent most mornings rowing crew. Within a week of sleeping together, he'd invited me to go camping near Lake Okeechobee the week before Christmas. Robert already considered me a part of his future, too.

I spent many nights perched on that same barstool at Dan Marino's, waiting for his shift to end. Watching his golden curls bounce across the dining room, I sipped sweet cocktails, relishing the pleasure of my independent existence in a new world. A White Russian's rich flavors of vanilla, coffee and cream were the perfect replacement for my favorite comfort drinks back home: root beer and chocolate milk. Little did I know, sweet cocktails branded me—too immature to be a bonafide barfly, too inexperienced to drink the classics. Robert never tried to upgrade my taste; maybe *that* was a sign.

MY PHONE RANG on a Sunday morning. No surprise there. My mom called me every Sunday at 9 a.m. sharp after she got home from early Mass—right before my brunch shift. I dropped my white oxford on the ironing board and grabbed the receiver.

"Thank God I found you." Robert's voice charged through the line. His breaths trembled between every word. "I need your help." My hand gripped the receiver. My throat got tight. *Help?*

"What's going on? Are you okay?" I shrieked from the shock. I stood frazzled in the middle of my apartment, wearing only panties and a bra.

"Alicia isn't there, is she...is she there?"

"No," I replied, my mind dashing. "Why?"

"Good. I don't want her to know. You can't tell her I called."

I felt as if I'd been parachuted into a soap opera love triangle. *Are they pulling a* Three's Company *on me?*

"You're scaring me." My voice wobbled. He'd been trying to get her to "bless" our relationship for weeks. The morning after his first sleepover, Alicia had said, "Too cute. He's trouble."

"What does she have to do with anything?" My voice cracked. Gorgeous Latinas like Alicia were always requesting Robert's station at Dan Marino's. I pictured the two of them having beers at Loggerhead while I was still closing my station at the restaurant. Maybe they went out back to smoke some weed. *I know where that leads...*

"I don't know. I don't know..." Robert's chaotic voice trailed off. The hum of the silent phone line crowded my racing brain. "I just don't want her to know." I looked over at Alicia's empty futon. My tongue felt like a rock.

The fear plunged deeper into the pit of my stomach. "Know what?" The silent line hummed so long, I could only hear my heart pounding.

"Robert, are you there?" I pressed the receiver so close, my earlobe throbbed. Adrenaline pumped through my anxious body.

"Shhhh...wait," he whispered. "I think someone is follow—" His last words were cut off by the beep of my Call Waiting. I growled. *Not now, Mom!*

"What did you say?" I gasped. "Damn Call Waiting."

"Who could be calling you right now?" His voice shrilled at the pitch of a fighting tomcat. "Who knows you're home?" I looked down at my tanned body. Happy thoughts of my first winter without thermal underwear were replaced by fear. It felt like I'd been tossed into a Wes Craven movie.

"It's my mom," I replied, pacing. "What is going on? Where are you?"

"I don't know where I am!" Every word was draped in panic. "Someone is following me. Please come get me. I need you." The sound of Robert's shaking breaths filled the line.

"I'm right here," I replied with the calmness of a 911 dispatcher. "Take a deep breath." Visions of kidnappings and ransom notes poured into my head.

"What do you see around you?" My instincts from watching years of *America's Most Wanted* kicked in. "I need you to tell me details of your surroundings, so I can figure out where you are. Street signs, house numbers, papers. Anything."

"I'm in someone's apartment." He raced through the words. "I did an eight ball at Liquid. I haven't been to sleep yet."

"You did a what?" I sounded as sheepish as an 80-year-old grandma who'd just seen her first computer. "An eight ball?" The vision of the black ball on a pool table rolled through my mind. If I'd spent the last twenty years living under a rock, my knowledge about illegal drugs and men would have pretty much equaled what I'd learned growing up in rural Kansas.

"You know. Blow. Cocaine?" Robert paused. "Oh, you don't. You are too cute." My ear began tingling against the humming receiver. Shock slammed through my chest. "My head is going to explode. I don't ever want to feel like this again. Why didn't I just go to your place last night?"

"Why?" I whispered, my head reeling. My whole body shuddered. It was seventy-five degrees outside, and my windows were open. I needed a blanket, and I no longer owned one. I thought of Jami Gertz snorting coke with a rolled dollar bill in *Less Than Zero* and gnawed my thumbnail.

"Babe, this is Miami Beach." Robert's tone was smug. "It comes with the territory. It's not a big deal."

The hum of the phone line filled my ears. My lips trembled. "I guess...I...I didn't know." My mouth hung open from the shock. The underbelly of big city life had just been served to me—straight up with a twist. Coke was way beyond my discomfort zone with marijuana.

"You're so good for me." Robert's voice boomed in my ears. "I won't do it again if you don't want me to."

I squeezed the phone cord, my heart sputtering.

"Nevermind. Everything's cool. I'll call you later, babe. Love you." The phone clicked.

My mind began a tailspin. My boyfriend just told me he did coke and he loved me all in the same phone call. I threw on my work shirt and raced up the buttons. *My life is becoming a* Miami Vice *episode. All that's missing is the boat and some guns.*

I stepped in front of my bathroom mirror and stared at my tan face—the strong jawline, high cheekbones and jagged forehead scar. *Robert loves me. All of me.* I ran a pick through my curly hair, letting our whacked out conversation sink in. This beautiful, troubled man loved me, and he'd said *it* first. Guys didn't drop the "L" word unless they meant it.

My thoughts ricocheted from walking on the beach with Robert to fishing ponds with my dad. After he'd returned from the Navy, Dad had started going heavy on the beer—Busch was his can of choice. Mom had begged Dad to join Alcoholics Anonymous (AA) for years, but he never did. Before I'd hit puberty, our familial bond had already dissolved faster than a sand castle at high tide. A five-hour car ride to college seemed like enough distance from the situation, and then I'd moved halfway across the country. My interactions with him had been limited to a monthly phone call.

I should have tried harder with my dad.

If I stand by Robert, I can at least make one wrong right.

I grabbed the phone book and scanned the yellow pages. *New Jack City* had taught me everything I needed to know about cocaine: It was addictive. It killed. It made grown men dry hump stuffed rabbits. I needed to be prepared for the worst. I circled all the crisis clinics, addiction centers and hot lines. I plotted my plan while The Cranberries chanted about zombies from my stereo. I'd help him pack his suitcase. I'd hold his hand. I'd visit him every day. I would be the most positive influence of all.

ROBERT MOPED INTO my station at Cheesecake. He paced around a cluster of areca palms while I stood at table thirty-nine, scribbling a Cuban couple's order on my notepad. My heart sank. His golden curls were ratty and dull. His golf shirt was wrinkled. *Oh, my messed up Robert.* Hours had passed since the cocaine call. I grabbed his hands and led him to the fancy wood payphone banks by the bathrooms, feeling the weight of his addiction on my back.

Robert pecked me on the lips then squeezed my shoulders with both hands. "I don't know who I am anymore." His blue-green eyes darted around my face.

"I do." The hum of the busy dining room buzzed in my ears. "This isn't you." His blood-shot eyes watered. He dropped his head like a defeated athlete.

My tongue felt like an inner tube. "I will help you get through this." My hands squeezed his as I stared at the Spanish-tiled floor. A fellow server had cued me in on the symptoms of addiction—high energy, insomnia, confidence and paranoia—which I'd grown to love as Robert's personality.

Robert's eyes ricocheted from my face to the bustling dining room. His body jerked from side to side. He looked like a wild animal caught in a cage. "You'll help me keep away from bad influences?" He gripped my fingers tighter. "You'll keep me out of the clubs?"

I nodded, rubbing his knuckles. It meant steering clear of Jessica, his long-time friend, who lived walking distance from CocoWalk. She had long, red hair and bewitching green eyes and did lots of drugs. Robert used to crash on her couch before he'd started sleeping in my bed.

Robert ran his hands through his messy hair. "It's my addictive personality. I just can't do anything once. I just keep tempting myself." He began pacing, looking down at the octagon tiles.

I wrapped my arms around his waist. "Don't worry. I will be here for you." He dropped his head onto my shoulder and squeezed me tight, like a child hugs a parent. His vulnerability made me feel strong and needed, helping me press through the fear of dating a guy who described himself as "addictive." My father didn't think he had a drinking problem either. "I won't leave you." My voice shook. I wouldn't run away from him like I'd done with Chris. I wouldn't desert him like Dad.

Robert pulled away from me, his face twinkling like a Christmas tree. "Then we have something to celebrate." His somber tone flashed to bright. "Last night is never going to happen again." He gripped my shoulders. "We should drink to that."

OUR CAMPING TRIP fizzled out before the ghetto campfire was even lit. Robert and his friends gathered around the flaming garbage can, rolling and passing joints. Seven days had passed since his sober declaration, and he'd already fallen off the wagon. I scurried off to our cabin and silently bitched him out from inside my borrowed sleeping bag. *Why do I love him so much? What have I gotten myself into?* I'd given pot a chance—and all it had given me was the urge to motorboat a chocolate Bundt cake.

I FLEW HOME for Christmas, and the chill of a Kansas winter felt deeper and darker than any memory.

One afternoon, I went to the American Legion to shoot pool with my dad—our primary way of bonding. Dad paced in a light haze of stale smoke and filtered sunshine, fidgeting with the flip-top on his can of beer. His flannel shirt and Levi's jeans seemed to sag on his bones. He was always a lean man, standing just 5-foot-9 and weighing maybe 160 pounds, but he looked frailer than ever before, even though he always sported full-body long johns under his winter clothes.

His Bass Pro Shops ballcap hid his crystal blue eyes, as he sharpened his cue. "I screwed up this time, Pooh," he said, shaking his head of wavy brown hair. He often called me by my childhood nickname, born from my early obsession with Winnie the Pooh.

"Dad," I said, as solemn as a trial judge. "You have to move on."

"I had everything." He leaned over the green felt table and rocketed a stripe into the corner pocket. "I threw it all away." The words mumbled from his thin lips, ever hidden behind a thick moustache.

I stood in silence next to the jukebox, watching the remorse whitewash his face.

"Maybe I can just wait until he dies and get her back," he said, circling the table for his next shot. "He's pretty old." Most conversations with Dad revolved around the demise of his marriage and his metastic remorse. At the time, my parents had been divorced for about three years, and Mom'd been remarried for six months. My stepfather is thirteen years older than my mom, and was a chain smoker and heavy vodka drinker for decades, so an early death seemed inevitable to all of us. (He's still crushing life at age eighty-two, by the way.)

"Dad, that's not the way to live your life." I watched as he continued to knock stripes in pockets, one by one, mumbling about his mistakes as a husband, wading deeper into his own self-pity. The delicate balance between being self-absorbed and self-aware was one my father never mastered.

I took my turn at the table, trying to focus on the solid purple ball near the corner pocket. Shooting pool at the Legion or hunting in the woods: those seemed like the only ways to get close to my father. He'd usually pop back into the house just in time for breakfast or dinner, but otherwise didn't seem comfortable being at home. He never really engaged in my personal life. He attended a couple of my softball games but stayed in his truck at the far end of the field, and never came to one of my cheerleading performances. Sitting on a barstool or walking alone in the woods was much more palatable than descending into a public place. He was the present participle of parents—always in motion, but easily replaced and lacking clear definition.

Dad ordered another can of beer and continued to mumble about missing my mom. I'm pretty sure he never asked about me—and there was so much to talk about with my new job, my new apartment, my new boyfriend and all of my new friends. Little had changed since I'd left, except my feelings about the meaning of the word "home."

I RETURNED TO Miami and threw myself into work. But, I kept one eye fixed on the restaurant's front door, expecting Robert to bounce in and apologize for the camping trip. Waiting, more waiting. Four days later, I finally got the nerve to walk upstairs to Dan Marino's and call a truce. I missed our nocturnal expeditions; any bad memory had been smothered by my loneliness.

The bartender said Robert had not shown up for his shifts in three days.

The shock felt like a barstool had hit me in the gut. I spent the next two hours marching into every bar and restaurant in CocoWalk and Commodore Plaza, scanning the crowds. I was one White Russian away from shoving his picture in strangers' faces like the psycho cop in *Terminator 2* and saying, "Have you seen this boy?"

Robert had vanished.

For two days, I paced in my apartment, burning tracks in the living room carpet. *Should I call the police? File a missing person's report? Had I learned nothing from* America's Most Wanted? My desperation turned from helplessness to denial to resentment by day six. I'd told him I'd be there for him. He'd slept in my bed. He'd taken me camping. I'd dedicated more time and energy to his addiction than my father's, and I'd known Robert less than one month.

¶¶¶¶¶

LOOKING DOWN AT a stack of napkins on the empty veranda at Cheesecake, I practiced my Robert break-up speech. Each precise crease my hand pressed into the white cloths revealed another layer of his disrespect and desertion. He was less than a zero.

"I just can't let you go on like this," a fellow server named Mark said in his gruff, nasally tone. He collapsed into the booth seat across from me, letting his long legs dangle in the aisle. Mark had been hired about four weeks after the restaurant had opened. He'd lived in Wisconsin as a closet homosexual until age thirty then moved to Miami to liberate himself.

I paused mid-fold and looked over at his 200-pound frame filling the booth. He was blond and hairy with a crooked nose from multiple sports injuries—not an ounce of femininity.

He palmed the stone tabletop with his thick fingers. "I saw your boyfriend."

My eyes practically shot from their sockets. I lunged across the table at Mark. "Where? When? What the hell happened? Is he okay?" The questions fired from my mouth like bullets.

Mark smirked and laced his fingers around the back of his head.

"You're being an asshole!" I pulled my check presenter from my apron and threw it across the table, smacking him square in the chest. Receipts fell like confetti onto the tiled floor.

Mark loosened his tie, coolly. "I'm not sure I should tell you."

"Stop it with the stupid games." My voice hissed.

Mark stared down at his beefy fingers and began gnawing on a jagged cuticle. "I saw him at Jessica's house a couple nights ago." There was an Octomom pregnant pause. My legs began to quiver. "We shared an eight ball." He looked at my aghast face then out the window. "Then we played a little game I like to call 'Three's Company.' He's quite the catcher." He grinned and raised his index finger playfully to his thick lips. The words rolled nonchalantly off his tongue as if he were recounting a dinner order for table nineteen.

My mouth hung wide open in the air as my hands flew to my ruddy cheeks. I looked like the dude in "The Scream" painting. *Holy shit cows!* I couldn't stop the mental picture from forming. I saw my beautiful boyfriend bent over the arm of some couch, his face in Jessica's crotch—while Mark pumped him from behind. My eyelids snapped shut. Vomit stirred in my stomach. I flew from the table into the bathroom around the corner, hearing Mark's voice trail off through the glass veranda door: "Now you know why I didn't tell you sooner."

I stood above the wall of fancy copper sinks, splashing water on my tan face. The violation made me feel like raw meat exposed on hot pavement...under the blazing sun...for a day...being stepped on with dirty feet...until rotting bacteria turned me green and purple. We'd never used a condom once. On the first night, he'd said, "I know I'm clean, are you?" The question made me feel as uncomfortable as a pelvic exam. I was on the pill, which seemed safe enough. I would never drive a car without a seat belt, so why did I have sex without a condom? My brain was missing a safety gauge. In high school, my parents' idea of talking to me about the birds and the bees was sending me to Catechism. We were Catholic. We weren't supposed to have sex before marriage, and taking birth control was a sin.

I darted into the last stall and kneeled in front of the toilet in my white uniform. My fingers laced over the cool toilet seat. A restaurant bathroom?

Close enough to a confessional booth for me. *Hello, God. Are you there? It's me again...*

I returned to the row of sinks and mirrors and gripped the granite countertop with both hands. I looked deep into the reflection of my blue eyes, feeling drops of clarity seep into my bones. It was like staring into a swimming pool that hadn't been touched all night. Our relationship was a horrible chain of events that would scar me for life as wife worthy. *What man would marry a girl with my sexual history?* I'd hit on a stranger in a bar, who happened to be a model, who happened to talk me into having unprotected sex, who happened to smoke weed, who happened to snort cocaine, who happened to fancy an occasional dick in the ass. Not quite the "broadening of my cultural horizons" I'd had in mind.

"Why me?" I whispered to myself in the mirror. The shock numbed my love for Robert, but it couldn't kill it instantly. He'd battled the demons I'd grown up around. Only a girl with my upbringing could see beyond his beauty and accept his faults. My greatest fear had been losing him to a Victoria's Secret model—not to a burly rugby player.

I pulled paper towels from the dispenser and wiped my eyes. My stomach spun like a blender. *What kind of microbial parting gift is growing inside me?* I'd dodged a half-dozen pregnancy bullets in high school and even a STD scare in college. Mainstream awareness of AIDS and HIV was in full swing, thanks to Magic Johnson and Pedro Zamora from MTV's *The Real World: San Francisco*. Birth-control pills wouldn't save me this time. My luck had finally run out.

🍾🥂🍸🍷🍹

FEAR AND DISGRACE kept me confined to my apartment and the restaurant for at least a week. I sulked from table to table and avoided the bus stations where coworkers gossiped. *Sex is going to kill me.* I didn't want to die young. I wanted to be the first woman in my family to graduate from college. I didn't want to be the butt of jokes, either—the girl whose boyfriend dumped her for a guy. Lou Diamond Phillips had taken enough of a beating for hetero mankind when his wife left him for Melissa Etheridge.

I finally visited the holy temple that could end my angst: Planned Parenthood. The nurse's aide ran tests for every sexually transmitted disease possible. Then I waited for the results, biting my nails down to the quick.

My anxiety morphed into an eight ball of anger within days. Robert resurfaced faster than a tennis ball in water once the threesome secret was revealed, and I wanted to crawl into a conch shell at the thought of confronting him. Facing my own demons and his required reinforcements. So, I slammed two Jell-O shots and a White Russian at Fat Tuesday before marching upstairs to Dan Marino's.

Robert counted tips at the bus station, looking hot in his turquoise blue work shirt and khaki shorts. I wore a striped blue T-shirt with my white work jeans and sneakers. My curly hair was bushy and wild—just right for a fight.

The entire scene moved in slow motion. I took two steps toward him, and my legs felt like boat anchors. His head turned toward me. *Crap!* I ducked behind the island bar and grabbed a stool.

The bartender recognized me, and we exchanged smiles.

"The usual?"

"No." I pushed my fake ID across the bar, and he waved me off. Our routine. "I'll have a glass of sauvignon blanc and a water, please." I laced my fingers tight. *Time to change.* My knees twitched with fear under the bar. I didn't want to be that same naïve girl who'd sat on that same barstool and had gotten into this hot mess. I was too sweet—the same way I liked my drinks. Maybe drinking wine could introduce me to a world far away from my bisexual boyfriend.

"Oasis's song, "Wonderwall," drifted from the overhead speakers. *Was I really the one who was gonna save him?* I snarled at the irony. I'd wanted to save Robert. Me, the girl who'd slept with her mom well into middle school, thought she could save a promiscuous drug addict. My priorities in life always mutated into whatever seemed best for my boyfriend—not for me.

"Hey, you." Robert's voice rang in my ears. I looked up from my wine glass to find his sculptured face inches from mine. I stared into his beautiful eyes. My hands began to tremble.

"Hi." My voice shook. His sexy, citrusy smell filled my lungs. I gulped back half of the sauvignon blanc, feeling the alcohol find its comfortable home in my bloodstream. My eyes darted away.

I grabbed the skinny straw in my water glass and started stabbing the ice cubes like an enraged killer. "How? How?" My mind sped through all the pre-rehearsed statements, but my lips could only form one word.

Pull it together, Lisa. There was so much to say. He'd taken Mark's meat. He'd put my life at risk. He'd told me he loved me. That was a strong word—one that men in my family did not toss around often.

Robert looked down at me, stunned. His jaw opened, but he didn't say a word.

I jumped off the barstool and felt the room start to sway. As I stumbled toward the door, tears dribbled down my face.

My Z-24 roared out of the CocoWalk parking garage. I gunned the gas pedal, squealing onto Tigertail Avenue. *Get me far away from this sausage fest!*

Blue and red lights flashed in my rearview mirror. *Holy shit!* My heart hammered against my rib cage. *How many drinks did I have? Three?! I'm going to get the first DUI in my family, seriously?! Take a chill pill, Lisa.* I forced cleansing breaths like a Lamaze class student and kept pumping my brakes. The cop bleeped his sirens at me. *Think, think.*

I grabbed handfuls of pennies from my center console and stuffed them into my mouth—an urban legend about fooling breathalyzer tests. I fumbled my radio dial to a classic jazz station and turned on my blinker, looking like a chipmunk storing nuts. I sucked the copper coins faster than a streetwalker on the job.

By the time the police officer reached my window, the pennies were gone and tears streaked my cheeks.

"I'm so sorry," I sobbed, rubbing my mascara-stained face. I launched into my impromptu explanation, wailing about just breaking up with my boyfriend after a long shift at work, how I was stupid to let my emotions get the most of me while driving. *Thank God I am still wearing half my uniform.*

"License and registration, ma'am!" The officer's voice barked. He had short, black hair and a goatee. I guessed he was Cuban and in his thirties. He filed back to his patrol car with my documents. The hair on my neck stood up. I helplessly watched the officer in my side-view mirror while biting my thumbnail. Crying to cops had gotten me out of three speeding tickets in high school and college, and I prayed it would work again. My driving record, unlike my dating history, was spotless.

He grabbed a metal clipboard from his dash. My pulse pounded while my mind raced. *I cannot get arrested. Who would possibly bail me out?* He began marching back to my car. My hands choked the steering wheel.

The officer leaned down to my window. "Miss, I am giving you a warning." His shoulders squared. "And I think I should escort you home." His voice was stern. The crippling fear loosened its grip as he handed me the clipboard.

My car crawled slower than a float parade the entire eight blocks home. My eyes bounced frantically from the odometer to the rearview mirror. The bright lights of his black and white patrol car trailed close behind me. *You're not off the hook yet. He could still arrest you.* I pictured myself in a jailhouse jumpsuit, awaiting my *Deliverance* moment. *I'd look hideous in orange scrubs.* Tears trickled down my cheeks. I sucked more pennies.

When we reached my apartment building, I pulled onto the grassy parking area. His car inched up next to mine, and I gripped my steering wheel tighter. My nerve endings prickled. *Breathe, just breathe.*

He stepped out of the cop car and marched toward my trunk. I sheepishly opened my door, which felt heavier than a block of concrete. The officer fiddled with his Batman-like belt of weapons; his movements were sharp and stiff like an army sergeant's. I dawdled back to my bumper, faking a few sniffles. My breath reeked of vodka and wine. *Don't breathe, just don't breathe.*

I rubbed my raccoon eyes with both palms. "Thank you for being so kind." My voice quivered.

"You seem like a really nice girl," he said, adjusting the chirping walkie-talkie on his shoulder. "Keep your chin up. Not all guys are jerks." His dark gray uniform looked black in the night.

"I know." My head dropped. "I just have really bad luck with men." I shrugged my shoulders. *I'm officially on the Elizabeth Taylor plan.*

The officer glanced up at the dim streetlight then back to me. "I have something I want to ask you."

My lungs fought for air. *Oh, shit. Here it comes.*

He kicked a few rocks under his black boots. "Would you be interested in having dinner with me some time?"

My jaw locked. I'd been trying to give an Emmy-winning performance to get out of a ticket, and he just wanted to get in my pants. I waited for someone to jump out of the bushes and scream, "Smile! You're on Candid Camera!"

I looked down at my white sneakers. "I can't even think about dating right now." My body began shivering. *This guy is at least ten years older than me, and I look like Alice Cooper. Double gross.*

He stepped closer to me. His eyes meandered from my face to my chest. I took a shaky step back. I was officially creeped out and scared shitless.

"I figured as much." He readjusted the black club on his belt. "Well, if you change your mind, you know where to find me." The CB radio in his patrol car clicked and beeped. I listened to his dispatcher's voice echo as he drove off into the night.

A sigh the size of Lake Okeechobee left my lungs. I stepped into the courtyard of my apartment building and looked up at the moon shining through the branches of a lumbering banyan tree.

How many bullets did I dodge this month? The wake-up call rang out in my head. No more hitting on strangers in bars. No more druggies. No more drinking and driving.

I crawled into my bed and counted my lucky stars—all before midnight.

MARCO
The Shots Days

I stood in the dim hallway, fumbling for my keys in the bottomless black hole of my purse. It was one of those warm, January nights when the ability to wear a sundress made me feel invincible. The three peanut butter and jelly shots didn't hurt, either.

Marco grabbed a fistful of my curls from behind. "Hurry up." The words breathed raspy from his thick lips as he nibbled my neck. Goose bumps rippled down my arms.

I moaned, drinking in his touch outside my front door. "You just wait." I threw him a sassy look and continued digging through my purse. His teeth fondled my earlobe, making my whole body quiver.

My key poked at the dead bolt. "Stop it! I need to concentrate." The scene made me feel even more light-headed than when we'd left the nautical-themed bar.

"You're smashed." Marco's lips tickled my neck. The smell of fancy beer on his breath filled my nose as my key finally slid into the lock.

I shoved open the door. "You think you know me, but maybe you don't." The alcohol coursed through my bloodstream, making my confidence rise. Hanging with a guy like Marco required my palate to venture back to the land of shots. His post-shift drink after a rough night was a shot of Jägermeister with a Johnnie Walker Black and Coke chaser. Drinking Scotch and Jäger was as painful and confusing as watching Björk's music videos for me, so I stuck to the sneaky-sweet shooters.

Marco staggered into the apartment, his deep-set eyes squinting. His brown, curly hair cast a Chia pet-like shadow on my dark living room wall. I choked back a snicker. He wore a white cotton tee and blue jeans, both über-tight—a Fonzie-meets-Asian-teenager look.

I tossed my keys on the counter, smelling his beer breath over my shoulder. My roommate was at work, giving us plenty of privacy. He wrapped his muscular arms around the waist of my baby-blue sundress and squeezed me like precious stuffed animal. My heart melted from his affection—always deliberate and longer lasting than a typical guy hug.

I pushed him away before grabbing his belt loops and tugging him back. His full, soft lips landed on mine. My mouth inhaled his like a sampler bag of chips. The salty taste of Jamaican beer lingered on his breath. We'd just finished a very refined, liquid dinner at the Coconut Grove Loggerhead: six Red Stripes as appetizers and six PB&J shots for dessert. Chambord is French and Frangelico Italian. Could a drink get any more dignified than that?

Marco wrapped his toned arms tighter around my waist. "What happened to the sweet girl from Kansas?" We stood in the middle of my living room in the dark, wobbling in each other's arms. The streetlights outside my bay windows gave the entire apartment a gray glow.

My fingers twisted through his curls. "Oh, she'll be back soon. She's still at work, delivering your piña coladas again, you slacker." I kissed him playfully, letting my long curls brush against his face. Marco had started wait-ing tables at The Cheesecake Factory a month before—precisely when my shape-shifting began. A substitute-teaching gig had fallen through for the new year, so Marco went back to working at restaurants. He always smiled in the face of restaurant chaos; I assumed the stress of juggling four tables paled in comparison to coaching bilingual third graders all day. Marco had graduated from University of Miami with a degree in biology and wanted to be a middle school teacher.

He laughed. "I'm not that bad." He brushed my hair off my shoulders and pecked my lips. "I was a star server at Friday's."

My eyes met his. "You wait tables about as well as Pauly Shore acts." Marco's frozen drinks often "died" on the service bar while he played patty-cake with kids in his station. The man was different from the other male servers—more caring, more father-like. Falling in love at work again was as easy as riding a tricycle. Shifts lasted longer than the night's sky. We shared the obligatory after-work drink. Sparks flew over squatty bottles of his fa-vorite Caribbean lager.

His fingers glided down my arms, hushing my inner smart-ass. The veins in his smooth, muscular arms bulged. Marco spent most mornings surfing off Miami Beach and his Caribbean-European heritage further deepened the color of his olive skin. His type was as alien to me as grüner veltliner.

"Friday's isn't Cheesecake," I said, as he tugged me toward my papasan couch. Marco was all mine...the hot surfer, but pathetic waiter. He never wrote down an order. He forgot to starch his apron. I'd trained him to work the floor at the hottest restaurant chain on the East Coast, and he acted like we were serving milkshakes at Johnny Rocket's.

Marco's thumbs rubbed my hands. "I know when to apply myself and when to slack off." His big eyes locked mine. "All great teachers do." I stared at his handsome face in the darkness. My brain hurt trying to analyze his affirmation.

"I still have no idea how you passed the final." My fingernails skimmed down his T-shirt. Marco fell into my papasan couch, laughing as the wicker frame creaked. I staggered awkwardly toward him like a newborn duckling and tried to sit upright in the oval pod. Worst furniture purchase ever.

"But I never get tired of picking up your slack." The words slurred off my tongue. Marco had flipped my attraction switch the first time he'd called me "hon." When I'd refilled his empty bread baskets the first time, he'd brushed his thumb across my chin and said, "Thanks, hon. You're a doll." I'd felt like the only girl in the restaurant. Our flirting match had ensued. I'd begun scurrying around his station, delivering his orphaned drinks, desserts and espressos. As a kid, I'd raised a dozen baby chickens, two rabbits, a guinea pig and one raccoon. I could handle Marco's station and mine, *no problema*.

"You are a piece of work." Marco grinned at me from his shallow grave in my papasan. He stretched his muscular arms to both sides like a sacrificial animal.

I hiked my sundress to straddle him, channeling my alter ego. "I'm just doing what comes naturally." I could smell the lie, and the Frangelico, on my breath. *Yeah, what comes naturally after six drinks.* I smiled through my nervousness. Big city boys liked exotic, sensual women. Every ex-girlfriend Marco had mentioned was South American, a.k.a Miss Universe land. Latinas and me—we had about as much in common as Vanilla Ice and Ice Cube.

Marco leaned up to kiss me. "I didn't know Midwestern girls were like this." His tongue dangled from his gaping mouth. The tiny room felt like it was closing in around me. *Ummm, we're not.* Ms. Land of Oz? I was as exotic as a leather sofa from Jennifer Convertibles. I didn't know what a

Brazilian wax was, and I was too embarrassed to ask the South American waitresses at work. If it weren't for my Colombian roommate's divine undergarment intervention, I would have still been wearing granny panties. Shots seemed essential.

I bent to his ear. "Miami changes people. You know that." Five months of cultural immersion had slowly begun working its magic. I could say chicken, pork and rice in Spanish. I drank Jamaican beer. I wore thongs.

"I like you like this." Marco planted a passionate, wet kiss on my lips. My heart lurched into my throat, feeling his tongue dance with mine. He pulled away, leaving me breathless.

His thick hands palmed my butt. I felt my thin sundress rise up my thighs. He squeezed both of my butt cheeks. I squealed like a teenybopper. *Dorothy, you're not in Kansas anymore.*

"Are all Latin men like you?" I asked with a purr before kissing him again. Marco was a cultural melting pot—half-Cuban, half-Italian and 100 percent macho. I found this refreshingly reassuring, post-Robert. Cubans made up about fifty-nine percent of the Miami population back then, so I'd embraced the odds that I'd end up with a Cuban boyfriend sooner or later.

Marco panted, his chest fluttering. "*Sí.*" His eyes hopped around my face.

I leaned my weight into him, kissing his lips softly. The alcohol kept surging through my bloodstream, helping me play the role of aggressor. I'd also been getting dating advice from an Amazonian blonde server at Cheesecake named Christina who encouraged me to keep shaving my crotch and said, "Great sex is like waiting tables. Women do all the heavy lifting."

"We should do this more often on our day off." Marco pulled my hips closer to his.

I caressed his face, my bruised ego rejoicing. *He's not the kind of guy who will switch teams.*

His tongue chased mine. He smelled of beer and cigarettes, and only a tipsy college girl would find that physically attractive. Without leaving his lips, I guided him off the couch into my adjoining bedroom. Excitement and nervousness surged through my body.

Shadows of craggy banyan trees outside the windows covered my bed. I pulled away from Marco, stumbling through the dark and bouncing off every piece of furniture like a pinball.

"Don't mind me." I turned my back with a smirk. "I know where I'm going." My hands tugged the mini blinds shut, sending the room into darkness. I took a deep breath and closed my eyes; the room began to spin. *I am just being myself, my new self. Shedding my Midwest inhibitions. Taking control of my sex life.* Miami in the mid-1990s was a fondue fountain of sexual energy—just add chocolate and alcohol. I couldn't go a day without seeing men's glistening chests on the street or women's huge breasts popping out of their bikinis at gas stations. It was a special place to be young and hormonal.

Marco stepped behind me and lifted my hair off my neck. He plunged his teeth playfully into my shoulder, making me moan. I ran my fingernails through his thick, brown curls before turning to face him. My fingers moved slowly over his face in the darkness like a blind person reading Braille.

I pushed Marco away and laughed. The little voice in my head began scolding my naughty nemesis for deserting my morals—then my blood alcohol level drowned out the voice. I sauntered over to my new JVC stereo and tapped "play" for preloaded disc one. *Premeditated sex. Another Miami first.* The electric pulse of the drumbeat filled my bedroom. I turned and slinked back to Marco. My chest thumped to the bass line of Nine Inch Nails's "Closer."

His athirst eyes watched me in the darkness as I concentrated on un-buckling my sandals and not taking a header into my bookcase. I pulled off his sneakers then slipped my spaghetti-strap dress over my head. Marco's eyes bounced hungrily from my teal satin bra to my matching lace panties. I ran my fingers through my hair, keeping my eyes locked on him.

I pounced, straddling him like a tiger about to devour her prey. He began squirming and grabbing at my legs. My body wobbled over him. I looked like a drunken spring breaker trying to ride a banana boat.

"You Kansas girls are all that." Marco's eyes bulged in the darkness.

"And a bag of chips." I slipped the black leather belt off his jeans as the sexy song blasted through my apartment.

He pulled off his T-shirt, revealing the kind of six-pack I'd only seen on *Beverly Hills, 90210*. My tongue flew from his chest to his stomach. I frantically lapped away at his tight muscles like a thirsty puppy. A little sliver of self inside me whispered, "This isn't you. It's the shots." I shooed it back into the deepest corner of my cloudy head.

Marco slipped off his pants faster than a horny teenager. My fingers gripped his thighs, and I froze like a mannequin Kim Cattrall.

He shaves his legs?! I felt like an old woman groping a preteen boy. The music pulsed from my head to my stomach. Gaydar. Red alert! I'd never seen a guy shave his body before moving to Miami, but manscaping was commonplace—whether guys hung out at 10th and Ocean on South Beach or Gold's Gym in Coral Gables. It still freaked me out a little bit. Only four weeks had passed since Robert had taken it in the butt. And he didn't shave his legs!

I collapsed beside him on my bed and stared up at the ceiling. *My legs have more stubble than his.* The room began to spin. *Please, God. Don't let me puke.*

We spooned in the darkness, not saying a word. Marco tugged me around to face him again. "I'm Cuban-Italian. I have no choice." I turned to look at his muscular silhouette lying on my bed and pictured him turning into Michael J. Fox in *Teen Wolf.*

My chin rested in his armpit. "I'm sure I'll get used to it." My bedroom continued to spin like a Ferris wheel. I forced my eyes to lock on a bookshelf. I'd puked on a boy—while making out in his bed—my senior year of high school. It was a Hallmark moment I didn't want to relive.

I rushed to the kitchen and chugged a glass of water.

"You're dating a *gringa*, and you've adjusted *muy bien*." The foreign words slurred from my lips. My Spanish vocabulary had risen from zero to twenty words in three months. I wanted to be chatting up the Cuban busboys before summer. I also wanted to throw up.

"I like different." He smiled at me from across the room. The music stopped. I scurried over to my stereo and hit "rewind."

The electronic pulse of the music bounced around us. Marco reached for his jeans and fished a condom from his wallet. My mind rejoiced. Robert had scared me straight about unprotected sex.

I slithered up and down Marco's tanned body to the beat, feeling like the biggest fraud since Milli Vanilli. But hey, I was twenty, single and living in one of the country's sexiest cities. Blend in with the locals. Fake it until it feels natural—my new motto.

🍸🍸🍷🍸🍸

"SHULA'S HAD A GREAT run, but it's time to pass the torch," Marco said to one of the bus boys in the main bus stand. I pictured his smooth legs under his wrinkled apron. Two days had passed since the shots sexcapade. Like most straight guys at work, Marco loved to talk football. I liked to play along.

I stuffed two plates in a bus tub. "If it wasn't for Zach Thomas and Jason Taylor, Shula would have been canned two years ago." I continued spouting off statistics about Thomas's sacks like an Al Michaels protégé. My older brother and I had shared a Dallas Cowboys-themed bedroom until fourth grade, and it didn't take me long to trade in my Barbies for a pigskin.

"This girl is unreal," Marco said to the busboy then winked at me. I blushed and grabbed four water mugs from a rack. *Touchdown.*

"Did you see the rack on that lady at thirty-one?" I asked, pushing the glass rack back under the counter. "She could smuggle a whole cheesecake between those things."

"Bullshit!" Marco darted over to survey her cleavage. Enter the country girl who could talk football and boobs and do a keg stand—the buddy with a vagina—every macho man's dream. My secret weapon had been deployed.

SUPER BOWL XXIX CAME to Miami in late January. I couldn't afford tickets, of course, so I bought us two passes to the NFL Experience at Joe Robbie Stadium. Marco and I scurried around the stadium, playing games like two grade schoolers at the county fair. The relationship was sweet, playful and a little dangerous—like the Slippery Nipple shooters we often downed together. We'd spend afternoons hanging out at his apartment or mine on the rare occasion we weren't both scheduled to work. He invited me to spend the night at his place and cooked me a bona fide breakfast: cheesy scrambled eggs, made with Kraft singles and Jimmy Dean sausage—the fast lane to a Midwest girl's heart. We shared smoothies (same straw) and salads (same bowl, same fork) before our work shifts—the tell-tale sign we were serious. I bought him a Miami Dolphin-colored Nerf football so we could play catch in the street.

Then I went out of bounds.

I took a vacation.

Alicia, Christina and another server named Brent had been planning a road trip to Mardi Gras in New Orleans for almost two months and invited me to tag along. The legal drinking age in Louisiana was still eighteen at the time—an added bonus. The idea of leaving Marco for five days, however, made my stomach squirm. *A Latino man's eyes never stop wandering*, my roommate said. I'd never worried much about getting dumped too soon before moving to Miami, but leftovers from Loggerhead seemed to last longer than my relationships with Floridian men.

🍺 🍶 🍷 🥂 🍸

WE DROVE BRENT'S mom's minivan fourteen hours straight to New Orleans, switching drivers along the way. Before college, my idea of a vacation involved a twelve-pack of hot dogs, a can of bug spray and a twenty-minute car ride to Farlington Lake.

"That'll put hair on your chest, eh?" Alicia asked, watching me sip my first frozen Hand Grenade at Tropical Isle's weathered-wood bar. I sucked the sweet melon cocktail through a straw until brain freeze set in. It was Alicia's third trip to Mardi Gras, and she knew the best bars for drinks, the best clubs for jazz, the best diners for Cajun food and the best street vantage points for each float parade.

I slammed the grenade-shaped cup onto the counter. "Thank you, sir, can I have another?" Purple and green beads bounced around my neck, tangled in my hair. I could handle my liquor; my dad's ancestors were German and Czech. Since leaving Chris, I'd spent one-third of my tips on booze each week. I'd dived head first into the restaurant lifestyle and hadn't come close to hitting bottom.

"Dorothy's gotta learn how to pace herself!" Alicia pulled a $20 bill from her jeans pocket. "We've got four days of partying ahead of us." *Pace myself?* I rolled my eyes and kept sucking the potent, fruity concoction through my straw. New Orleans was a one-stop shop for my three favorite things—delicious food, stiff drinks and live music. I felt like a crack addict who'd just been dropped off in Skid Row with a $100 bill. We devoured spicy shrimp po' boys at Mother's on Poydras Street. We downed fruity hurricanes on the brick patio at Pat O'Brien's and danced in the street alongside a roaming, five-piece band. We ate king cake for breakfast, paired with frozen strawberry daiquiris. My taste buds rode the heavenly high straight through to the gigantic parade floats and flying strings of beads. Alicia flashed her huge breasts to get tons of necklaces and slipped every other string over my head. *Boobs. That's what friends are for.*

🍺🍸🍷🍴🍹

ALICIA CALLED THE Cheesecake Factory to check the upcoming two-week schedule. It was Sunday afternoon, and Mardi Gras revelers were dancing in the street below our hotel room window. Our server manager posted a new fourteen-day schedule every other Sunday, and even though we'd requested time off for our entire trip, we wanted to be certain there were no issues. We sat on the floral-print sleeper sofa in our cheap hotel living room, watching Alicia's eyes bulge with the phone receiver pressed to her ear.

"We're all scheduled on Monday?" Her face contorted as she twisted the phone cord between her acrylic nails.

My jaw dropped. Monday was twenty-four hours away.

"You gotta make me understand what happened here, Richard." Alicia launched into her "Jenny from the Block" routine with bobbing head and nasty tone. She'd grown up in New York, and made sure everyone knew it. When her tanned face turned red, Brent grabbed the receiver and tried smooth-talking our boss like a used car salesman. Alicia rolled her eyes. We huddled around the phone in Brent's hand, listening to our boss explain how he didn't have enough bodies to cover all the shifts we'd requested, so he'd scheduled us all on Monday, because that would be the easiest shift to cover.

My body felt paralyzed by fear and helplessness. My eyes darted from my duffle bag on the bedroom floor to the dead bolt on the front door. Fourteen hours of interstate highways and turnpikes stood between the Dade County line and us.

Our manager placed us on hold.

Alicia fumbled for a cigarette lighter in her jeans pocket. "Screw him!" The words spit from her full lips. "How the fuck can he be so disrespectful to some of his best servers? We've been there since day one." Her wavy, black hair whipped around the shoulders of her New York Knicks jersey.

Christina collapsed onto the queen bed in the adjoining room, feeling the pain of a hangover and the remorse of screwing a stranger the night before.

"What an ass wipe!" Christina stared up at the popcorn ceiling. "He can't be doing this to us." She reached for a pack of Marlboro Lights on the nightstand.

Alicia exhaled a perfect ring of smoke. "He can kiss my ass." She shoved her lit cigarette toward the door. "I'll go bartend on South Beach and make twice the money." Christina cheered from the next room, cigarette dangling from her mouth. Even Brent nodded and flipped off the phone. He was five years older than me and had a college degree. It felt as if I was watching fifth graders on a playground standing up to the class bully.

"Maybe you guys don't care about getting fired," I snapped the words, standing in the center of the tiny living area, "but I do." I crossed my arms over my new Mardi Gras T-shirt. I wore a checkered flannel shirt wrapped around the waist of my intentionally ripped Gap jeans and black Army boots...the grunge band look.

"There are plenty of good jobs in Miami, Dorothy." Alicia pointed her French-manicured nails at my nose. "You haven't lived there long enough to realize it."

"I'm not losing this job!" Beads jingled around my stiff neck. "We can drive home now and be there in time for work tomorrow." My heart hammered in my chest. The room was as quiet as models on *The Price Is Right*.

Alicia took a long drag and exhaled. "We're not driving home now." She twisted her stub in the ashtray on the coffee table. "It's not even Mardi Gras yet." Her shoulders squared. My hands began to shake. The only fight of my life had involved my best friend from grade school, a swing set and two packs of Slim Jims.

"I'll find my own way home tonight if I have to!" I boot-stomped over to my duffle bag. "Maybe losing a good job doesn't mean much to you guys, but it means a lot to me." Having a five-month stint on my résumé seemed like the scarlet letter, and the loss of my job would strip me of my only security blanket: money.

"Maybe you should talk to him then," Alicia hissed.

"Fine." I plucked the phone from Brent's chest. I had a good relationship with our supervisor. He'd recently promoted me to senior trainer.

"Lisa, I like you," he said firmly after listening to my plea. "You've been a great employee, but if you can't cover your open shifts, I will fire you all. You leave me no choice." My voice trembled as I asked him if he could give me a list of every person not scheduled to work on Monday. I jotted down every name and phone number on a hotel notepad. My fingers shook in cadence with my breaths. One by one, I spoke to seven people on the list. Brent left Alicia's side on the couch and joined in my pleading cause. Thirty-five minutes, $200 cash and four I.O.U. shift-trades later, the crisis had been averted. But the big save didn't make me feel like doing cartwheels.

I looked down at Christina and Alicia sprawled across the couch in our messy hotel room with cigarettes dangling from their mouths, the weight of reality hanging over our heads in their cloud of smoke. There was an invisible line that divided employees at the restaurant back then: You were a lifer or a temp. Waiting tables wasn't considered a viable career like it is today. Lifers like Christina were hooked on the quick money and the lifestyle. College students like me were the temps. *Why am I trying to cross to the other side?* I'd planned to build my life around five steps: take one year off, get my residency, save money, pay down debt and go back to college. My credit card debt had ballooned to $750, and my checking account had dwindled to $100. The only serious decisions in my life had become draft or bottle, frozen or on the rocks. My choice in friends and drinks had shaped the new me and left an unpleasant aftertaste.

🍺🍸🍷🍴🍷

I RETURNED TO work with a newfound purpose—and a rock in my stomach. *Will my boss still be mad? Did Marco miss me?*

Marco coasted right past me on his way to the bakery. "Hey, kiddo," he called out over his shoulder. His eyes never met mine. The sweetness in his voice was gone, along with the "honey." The rock moved from my stomach to my throat. For days, I'd been thinking about how much I missed him, how I wanted to erase all the bad things that had happened in New Orleans and start my life over. I juggled my four tables with ease and tried to make small talk at the POS system. He was one step ahead of me every time.

At the end of our shift, I spotted Marco near the main bus station talking to Gabriela, one of the new servers. She was Brazilian with a body like Beyoncé and a brown mole on the tip of her nose. She had cat-like eyes and thick, brown hair that tumbled down her back. She loved to dance salsa just like Marco. Her cheeks plumped when he talked to her. She lifted a spoon from her cup of soup to his lips, and my mind screamed: *No! Not the telltale sign!*

I rushed into the back hallway break area and found my friend, Linda, drinking a soda amongst the cluster of milk crates-turned staff stools. We were the same height, same build and had the same hairdo. We'd also tied for the highest score on the Cheesecake training final. She never partied with us after work and was always the voice of reason.

"They've been making goo-goo eyes at each other since you left town." Her brown curls bounced as she rolled her eyes "They've been going to raves. Rolling like crazy."

"Rolling what?" I asked with a puzzled face.

She shook her head in disbelief of my ignorance. "Let me explain, Dorothy..."

My jaw fell when the word "drug" left her mouth. Coke. Threesomes. Shots. Ecstasy. *Is this normal for most big city restaurants?*

I stamped my sneaker on the concrete. "Goddammit. Not again!" My chin dropped to my chest. *Why is life in the big city so damn complex?* Rave was a brand of hairspray, not a dance party for druggies. Rolling was what Chris did to make homemade joints. Linda told me that several coworkers took hits of a drug called Ecstasy at "raves" or "rolling parties." People popped the pills and pawed each other like cats for hours. I couldn't believe Marco had fallen prey to the party drug scene, too. Marco was a schoolteacher, a mentor to small children. My squeaky-clean picture of him began to shatter.

"X will screw up a person's nervous system for life," Linda said, perched on her milk crate with ankles crossed. "Those two have rolled at least three times this week." I sighed deeply and looked down at the floral-print tie on my flat chest. Gabriela hated football. She loved shopping. She and Marco had little in common. *It must be the boobs.*

I buried my elbows between my knees. Marco had been fully vetted. We'd spent at least fifty hours a week together at the restaurant. We'd hung out during pre-shift and grabbed drinks after work. I knew his full name, where he lived, his favorite color, his previous jobs. He was a schoolteacher! Can a man get any more wholesome than that? *Suddenly, he's popping pills with Miss Brazil.*

I felt like the Tasmanian Devil cartoon—spinning in circles, devouring men, exposing my dimwit. Meet guy at work, fall quickly in love, have sex, become a couple, be shocked when he does drugs and cheats...the end. My love life, abbreviated. It was duplicating more times than the syllables in Hawaiian.

🍺🍷🍸🥂🍹

COCONUT GROVE PLAYHOUSE hosted a senior citizen's discount day once a month. It was the shift every server begged to get off but few succeeded. I will never forget the first Playhouse shift after Mardi

Gras. Two Greyhound busloads of Boca Raton snowbirds poured into the restaurant as soon as we opened the doors. Every table was filled with blue-haired, old ladies with gaudy jewelry and huge handbags. We deplored waiting on old women. Their demands and special orders were relentless—and this was long before gluten-free diets and the vegan craze. Hell, the South Beach diet hadn't even been invented yet.

I marched back into my beehive of a station, quadruple-sat, still fuming over my first Gabriela glance of the day. She was wearing Marco's Jerry Garcia tie! They'd become surfing buddies. She'd helped him wax his board—and his chest!

I scuttled over to service bar with sixteen drink orders—decaf coffees with low-fat milk (not cream), hot teas—the kind of high-maintenance shit that would piss off any server. Every hot teakettle was already in use. Four coffee machines were brewing new batches after being wiped out in the first five minutes of the shift. I huffed and shoved the last three creamer cups in my apron like a soldier storing ammunition. It was February and seventy degrees outside.

"Take your coffee and your big hair," I hissed under my breath far from my station, "and go back to New York and shovel snow." The mere idea of drinking coffee in Miami infuriated me. I painted on a sweet smile as every little old lady at my tables ordered egg white omelets with no oil and no butter, each with a different type of toast and side dish.

"I ordered pumpernickel bread," one of the old ladies snarled. "Change this." Her bony fingers pushed the plate to the center of the table.

I forced a smile. "I'll bring you a side of whole wheat. That's the only brown bread we serve." *Know-it-all, hag.* I plucked two dirty sides plates from the table and marched back to the line. My neck felt stiff and hot.

"Fresh side of wheat baguette toast, pleeeezzee," I said to the expediter. The warming lamps in the kitchen service window made my head feel like a pressure cooker. I stood up against the wall of mirrors by the kitchen with dirty plates in hand. At the bakery counter, Gabriela and Marco were giggling, squirting whipped cream out of the canister on top of two lattes in a slow, suggestive way. *Get a fucking room, people!*

I stomped over to the main bus stand. Standing over the stainless-steel trash shoot, I smashed the side plates together like marching band symbols.

I glared at the dirty plates in my hands. "Does anyone in this place have respect?" My voice boomed like a sportscaster's. The line of servers at the bread station turned and stared. The whole shitty situation had reached a boiling point. I wanted to skewer Gabriela and serve her to the blue hairs with a side of "fuck you."

I growled and banged the plates harder against the trash bin. Clank! Silence blanketed the restaurant. The jagged pieces of ceramic felt like rocks between my fingers. Cooks and servers glared from both sides of the kitchen's heat lamps. My cheeks felt on fire. I dropped the last two broken chunks into the trash bin before storming into the back hallway.

I SAT IN a booth by myself at the end of the shift, stacking napkins and chewing my nails. Our manager, Richard, marched over to my table. "I need to have a word with you."

I followed him into the empty veranda, my arms cinched around me like a straitjacket. He shut the heavy glass door behind us. Nausea whipped through my stomach as he grabbed a wicker chair. We sat down at a table with a view of the street. I wanted to jump out the window.

He leaned back and ran his fingers through his short, brown hair. "I don't know what has happened to you." Every syllable shot out of his mouth like rounds from a pellet gun. "You were one of my star employees."

He paused, lacing his hands on the stone tabletop. "Then there was the Mardi Gras trip and the scramble to cover your shifts." His eyes were anchored on my face.

My wicker chair creaked. My throat felt like sandpaper. I hadn't felt that embarrassed since a boy depantsed me in eighth grade study hall.

Richard's head shook from side to side. "And now this." His eyes bulged. "You throw plates. You yell. You storm out of the dining room. You are not the Lisa I hired."

I looked down at my hands cupped in my lap. My breaths trembled as tears swelled in the corners of my eyes. *Say something.* I watched my fingers shake. My vocal cords were tangled by the shame of hard truth.

Richard leaned over the table. "I don't know what is happening in your personal life." He furrowed his eyebrows. "And I don't care. We're adults, and this is a business. You're here to do a job and do it exceptionally well."

"I am...I'm sorry." The words stumbled from my quivering lips.

"I like you," he said in his ever-hurried pace. "I think you're a good kid with a bright future. Six months ago, you were a different person. You had a plan. You were following your dreams. I don't want to see you mess up your life." His green eyes pierced mine. "Some people can't handle the lifestyle of working in a restaurant. Don't let yourself become one of them."

I wiped the tears from my cheeks, too shocked to feel the magnet pulling me down my father's dark path. I was the anchor in a relay against myself. I'd lost all the ground I'd gained since leaving home.

"I know." My shoulders caved, and my necktie fell onto the tabletop. "This isn't like me." My epiphany during the Mardi Gras trip flashed through my mind. My good intentions had drowned in a Bourbon Street Hand Grenade. I was one broken plate away from being fired from the best job I'd ever had—all because of a slacker who shaved his legs.

Richard stared me in the eye. "I'm giving you one more chance." I looked at his hard face. Rays of sunshine poured from the French windows behind him, lighting his silhouette. He looked like Moses reading the Ten Commandments. "But that's it." He slid a white sheet of paper across the table for me to sign. "This is a disciplinary form. Please review and sign."

My gut squished wildly like I'd just scarfed down an entire shepherd's pie. My hand shook as I signed and dated the scarlet letter for my employee file. "Thank you." I rubbed my cheeks to blend in the trail of tears. "I will get back on track. I promise."

I opened the veranda's glass door and stepped into the empty dining room. Fellow servers in white uniforms with loosened ties counted tips and folded napkins in the booths just outside the door. All eyes flew to my face when the door shut behind me.

I turned and scuttled to the service bar. *So much for my new family.* I'd been given one more shot. And I could not drink that one away.

MATTHEW

The Imported Beer Days

I buried my nose deeper in the book, searching for answers. Tiny, turquoise waves patted against the shore of the empty, barrier island beach. The blazing sun baked my back. I lay sprawled out in reverse spread-eagle on a towel, wearing a floral bikini—prime target for a seagull shit missile.

A sharp, scraping sound poured into my ears. My head flew toward the water.

A shirtless man tugged at the ropes of a Hobie Cat sailboat, as his fiberglass bow dug into the sandy shore. The boat coasted to a stop yards from my beach towel.

My eyes scanned the empty beach. Of all the places this guy could dock, he chose here. Intentional grounding?

I rose to my jellylike knees. "Is that a rental?" I plucked my sandy towel off the ground and wrapped it around my sweaty body. It seemed like a covert way to determine his status: tourist or local.

His head shook in a huff. "No. I know what I'm doing." He spoke with a serious, yet artificial tone like an emergency room doctor on a soap opera. Mr. Smooth Sailor wore only sea-green board shorts and a Miami Hurricanes baseball cap; his muscular chest glistened in the sun. We're talking beach sexy with a capital "B."

"I'm Matthew." He extended a callused hand. A sliver of a smile parted his thin lips. He had strawberry-blond hair and a cleft chin.

I looked up at his dark, auburn eyes and wiped my dirty hands on the beach towel before accepting his handshake. He gripped my gritty palm tightly. I felt a tingle of excitement in my sweaty chest.

"Sorry if I startled you." Matthew's eyes peeked out from under his cap. "This seems like the best spot to come ashore." His stern voice had a rhythmic cadence.

"Lisa," I replied coolly, pulling away from his handshake. The entire scene felt hopelessly romantic to my lonely soul. After my encounters with Coke Boy and Professor Ecstasy, I yearned for a normal guy to *walk* into my life.

Matthew reached down and grabbed my book from the sand. "Deepak Chopra." He shook granules from the pages, smiling. "That's pretty deep." Beads of sweat trickled down his ripped stomach. I inhaled deeply, trying to stay cool.

"That's what I was hoping for." I grabbed the book from his hands. "It's very uplifting. Very spiritual."

My fingers squeezed the hardback. "I like the positivity of his beliefs." My spiritual guide, Jorge, who doubled as my hairstylist, had given me that book. Jorge had challenged me to rid my life of toxic relationships in less than thirty days, yet it took him two years to convince me to stop perming my hair.

I ran my fingers over the sandy book cover. My bad choices included the proud addition of a drunken hookup on my twenty-first birthday with a fellow Cheesecake waiter who owned a Harley, wore a bike-chain bracelet and strutted around the dining room singing Splack Pack's "Scrub Da Ground." A real class act. I desperately needed to find inner peace, and Chopra's affirmations were working serious magic on my mojo.

"I'd like to read that someday." Matthew slid his hands into the pockets of his shorts. The afternoon sun cast a fiery glow around his muscular, lean body. His deep eyes almost matched the color of his hair.

I looked down at my sandy toes, trying to keep my heart from melting.

"How often do you come here?" Matthew asked. Australian pine branches rocked in the wind above us.

I pressed my toes deeper into the warm sand. "Every day." The blazing sun baked my shoulders as I inhaled deeply, the familiar scent of fresh, salty-sweet air filling my chest. "I love how peaceful it is. Well, how peaceful it *usually* is." I smirked at him. During the spring of 1995, most of my afternoons were spent on Virginia Key, a tiny island between Miami's mainland and Key Biscayne, reading Chopra while soaking up sun and solitude. A halo of optimism always floated over me in the blue skies of Biscayne Bay. The island felt like my own secluded, holistic retreat. Who needed Prozac? I had access to 250 days of sunshine per year, a motivational book and the will to heal my broken self. When it came to dating, my moral compass felt like it had been run over by a rickshaw, and spending time alone at the edge of the ocean was my recipe for finding strength, for rediscovering myself.

Our conversation flowed as smoothly as rum runners on a summer night in Islamorada. I tried not to think about my sweaty face or crooked ponytail. "Do you have plans this evening?" Matthew asked as the late afternoon sun began to sink into the horizon.

"LAST CALL!" THE bartender yelled from behind the worn-wood bar. I looked into Matthew's dark eyes then down at my Bulova watch. We'd been talking for five hours at a dive bar near the Coconut Grove Playhouse. It felt like fifty minutes.

"It can't possibly be closing time." Matthew threw back his head. "We're not leaving yet." His bravado made my ego do a headspin.

A big smile spread across my face. "Nights off always go by too fast, you know." I sat on my barstool with my back straight, sporting my favorite teal tank and new pair of button-fly Levi's. My chest felt damp and my hair flat—a small price to pay to never endure a blizzard.

My eyes lingered over my half-full mug of Corona Light, waiting for his next move. I'd already gathered a boatload of information about Matthew: First, he liked imported beer—and only the light kind—which seemed like a sign of a well-traveled, mature man who also cared about his body. He was gainfully employed with a real career (Navy SEAL), liked to go fishing in the Keys (bonus!), didn't appreciate the high-rolling, party city Miami had become (ditto) and had a penchant for drawing award-winning sketches of water birds (jackpot!). Matthew was pushing all my buttons, but there was a catch.

He lived in San Diego.

The first normal guy I'd met with a dollop of potential, and he was almost as geographically undesirable as a Frenchman. At first, the disappointing news felt like a piece of coral reef resting on my chest. Then I remembered my pen pal from New York back in fifth grade. We'd kept our friendship thriving for two years and had never met in person.

Maybe we have a chance.

His beer crossed my lips again. The pale lager tasted thin, bitter and dry. Drinking beer seemed like an unpleasant chore that came along with most dates. The only guy I'd ever met who didn't drink beer was Robert, and look how that ended.

"Come with me." Matthew's voice rippled through the thick, muggy air. My eyes moved from my yellow beer to his serious face.

I took a sip to fill the uncomfortable space. *No more getting involved with men who don't really care about me.*

His hand moved across the table and grabbed mine. "I'm not ready to say goodbye." My eyes darted from his face to the handle on my mug. His flight to California was departing at 7 a.m. *Was this the beginning, or the beginning of the end?* My little voice told me to say my goodbyes and walk home. *Can a pitcher of beer lead to anything good?*

"I...I can't." I looked down in a blush. "It's not a good idea."

He leaned into me. "Just for a few more hours." The humid air around us jumped five degrees. "I just want to talk." His words chimed in my head. My chest began throbbing. I grabbed my beer and chugged longer and harder than a Lambda Lambda Lambda pledge, stalling, battling my inner demon who never wanted to say "no" to anybody.

We walked down Main Highway in the dark, past the towering banyan trees and coral-rock gates of the private schools. I jabbered on about work to calm my nerves. Matthew reached for my hand and electric currents flew up my arms. He led me to his friend's house, a tile-roof bungalow nestled in a tiny jungle.

We sat on a couch in the den with the lights off, caressing each other's hands. Matthew talked about the emotional strain of military service, the thrill of international ops and his love of art. I told him about my passion for writing, my love of South Florida's weather and my plans for college. As we sat in the dark baring our souls, he pressed his firm lips to mine, sending shock waves through my body. His kiss had a lightness that made me feel five inches off the ground. Matthew held me in his muscular arms until sunrise. Never once did he try to get up my shirt or down my pants. I couldn't help but think: This guy is worth the distance.

WITHIN A WEEK of meeting Matthew, I began trading my lunch shifts in the busy stations near the bakery for early-closing stations on the veranda. Getting "cut" after the lunch rush gave me just enough time to meet the postman in my stairwell. Matthew was often at sea on missions, so the only way we could communicate regularly was pen to paper, envelope to mailbox. Every five days, a thick, white envelope arrived. Dating B.E. (before email) built up more anticipation than the first season finale of *Friends*.

I always sat on the corner of my bed reading his poetic prose with wide eyes while Florida sunshine spilled into my bedroom. Letters were always three pages double-sided—never more, never less. The papers felt as glamorous as a bouquet of calla lilies between my fingers. My eyes danced across every hand-written sentence, words aligned perfectly with the thin, blue lines. A typewriter would have been hard-pressed to reproduce Matthew's precise penmanship. Reading his love letters filled my heart with more passion and excitement than any relationship before, and we'd barely gotten to first base. I knew I could learn a thing or two from a disciplinarian like Matthew.

His compliments rose from every page and caressed my ego: The beaches of San Diego constantly reminded him of the day we met. He was so glad he'd "glided" that catamaran to the sandy shore near the blonde in the bikini. He couldn't wait to teach me how to surf. *Take that, Marco!* The Pacific

Ocean could never be as blue as my eyes. Only I could distract him from thinking about his next mission. He'd grown up in Miami and meeting me had made him realize he belonged back in South Florida. I felt the blood rush to my cheeks as I read every sentence twice over. His words floated around my apartment, making everything bright and sunny until the next batch of mail arrived—and my roommate yelled, "Gag me with a spoon!"

This man was more than words. Matthew sent me cardboard tubes filled with colorful drawings of pelicans, black-winged kites and seagulls. He was like Bob Ross with a bird fetish. I created a shrine of Matthew's love letters and artwork on my bookshelf alongside *The Sailors' Handbook*, a gift Matthew had given me on the doorstep of his friend's house. My life felt like a Harlequin novel.

No man had ever bared his emotional side to me—not an ex-boyfriend and definitely not my dad or my grandpa, who were both hobbits in the expressing feelings department. They were my guideposts for how men treated women. Hugs were reserved for special occasions. Conversations usually centered around food and money. Women worked, cooked, cleaned and paid the bills. Matthew was custom built for an attention-starved girl like me—someone who saw a slice of Prince Charming in every fruitcake that walked, served, drank or sailed his way into my life.

For every letter Matthew sent me, I wrote a reply, just as long and loving as his. I sat on my bed, scribbling away on a pad of paper while Everything but the Girl's "Missing" blasted through my apartment. I told him everything happened for a reason. I told him I believed in fate. My deep longing for Matthew had my inner artist working overtime, and I hadn't written any poetry since Lance. With every letter, I included a new poem written while sitting on Virginia Key in the exact spot where we'd met. "Someone" is still my favorite:

Is that someone out there really true?
The one who knows exactly how you feel,
When you hurt inside?

The one who makes you smile for no reason,
And wants to be there,
When you need him most?

Does fate take two strangers,
Who have fought the same battles and join them,
So they can learn from each other?

Is there someone who shares your hopes, ambitions and dreams,
Because you've traveled the same path,
And met at a crossroads?

The long-distance romance with Matthew aided my much-needed transformation. After years of under-age drinking, I had no interest in hanging out in bars, slurping frozen cocktails and doing shots *legally*—especially when my man was on the West Coast preparing to defend our country. Instead of wasting away mornings sleeping off hangovers, I watched the sunrise while Rollerblading up and down on Key Biscayne's boardwalk with my Sony Walkman. Then I'd change into my OP bikini and read Chopra on the beach. My body had never been so toned or tan, my head never so clear. I spent afternoons by my kitchen window, painting bright, geometric patterns onto empty Robert Mondavi Woodbridge Sauvignon Blanc bottles. I'd stopped painting after high school and hadn't worked out since K-State. I liked the way Matthew brought out the good in me without even being in the same time zone.

The distance between us strengthened our connection more than any of my past physical relationships. Sure, there was the frustration that came with opening a mail slot and finding only a pizza delivery flyer. But I knew how I'd feel when one of his love letters did arrive. It was the thrilling era of pre-cell phone and pre-Internet dating, falling in love with a military man who was often at sea, assigned to a secret mission he couldn't discuss. The raw sense of anticipation was always wrapped in a ball of complete helplessness. *Do wives of Desert Storm soldiers feel the same way?* I needed to be strong for him. He'd earned my love and my trust, and had the writer's cramp to prove it.

I BOARDED MY first cross-country flight at Miami International Airport, bursting with more excitement than a dozen Puerto Rican girls at a Menudo concert. I'd only traveled west of Kansas once in my life—a sorority road trip to watch a K-State football game—and my only real vacation involving an airplane had been the France trip in high school. Flying home to Kansas for the holidays felt more like an obligation, not a destination. But, it meant access to free flights for giving up my seat. A long weekend in San Diego seemed like the perfect way to cash in my first, coveted flight voucher. Matthew had secured permission to go "off base" and suggested we meet in Los Angeles because there was "more to see."

After takeoff, the pilot made a loop over the Miami Beach coastline to head west. It was just after sunrise, and from the wing view, the sand looked painted gold. A wave of awe and profound gratitude rolled through me. *What a beautiful place to call home.* I thumbed aimlessly through the *Sky Mall* magazine, relishing the forgotten thrills of airline travel—fitting everything needed in life into a carryon, settling into a seat next to a stranger, walking into a buzzing terminal and feeling my internal compass awaken. I became acutely aware of my precise location on the planet—how marvelous it felt to begin a journey in one time zone and arrive in another—all on the same day. The airplane was more than a flying bus. It was a slingshot into the unknown—a portal to learning more about the world and myself. The seed of wanderlust had been planted...with Miracle-Gro.

When I stepped into the bustling terminal at LAX, my eyes locked onto Matthew immediately. (How I miss the days of airline travel before 9/11.) He stood at ease in the middle of the crowded walkway by my gate, his hands cupped below the waist. He wore a chambray shirt and khaki dress shorts that showed off his lean, muscular frame. A sweet smirk splashed across his face. My sandals felt like ten-pound weights as I raced toward him, my linen backpack bouncing on my elbow. I launched myself into his arms, hanging on like Spiderman clinging to a wall.

"It is so good to see you," he said softly, twirling me in the air. The edges of my floral skirt danced around my tanned thighs.

I looked into his auburn eyes. "I missed you so much." I nuzzled his chest. We still had our mojo.

🍺🍷🍸🍾

"I THINK I'LL have a glass of wine," I said as we sat in a booth at The Cheesecake Factory Woodland Hills thumbing through the book-thick menus. I couldn't wait to share the exotic foods and décor of my workplace with Matthew, who'd never eaten at a CCF. My eyes bounced from the wine list to Matthew's head buried in the book. "Maybe I should try something new." Matthew was five years older than me, so I wanted to show him how mature and refined a young waitress could be.

Matthew aimlessly flipped the laminated pages. "I'm getting a Corona Light."

"Why do you like Corona so much?" I asked, remembering its thin body and subtle musky flavor—not much different from the big brands of American beers. Back then, restaurant beer lists were just as short on choices as they were on taste.

"It reminds me of the beach." His eyes stayed glued to the thick menu. "That's where I belong."

I pictured him on the sailboat in Miami as my heartbeat fluttered. "Oh, I'd never thought of it that way." My fingers flipped through the pages, reflecting on the idea of drinking an alcoholic beverage to relive a memory—a new concept for a twenty-one year old. "Well, since it's my first trip to California, I should get a glass of wine then." I had no idea how far we were from Southern California wine country, but it was the closest I'd ever been to a vineyard.

A thin waiter sashayed over in his all-white uniform and announced the daily specials in the bubbly Cheesecake way.

My eyes moved to Matthew as our waiter bounced away. "Did you see his wine key? It has an ivory handle. Very impressive."

Matthew shot me a perplexed look. "A wine key?"

Oh, he doesn't know.

"Sorry." I closed my menu. "A wine key is what servers call corkscrews." It was the first time in months I was dating someone who didn't work in a restaurant. I liked the way teaching Matthew about wine made me feel. "In our training class, the distributor rep told us that wine is a living, breathing thing. A prisoner in a bottle, waiting for that key."

Matthew's lips curled. "You're just like you are in your letters." He paused. "Sweet, introspective, poetic." I felt my heartbeat zigzag with every word.

I looked up from my menu, blushing. "We have to get the avocado egg rolls with tamarind sauce." The word "tamarind" rolled off my tongue like a seasoned epicure.

"I'm in your hands." Matthew closed his menu, grinning. "Well, until we leave this booth, then the tables will be turned." His voice was playful and flirtatious. My eyes flew from the menu to his chiseled face. The ravenous look in his eyes sliced through my blushing cheeks. We stared at each other in silence, and then I went to work, planning our meal.

After lunch, Matthew drove us to Topanga Canyon. His blue Cutlass Sierra cruised through the city's busy intersections and residential neighborhoods before the road narrowed to a winding climb up the mountain. He glanced over at me every few minutes with narrow, hazy eyes. It was that horny look guys often give after dinner when they're hungry for *something* else. I grinned out the window, watching lush pine trees whiz by.

Matthew pulled off the road on a wide shoulder and guided me out of the car. We walked silently to the edge of the mountain ridge and stared at the sweeping views of the valley vista, flanked by the Sierras. My jaw fell in awe.

"I can't believe I've gone twenty-one years without seeing a mountain." My eyes fluttered from mountaintop to tree to high-rise buildings in the canyon below. I could feel the distance between Kansas and me: soy bean fields, the crumbling grain elevator towering over the town, the frozen foods for dinner, the evenings spent watching primetime TV, my dad sitting on an American Legion barstool wearing camouflage. I felt strong and alive, like Joan of Arc after a battlefield victory.

Matthew's hand stroked my long, curly hair. "And if we drive just five miles farther that way, we reach the Pacific Ocean." I leaned into him and rested my head against his chest. Wind kicked up dust around our feet.

"My world has always been flat," I said, looking down into the valley. "I thought there was no place in this country more beautiful than Florida. Until now." I'd always dreamed of living near the ocean and had followed Chris east. *Did I move to the wrong coast?*

Matthew stepped behind me. "There is no place like California." He wrapped his arms around my waist and tucked his chin to my ear. "You can surf in the morning, and snow ski in the afternoon. The people are real. It will never get fake like Miami."

I stood quietly, listening to the wind whistle, squeezing Matthew's hands so he wouldn't read my mind. *Maybe he'll never want to move back.* Fate was throwing me another curve ball. Taking another year off from college to get my state residency in California wouldn't put me that far behind schedule. I leaned back against his chest and drifted into another daydream.

♀ ♀ ♀ ♀ ♀

WE CHECKED INTO the Good Nite Inn, a block of tan-painted cinder blocks not far from a freeway. His lodging choice didn't faze me. Where I grew up, the Super 8 was fancy.

Our room felt cold and sterile, more hospital than hospitable. A king-sized bed seemed to occupy the entire room once we were alone behind closed doors for the first time. I barely noticed the tiny, wooden desk or the bowl-shaped chair near the window. I felt like a comedian under a flood light with an audience of blank faces staring up at me, waiting for my act to begin. I had no idea how we could possibly make our first time romantic. There was no CD player. No candles. No alcohol. Just him and me. And two duffle bags.

Reality sunk in like a brick in a bathtub as Matthew slipped the lanky brass chain through the door lock. My heartbeat lunged into my throat. He marched over to the window and tugged the drapes, sending the room into darkness. Thoughts flooded my mind.

This guy could make me disappear. He is almost a stranger.

I couldn't fight back the evil thoughts. *What kind of statistic was I going to become? How long before housekeeping would find my body?* I pulled the wooden chair from the desk and sat down. I willed positive affirmations into my brain: *Matthew is normal. I am safe. No freak would spend hours writing love letters, right?* My guardian angel always had my back. I picked at my fingernail polish then rested my chin in my hands.

"What's wrong?" Matthew asked, setting his ball cap atop a stack of neatly stacked clothes next to his army-green duffle.

"Oh, uh, I don't know." I stared at the carpet floor, stalling. "I guess, uh, it's just that, um, I think I'm overwhelmed." I rocked my knees from side to side. "You. Me. Us. Finally together after all this time." The true reality of our relationship was unraveling in my head. We'd basically had a whirlwind romance over six weeks with less than a day of face-to-face communication. I'd never really took a step outside my head until that moment to realize how strange it felt to be in the physical presence of a man I'd grown to love purely on paper.

"I know how you feel." Matthew reached for my hand. He tugged me up from the chair and hugged me firmly. "Fate works in mysterious ways." He guided me to the edge of the bed. We sat down side by side.

I stared at our reflections in the mirror above the desk. "Do you need at least three thousand miles between us to open your heart?" Matthew had waited until we got into his car in the airport parking garage to kiss me. We'd kissed and hugged several times at the top of the mountain. But it felt like there was a barrier between us, though as thin as a bed sheet. *Fly-*

ing five hours for a first date is bound to lead to awkward situations, right? I made small talk about avoiding Marco, Gabriela and the Mardi Gras posse. My work environment had become as cold and isolating as an Antarctic research station.

I felt his eyes staring at the side of my face. "It's not that I don't have feelings for you." His voice was rigid. "I just need time to analyze my thoughts, screw my head on straight." The emotional rejection felt all too familiar.

He touched my face with the back of his hand. The warmth of his touch flushed through my entire body. I palmed his fingers and turned toward him. His eyes darkened.

"I don't expect you to understand this." His Adam's apple bobbed. "I've witnessed some terrible acts in my life." His jaws locked. "The world can be cruel." There was an eight-month pregnant pause. My chest ached with empathy, just sitting there, helpless, watching the man I loved share his pain. He cleared his throat twice. "Something bad could happen to me any day in my line of work. I've learned to put up walls. I need to be focused to stay safe." His eyes were heavy and dark; his tone swayed from bitter to tender, tugging my heartstrings. Tears swelled in the corner of my eyes.

I gently pressed my lips to his forehead and held the kiss until I felt the tension between us release. *Oh, Matthew. My very own prisoner in a bottle.* My love could hold the key to unlock all his troubles. I had no idea what secret-ops military life entailed, but if it was anything like *Full Metal Jacket*, I couldn't imagine the psychological baggage he'd be forced to carry for the rest of his life.

He grabbed my hands and squeezed tightly. "It doesn't mean I don't have strong feelings for you." His auburn eyes sliced through my fear. I exhaled deeply, raising both hands to cup his chin. *Strong feelings for me.* A wave of comfort drifted through my mind as soon as those words left his lips. It didn't really matter that he'd locked us in a cheap motel room instead of taking me to his house. Or that he couldn't talk to me about his life. My world was as it should be. Every relationship, every choice I'd made in life was driven by my belief in fate: everything happens for a reason. But, sometimes the reason is that you're stupid and make bad decisions.

My hands dropped into my lap. "We've just said so much without speaking." I shrugged my shoulders, staring down at my knees. "It would be nice to hear you say just a few of those things." His written words were like nicotine to my inner daydreamer. There really wasn't anything else to say but those three little words I'd dreamed of hearing within two weeks of meeting every guy I've ever dated.

"You know how special I think you are," Matthew said in his firm, calculated way. "And pretty." He laced his arms around my waist and rested his jaw on the crown of my head. My cheeks gleamed with pride. Words from his letters began flooding my head:

You are my guardian angel. I feel you watching over me during the most dangerous times. When you're farthest away, you are closer to me than you'll ever realize. The missions always come to an end. My feelings for you never will.

"My job makes it hard for me to express my feelings verbally," Matthew continued, brushing my curls off my shoulders. "I need to write to you." I could feel the hurt in his sober tone. The realization that writing and drawing were his only outlets for self-expression made me love him even more.

Matthew sat on the edge of the bed with his arms still wrapped around me. His conflicted feelings seemed to seep from his skin to mine as he squeezed. He breathed deeply into my hair. Heartache pried at my chest. My worst days were getting kicked off the high school cheerleading squad for drinking and being cheated on by a coked-up bisexual. I needed to buck up.

I pulled back to look him in the eye. "I will always be there for you, whenever you need someone to talk with or write to—no matter where you are or what you're going through." My voice trembled, fighting off the urge to cry. "I promise." I felt strong and totally helpless at the same time.

We reclined slowly onto the bed. A fleeting tenderness lingered in and out of Matthew's kisses. Every muscle in my body ached for him. I could feel his hesitation, as he kissed me firmly then softly then firmly again. I felt like a priceless bronzed statue he was protecting from the evils that existed in our everyday lives. He pulled off his shirt, exposing a jagged scar across his right pec. Tears began to build in my eyes again, and I choked them back.

"It's okay," I whispered, caressing the thick scar tissue on his chest. "I have scars, too." He stared into my eyes. I felt a tear trickle down my cheek; he wiped it away with his thumb, his eyes never leaving mine. I listened to our breath, feeling his wall begin to crumble—even if only for a moment.

Then Matthew lifted my flowery skirt and pressed me against the mattress.

Afterward, we lay naked on the bed side by side in the dark. I leaned over and kissed his shoulder. "I love you." I gazed into his dark eyes. Then I told him it was okay if he couldn't tell me he loved me yet. Where was Dr. Phil when I needed him? Twenty miles away, waiting for his first call from Oprah.

🍸🍷🍸🍷🍸

MATTHEW SURPRISED ME with a visit to the Los Angeles Zoo. It was a sunny, spring morning—the morning after our first time making love. The air was dry and crisp. *So refreshing compared to muggy Miami*, I thought. We strolled through every exhibit, arms locked around each other's waists. I wore an almost-too-short sundress and chunky heels; Matthew sported a golf shirt, camouflage pants and white sneakers. We looked as mismatched as RuPaul and Rupert Murdoch, but I didn't mind. With Matthew, I got my first glimpse of zebras, elephants, giraffes and camels. Discovery seemed to be a common theme in our newfound love, and I liked how cultured and smart exploration made me feel.

We spent the entire afternoon driving up and down Pacific Coast Highway, holding hands while I gazed out at the rocky cliffs plunging into the deep blue ocean. I couldn't believe how much my life had changed in just six months—from country bumpkin to cross-country jet-setter. I rolled down my window and ran my fingers through the cool air. My horizons were widening faster than I'd ever imagined. I could finally squash my *Wizard of Oz* hecklers like bugs.

Matthew parked the car near Venice Beach. Bright-colored Art Deco buildings lined the oceanfront street. A long boardwalk flanked by towering palm trees snaked along the sand, dotted with artists, street performers and the occasional panhandler. It reminded me of South Beach—only smaller and weirder.

We kicked off our shoes and walked barefoot along the promenade, holding hands and letting the afternoon sun warm our faces.

Matthew guided me onto the sand. Behinds us, the eastward sky was bloated with haze and unknown possibilities. *Can I afford to keep flying to California? How much will my phone bill be? How often will we see each other?* Matthew squeezed my hand tightly every few minutes, releasing my tension.

Matthew leaned down and rolled up his pants. "Let's walk along the shore. Just like the first time."

My chest felt like it was going to burst from bliss. A romantic walk on the beach—every girl's dream. The cool, salty air whisked around us. We strolled hand in hand until the sun began to set. I felt as alive as the day I'd snorkeled in the Atlantic for the first time.

My smile disappeared. "How long will you be at sea?" I looked down at my toes and pressed them deeper into the cool, soggy sand.

His face darkened. "I can't be sure." He gripped my hand. "Maybe four weeks."

An eternity. My nerves began reeling. Missions were always top secret, classified and thus dangerous.

"When will I see you again?" My words oozed with fear and desperation. Thoughts of AK-47s and car bombs flashed through my head.

He raised the rim of his baseball cap. "Don't worry. Have faith in us." I collapsed into his tight hug.

"Will you take my art with you?" For every drawing Matthew had gifted me, I'd sent him an empty magnum-sized wine bottle painted with my abstract designs.

"Of course." He rested his chin on the crown of my head. "Whenever you start to miss me, just listen to 'Come Monday.'" Matthew loved all the island-anthem songs of Jimmy Buffett.

"I'll open a Corona Light." My arms stayed wrapped around his waist. "And we'll be back where we belong."

♦ ♦ ♦ ♦ ♦

MY EYES SWELLED with tears at the airport gate. Matthew stroked my face and hugged me while departing flight announcements boomed from the overhead speakers. I stared into his somber eyes. Matthew stuffed his hand into the pocket of his camouflage pants and pulled out folded papers.

"I'm not sure when I'll be able to write you again." He handed me a thick, crumpled envelope. "So you might want to wait a few days to read this."

I clutched the letter to my chest like a new diamond necklace. "It's going to be even harder now." Tears poured down my cheeks. A physical connection was now bonded to our sizzling emotional one, and my personal life was in shambles. Alicia had officially moved out the week before my trip. She'd insisted I owed her a deposit she'd never paid then left threatening messages on my answering machine. I'd woken up the next morning to find all four of my car tires slashed, right outside my bedroom window. Welcome to the sequel of *Single White Female*. I'd changed the locks on my front door, but we still had to share the same restaurant bus station when I returned to Miami.

"I know, but you've got to be strong." Matthew brushed my hair from my face. "You are better than any of those people. Besides, I need to know you'll be there for me." His strong hands squeezed my biceps like a football coach calling plays to the star quarterback. I looked into his eyes, letting his words sink in. We stood together at my gate in silence, arms locked around each other's waist. Fate was in the captain's seat.

I cried myself to sleep on the airplane.

🍷 🍸 🍷 🍸 🍷

THE PHONE RANG at my apartment before I'd set my keys on the kitchen counter. I dragged my sore body to the bookshelf in my bedroom, still aching from trying to sleep on the red-eye. My head felt as if I'd drunk a bottle of NyQuil.

I fumbled the receiver from the phone. "Hello?" My voice cracked with curiosity and fear. I waited for Alicia's hiss to strike through the line.

"Hey." Matthew's voice, curt and authoritative as always, collapsed my tension. My heart began humming. Only eight hours had passed since we'd said goodbye.

"I thought you were leaving today." Every syllable danced from my mouth. I took a deep breath. His unexpected call made me feel needed all over again.

"There's something I need to tell you before I leave." His words marched through the phone line. My heart pounded so hard, I could feel it in my toes. I'd spilled my emotions—on paper and in person—but thought I'd have to wait another eight weeks, not hours, to hear those three words leave his lips.

"I am married."

The receiver felt like a rock in my hand. His words were like a Ginsu knife, carving through my heart with the same ease as a tree branch, a beer can, a block of frozen spinach. My lips couldn't move. My whole world dangled from the edge of a cliff, and I could do nothing but wait for the rocks to crumble to the sea.

"It's not what it seems." His voice drowned out the hum of the phone line. My body trembled from shock and exhaustion. I listened to him talk, every word piercing me like an arrow. She was from Colombia. They'd met in Miami just before he'd joined the Navy. He said he'd married her to help her get her green card. His stressful military life needed the "normalcy" only marriage could provide, too. They were getting a divorce. His words sounded like typewriter keys bouncing against paper. A Kung-Fu fight scene of emotions broke out in my head. I felt like I'd been conned by Thomas Crown. I sooooo wanted to believe Matthew. He was my ocean, the man I'd sail through life with and into eternity. But the knot that had formed in my stomach never untied itself during his explanation.

I sat on my bed in silence, listening to the low hum inside the phone receiver. His only deception was supposed to be those lime wedges he'd stuffed in Coronas to make the swill taste refreshing! The anger of betrayal bubbled inside me.

"Lisa, are you still there?" Matthew shouted, as if we were platoon members separated during battle.

I should have yelled back, "Ten-four, motherfucker."

My chest felt ripped open. His confession kept barreling through my head. The courage to react finally overtook the shock. My move? I pressed my index finger on the "END" button then dropped the receiver on the floor. My hurt was bottled inside as always, far away from my boyfriend's ears. Before the off-the-hook beep rang through my apartment, tears shot down my cheeks like guided missiles.

I collapsed onto my bed and cried through waves of denial and embarrassment. Sure, Matthew wasn't perfect in terms of geography or job, but he'd wrapped me in a blanket of romance and emotional intimacy I'd craved my entire life. He'd bared his soul to me, which could have been a super-sized helping of crap if he was a liar, a ruthless heartbreaker who got his kicks off having affairs with women at every international port where his ship docked.

I went out and bought a Jimmy Buffett CD. And come Monday, everything was *not* all right.

That pill is just as hard to swallow now as it was back then. I'm still not sure I believe Matthew was a naval Casanova. I loved the movie *Green Card*. The crippling blow that my dream guy was married made me feel like a second-hand sweater from a thrift store. I was just as dirty as a South Beach shoplifter. I'd broken one of the Ten Commandments—a major one. My grandma's rosary was tucked in my jewelry box under his heap of love letters, and for days, I considered pulling it out and creating a confessional on the living room floor. What kind of bad karma was cursing me? I gave granola bars to panhandlers. I fed stray cats. I deserved a happily ever after—not dating hell.

🍶🥃🍷🍸🍾

I TUGGED OPEN the metal blinds in my bedroom windows, flooding the apartment with bright light. The fiery morning sun warmed my wet face. Four dark days had passed since *the* phone call. Four days of tears. Ninety-six hours of soul-searching. As I stared down at my favorite saw palmetto in the courtyard, a bright thought sliced through the sorrow: *Life could be worse.* Chris could have gotten me arrested for drug possession. Robert could have infected me with HIV. Marco could have slipped me a roofie and shaved my whole body. I'd come too far since Kansas to remain involved with some guy who *possibly* collected women like Beanie Babies. He had plenty of chances to spill *those* beans before we'd climbed into bed.

True love was still out there—with an honest, local man. Damn you, *Sleepless in Seattle,* for making me think a cross-country romance could work anyway! There was no Google to upchuck a background check, no social media accounts to stalk. Honesty and trust had always been the first pillars in a relationship for me. I trusted men until they give me a reason not to trust them. Believing Matthew was the man he'd demonstrated on paper—a fellow artist and hopeless romantic who wanted and needed me and showered me with compliments—came naturally. When you're twenty-one and living alone in a metropolitan city, some red flags just aren't obvious without the magnifying glass of time.

His letters and phone calls stopped after about six weeks—long after my inspiration to paint and write disappeared. The wine bottles began to stack up, but I couldn't stay away from that beach where we'd met. It was right where I belonged—minus the Corona Light.

JOHN
The Sweet Wine Days

John's thin frame squeezed between the crush of sweaty people circling on the dance floor. The sounds of trumpets, maracas and drums pulsed through my torso. His soft hand tugged me, shooting tiny currents up my arm.

Oh, the anticipation of where he'll touch me next. I shimmied my hips to the beat and watched John's backside flicker under pulsing lights: the jet-black hair, the cherry-red silk shirt, the baggy, black dress pants. He looked a bit like A.C. Slater from *Saved by the Bell*, and I was dying for him to ring mine. It was *merengue* night at Baja Beach Club, a word that, back then, still reminded me of Mom's lemon meringue pie.

John turned to me in the middle of the dancing crowd. Overhead lights blinked to the music, making his face flash white then dark. "Could you wait here for a minute, please?" The sweetness poured from his voice. His perfectly trimmed goatee tickled my ear lobe, and I nodded, the smoldering fire inside me igniting. *He's taking a different route to my heart. I like that.* His politeness always brought a big smile to my face—just when I was beginning to believe there were no nice guys in Miami. The most-used words in John's vocabulary were "please," "thank you, "miss" and "ma'am." I couldn't believe I'd spent months letting Alicia brainwash me into thinking that all Cuban men were sleazy cheaters tethered to their mothers for life...by a string of plantains.

"Okay," I shouted back, bouncing to the music. My shoulders swayed while John's kind, brown eyes circled my face. I quickly glanced away, back toward the door.

John brushed the curls off my shoulder. "Who are you looking for?"

I bit my lip. "No one." It didn't know what was worse: the thought of Latinos' eyes burning yucca-sized holes in my head for invading their turf or having a bartender from work see me with my arms wrapped around a busboy. The unspoken rule of dating hierarchy at restaurants was servers date servers or line cooks, i.e. peers. No moving up the ranks to managers or down to busboys and dishwashers...lines I dared to cross.

"You'll be okay here?" John flashed a sweet, sexy smile. It was our first real date, though we'd skipped dinner and a movie and went straight to the club for Latin dance night.

"I'm a survivor." I cracked a smirk as he disappeared into the crowd. John strutted like a businessman with enough connections to bypass the waiting line at Joe's Stone Crab. He was not your Olive Garden-variety busboy.

I watched John's silhouette carving through the crowd, changing colors under the flashing lights. My eyes scanned the room. Every single person on the dance floor had dark hair and dark eyes—except me. The women had their quintessential Latina curves and the guys their goatees. John fit in so well, gliding up to the DJ booth. I wore a tight, black jumpsuit with billowing legs (the fashionable follow-up to MC Hammer pants). My long, blond hair fell over the shoulders of my white blouse—one of those frilly tops with cascading ruffles like Prince wore in *Purple Rain*. I felt like I belonged about as much as a vegan in a steakhouse.

Silence poured over the dance floor. The voluptuous ladies with their short, black dresses and long, black hair froze next to their men. All heads turned toward the DJ booth. John swaggered back through the crowd, his big eyes locked onto mine. My whole body began to tingle, turbo-fueled by his desire. A man's deep, sensual voice, singing *a capella*, poured from the overhead speakers. I watched John's full lips singing along with every word. Every Spanish word. He could have been saying, "Your ass looks big in those horrible pants" for all I knew. My Spanish was limited to restaurant basics—*platos, tazas, serviettas, cuchillos, sopa, pollo*. Just hearing those foreign syllables rolling off John's tongue made me want to declare Spanish as my minor in college.

John pressed my palm flatly into his tiny hand. "Just follow my lead." We stood eye-to-eye with our shoulders squared; John was just 5-foot-6 and probably made bantamweight. His butt was smaller than mine, which was reason enough not to go out with him, but the thought of kissing a guy without straining my neck was intriguing. *Prince was only 5-foot-2!* I reminded myself.

Our noses touched. "Like this." John guided our hands to shoulder level, elbows bent at a ninety-degree angle. My chest thumped along with the song's bouncing horns, as John's free hand slid up my back. I felt as awkward as big-nosed Jennifer Grey in *Dirty Dancing*.

"Make me look like a regular." I leaned into his ear, catching his spicy-sweet, mysterious scent. "Help me blend in." *I'm a white girl living in a Latina world.*

John pulled back and looked me in the eye. "Hey. I like it that you're different."

I whirled my eyes, feeling my blond curls glowing like a neon sign.

John pressed his hand against the small of my back, bringing our hips close together. Suddenly, he launched our bodies into cadence with the rhythm. The song was sexy, fun and unusual all at once—so Miami. We glided with the music, moving in large circles. The baggy legs of my jumpsuit ballooned around me as we picked up speed, dancing in unison with the rest of the sultry crowd. From head to toe, his body movements flowed like fine silk, draping every beat. Like most Cuban-American guys I'd met, sexiness oozed from every inch of John—the groomed goatee, full lips, perfect nose, dark-brown eyes and light skin. He looked so hot, his accessory choices couldn't even turn me off—the plastic comb in his back pocket, the thick, gold chain around his neck and the matching ring on his pinky finger.

Beads of sweat glistened on my chest. "How am I doing so far?" My thoughts hopped from concentrating on not stepping on his toes to wishing another *gringa* or two would appear from the shadows, making me feel less like an outsider.

John smiled. "*Bien. Muy bien.*" We stayed locked together on the dance floor, bouncing to the fast-paced music until my blouse stuck to my back.

I laced my fingers tighter with his. "I've lived here way longer than you, and you're the one taking me new places." We both started giggling. John and I had met his first day on the job at The Cheesecake Factory, of course, the epicenter of my social universe. Every person I knew in Miami, I had met in that dining room. The restaurant felt like a tiny island, and finding an escape boat never crossed my mind. After Matthew told me about his top-secret wife, I'd waited tables sixty hours each week, throwing myself into the service of strangers. I didn't yet have the energy to put my heart out there again, and picking up extra shifts meant less time to think about how Matthew's marriage had shaken me to the core. John was patient, persistent, sweet and at the right place at the right time.

John bounced to the beat. "I haven't had this much fun since Los Angeles." He laughed, brushing my long, curly bangs behind my ears. John had just moved to Miami from Los Angeles, where Cubans were a Hispanic minority—very different from Miami. He was born and raised in a middle-class suburb. He had fond memories of the LA Zoo and sweeping valleys of Southern California. I tried to find our common ground without oversharing what had happened between Matthew and me.

At the end of the song, he twirled me around like a jewelry-box ballerina, tucking his bottom lip. His eyes scanned me from toe to head.

My eyelids fluttered, shooing away his unspoken compliment. "I'm glad this is our secret." My hand squeezed his. We'd been talking at work for a couple of weeks, but I'd kept it professional and discreet.

"They're going to find out sooner or later because we'll be doing this many more times," John said with a playful purr. "Who cares?"

I let his words sink in as we danced. *Did I really care?* John wasn't like the other busboys. John never stood in the main bus stand talking with grand animation about the ladies' boobs at table twenty-two. And he never called out "*Oye, Mami!*" when I walked into CocoWalk's back hallway before each shift wearing my white tank top. John's first words were "Excuse me, miss," as he'd carried a tray of clean coffee cups past me. He filled bus tubs the way librarians stocked bookshelves, and he never missed a chance to grab a towering stack of dirty side plates from my arms. Forget the flowers and chocolates. Teamwork on the floor could attract the most seasoned server.

John pulled back and wrapped both arms around my waist. My eyes flew to his. I felt like the Space Shuttle *Discovery* was about to launch from the pit of my stomach. He pulled my body closer, and my lips locked onto his like a magnet. His kiss was soft, yet forceful. His mouth tasted like Big Red gum, which my father had always chewed, and I'd detested until that moment. John stroked my cheeks as his tongue moved with mine. The sensory overload from the music, cinnamon and passion barreled through me. Lost in that moment, I wouldn't have cared if he got demoted to dishwasher.

His facial hair tickled my chin, as he pushed his lips harder against mine. *Oh well, tomorrow's skin rash will be worth it.* I'd never kissed a man with a furry face; rocking a beard wasn't cool in Kansas unless you were Mr. T or ZZ Top, but in Miami, goatees were all the rage.

With that dance floor kiss, John had me addicted to his touch. I'm still not sure how kissing a Latino didn't make the list in *1,000 Things to Do Before You Die*. My high school make-out sessions with gringos were fast and furious, marked by wild, rogue tongues and fleeting lips (except you, Lance). I'd always wanted more kisses, more hugs, more attention—then came John.

🍷 🍸 🍷 🍷 🍸

JOHN ARRIVED AT my front door right on schedule for our first dinner date—another way I could tell he wasn't a native Miamian—and greeted me with his usual, "Hey, sweetheart," followed by a warm, endless kiss, replete with both hands cradling my jaw bones. My knees got shaky as his tongue chased mine. Every nerve in my body felt scrambled. The smell of marinara sauce and gooey cheese filled the air.

John glanced down at the hem of my short, blue sundress. "Don't you look cute?" My grin grew wider. I looked down at my bare feet on the carpet, feeling my cheeks flush. I pushed my spaghetti strap back onto my shoulder and scurried back into the kitchen.

"Smells delicious, baby." John rubbed my bare shoulders. I kissed him on the cheek then grabbed an oven mitt from my top drawer. My first full-blooded Latin lover had transformed me into a completely different woman. I craved empanadas and plantains, and started throwing the words "*oye*" and "*pero*" around more than the domino players on *Calle Ocho*. Even though my stovetop prowess didn't extend beyond a box of Hamburger Helper, I had invited him over for a home-cooked meal—a twenty-four-year-old Latino who lived at home and had a simmering pot of *arroz con pollo* waiting for him every night. My inspiration for the menu? A brick of Italian Velveeta with a baked spaghetti recipe on the cardboard box. Food is a part of our cultural identity, so I'd returned to the comfort of my gastronomic roots—the world of the Pillsbury Doughboy, Betty Crocker and processed cheese.

John circled me in the kitchen, sneaking kisses and touching my hair, cheeks, shoulders, and arms while I bounced from duty to duty: grabbing plates from the cupboard, placing multiple pieces of silverware at our place settings, lighting candles. (Dining etiquette class from my sorority came in handy.) When we weren't at work, I could barely take a breath without John petting, hugging, squeezing or kissing me. He didn't show his love with an ink pen like Matthew. I felt like a newborn baby ushered into the center of his affectionate world.

John led me over to my glass-top dining table then pulled out a high-backed chair. As I served a mound of baked spaghetti on his plate with two forks, he poured some Riunite D'Oro (today known as Riunite Trebbiano Moscato) into my new black-stemmed glasses, which I'd purchased as a birthday present to myself. Riunite was the only brand I'd remembered from back home, so I'd decided to buy the pretty, gold-tipped label for our special occasion. Little bubbles fizzed in the glasses as John poured. The guy at the liquor store said the wine was smooth and sweet. It seemed fitting for a guy like John.

I raised my glass with a smile. "To new beginnings." I had no idea how any wine would taste with spaghetti. My wine of choice was sauvignon blanc in a magnum bottle, and I'd only sipped it as a concert aperitif with Christina. The time had arrived to start appreciating the marriage of wine and food.

John's smiling face flickered under the candlelight as we toasted full glasses. The bubbles tickled my tongue, and flavors of sugary peaches flooded my taste buds. It was a far cry from swigging Boone's Farm in the front seat of Emily's truck in high school. The only time I'd ever felt so civilized was my birthday dinner at the Olive Garden in Topeka, Kansas, with Chris.

"Oohhhs" and "aahhhs" flew from his mouth after the first bite. "This is delicious, sweetheart." He wiped his mouth with the napkin. "I love it that you cooked something I've never had before." He reached over and petted my hand. My face was all teeth. A log of Kraft cheese had helped me straddle another aspect of our cultural divide. *Go figure.*

Shop talk quickly ensued, as it always did when dating restaurant coworkers: biggest tip of the shift, worst customer of the day, longest wait for a table, tally of hung-over servers that shift.

His eyebrows scrunched. "Are Marco and Gabby still bugging you?" His tone was jealous; I found it quite cute.

I twirled my pasta with a fork and spoon. "Not really." My eyes stayed on my plate. "It just takes so much energy to ignore them, you know? I wish I was better at being a bitch but I'm not. I don't like having enemies. I don't like conflict." Marco still played with Gabriela's hair in the back hallway before work. Alicia still snarled at me in pre-shift meetings. Mark kept over-sharing the gory details of his *ménage-à-trois* marathons with a couple he'd recently found to replace Robert and Jessica, who'd both vanished from nightlife in the Grove. The environment was about as comfortable as wearing corduroy jeans in July.

"It's like the set of a soap opera there." John rested his fork on the edge of the plate. "I've only been there a month, and I can barely stand it." John had never worked in a restaurant before and didn't realize drama was always the daily special. Because John was thin, Latin and knew how to dress, he also had to endure hungry looks from one of the gay servers, Rupert, who carried a Louis Vuitton purse and wore Versace cuff links.

John took a long sip of the wine. "They act like a bunch of teenagers. Life isn't just about partying and getting laid. There is a real world out there." He scoffed and stabbed his fork in the pasta.

I nodded like a Southern Baptist at a sermon. John's sharp words made my foggy place in life suddenly seem clear. When I'd arrived in Miami, I'd thought I'd meet lots of people like me: college students working hard to graduate and land real jobs. I'd made many friends at the restaurant from all corners of the globe who talked big dreams, but the exiled men with degrees from universities in Cuba were still emptying bus tubs, the servers who said they were going back to college had not enrolled for fall semester and the models still hadn't landed the big agency contracts. Many temps were becoming lifers.

His nostrils flared. "Everyone there seems to have forgotten about their dreams." He tossed one hand in the air. "They should aspire for more in life." His driven eyes fixed on mine. My head kept bobbing as I coiled the spaghetti. It was the most motivational speech I'd heard since Richard had nearly fired me.

John wagged his head. "I just can't take it anymore." He reached for my hand and squeezed it hard. "I need to be doing what I was born to do." I looked at him with caring eyes. We'd never really talked about dreams before, other than chartering a boat and sailing to The Bahamas.

"What's your dream then?" I lifted my wine glass to my lips. Two years at a junior college in Los Angeles was the extent of his higher education, which worried the husband hunter in me. Our relationship centered around a shared love of dancing and public displays of affection. I couldn't be in a relationship for a month without contemplating marriage.

"I want to make a difference in peoples' lives." His brown eyes danced around my face. "I want to be an emergency medical technician."

I grinned and nodded approvingly. His desire to save strangers made him even more attractive.

John continued to gush about a classified ad he'd seen for a job at a 911-call center, the perfect training ground for an aspiring EMT. I stared into my half-empty wine glass. My heart sank at the thought of not seeing his goatee in the dining area.

"So when are you going to move onto something bigger and better?" He leaned over and pressed his lips softly to my forehead. "You're smart. You're beautiful. You have determination. You can do anything you put your mind to."

I blushed and looked down at the last spaghetti strings on my plate. I've never been comfortable receiving compliments. *If I'm so pretty, why does every guy I date shit on me?* Conversations with my father had never scratched the surface of kudos or advice. I don't recall any adult other than a teacher or two singing my praises. Memories of the parents who wouldn't let their children play with me—the latchkey kid from the other side of the railroad tracks—were the stains that remained. I had to learn to believe in myself.

"This is pretty big for me, you know." I grinned into my half-full glass. Bigger and better back home was working at the mall in Joplin, Missouri. Three years later, I was living in a tropical paradise, spending afternoons Rollerblading on the boardwalk of Key Biscayne. *How could my dreams get any bigger?* I took another gulp of sweet wine, letting the citrusy bubbles coat my mouth. Fizzy wine didn't bring on the usual buzz—an enlightening discovery. John's words began to work their sober magic. *Did waiting tables with people who spent their days sipping mimosas at News Café do anything to advance my dream of being a writer?*

I lifted my chin. "Graduating from college is my dream." I swirled my glass with confidence. My state residency had been approved for the fall semester, and my checking account was finally stocked with enough cash to cover one semester's tuition at Florida International University. My sights were set on nailing a 3.75 GPA—a big middle finger to anyone back home who thought white trash was my destiny. I slurped the spritzy wine.

Success is the best revenge.

"But what about your work until then?" He stroked my hand.

"Restaurants. Bars. Working for tips." I stared at his hand rubbing mine. "That's all I've ever known." I'd never stopped to realize that working around food and booze was the only line of work I'd ever considered. I never wanted to be a cashier at a gas station or bowling alley. I found comfort in making small talk with strangers while filling their bellies and getting them tipsy. The restaurant grind was inked into my being like a first tattoo.

"Try something new," John said, covering his mouth while he chewed. "Take a risk."

I pushed the pasta with my fork. "I can't make enough money writing to live here and go to school." Besides carrying four cups of full coffee in one hand, writing was my only other talent. But my penchant for rambling and a feeble vocabulary crippled my progress. I credited my literary handicap to the fact that the only books my mom kept around the house were the Bible and an astrology ephemeris. Making $8 per hour writing obituaries for the local newspaper—as I'd done before moving to Miami—wouldn't even cover my monthly rent.

"Don't forget." I took a bite. "I have no one to ask for help." His parents lived down the hallway. Running out of money and returning home to enroll at the local university was not an option. Some force had been pulling me down a different path for years. Staying in control of my destiny meant working my butt off and never asking my parents for money.

After dinner, John cradled me in my papasan chair. His hands never slid up my dress. He petted my hair and continued to coach me to follow my dreams. When I finally agreed to research new job opportunities outside the restaurant world, he kissed me goodbye and left for the night—like a perfect gentleman.

🍷🍸🍷🍸🍸

JOHN CLOSED MY front door behind him. "I have good news, sweetheart." His luscious smile grew as he dropped his backpack by my entryway closet. He rushed toward me, planting an intoxicating kiss on my lips. My whole body turned to Jell-O. John spent a good minute brushing his fingers across my cheeks before releasing me from his soft embrace.

"What could be better than this?" I asked in a purr, grabbing his hands. I wore a blue cotton tank and khaki skirt—typical attire during the sweltering summer. We'd begun planning work shifts so that we had two nights off together each week. More than three weeks had passed since we'd started dancing together. I'd cooked him dinner twice. Things were getting downright serious.

John walked into the kitchen. "Do you have anything we can celebrate with?" I stood next to the half-wall by my front door, leaning against its counter and watching him. John opened the refrigerator and pulled out a bottle of Riunite D'Oro, which had become our go-to drink. Sipping sweet sparkling wine at my place made us feel more refined than drinking beer at a bar. Wine separated us from the lifers. We were going places.

Seeing John make himself comfortable at my apartment made my heartbeat flicker. Lisa Loeb's voice drifted from my stereo, warbling for him to "Stay." *How appropriate.* John had never stayed overnight out of respect for his Cuban-Catholic mother. I only understood the Catholic no-sex-before-marriage rule, which I'd been ignoring since dropping out of Catechism in ninth grade. John lived with his family in west Kendall, about thirty minutes south of the Grove, and he'd yet to invite me home to meet his parents. I figured that was a Latin thing, too. I decided not to rock the *flotilla*.

John cracked open the screw cap bottle in the middle of my kitchen and poured his news first: He'd landed the job with the 911-call center in Kendall. He fished two wine glasses from my kitchen cabinet while jabbering on about his new responsibilities. I stuffed my hands in the pockets of my skirt. His commute would be shorter, his hours normal and his wages higher. Training started in one week. *Great, just great.*

John's teeth gleamed as he poured the wine. "I can't wait to give my notice." He paused, watching the wine's frothy head subside so he could fill my glass to the rim. I stared at the tiny bubbles as he handed me the flute. My face drooped, a mixture of happiness and sorrow. I pushed my hair off my shoulders. He crooked his neck.

"I'm sorry, sweetie." He pulled me into a long, soft hug. "I didn't mean it that way. I'll miss seeing you at work every day. This is the right move for me, though. You know that." He stroked my cheek and reminded me that the FIU south campus was fifteen minutes from his new office.

I looked down at my bare feet. "I know. It's just that I'll miss you." We stood in the kitchen doorway, silently sipping our wine. I'd held back my feelings until then. Living with Matthew's ghost had taught me about having patience in romance.

"Any updates on your job search?" He took my hand and led me to the papasan in my living room. Our talk had encouraged me to try to find a way out of the hospitality rabbit hole. I'd studied the newspaper classifieds every morning, circling every job that piqued my interest: an assistant manager for a tropical plant nursery, a tour guide at Fairchild Tropical Gardens and Dolphin Harbor Staff at Miami Seaquarium. (Life before Craigslist had its inconveniences.) Practically every job opening had a requirement I didn't meet: bilingual. Knowing how to ask for cream and sugar in my coffee in Spanish would get me nowhere at a palm tree farm. I tried to suppress my inner Bindi Irwin. Those jobs didn't get me closer to a career in journalism or public relations. Sadly, there were no advertised positions at the *Miami New Times* or *Miami Herald*.

I rested one hand on his thigh and gulped a mouthful of wine. "I have some news, too." I smiled sheepishly as his eyes perked. Sweet, fizzy bubbles coated my tongue, calming my nerves. "I did get a job offer." My tone was slow yet firm.

He's going to shit an empanada.

"I'm going to be a bartender."

John's bushy brow caved, and the Champagne flute shot to his lips.

I bolted through an explanation of my rationale. As soon as I'd started looking for a job beyond the restaurant world, Mike, our bar manager, had called me into the back office and had asked if I wanted to join his team. He'd spent years tending bar at TGI Friday's—Marco's old stomping grounds—and could flip bottles like Tom Cruise in *Cocktail*. He wanted to teach me how to make bellinis and how to burn the well. I knew that I needed some sort of boundary between my work and personal life. Two feet of granite countertop at the bar seemed like a good start, a clear separation from my dating history on the floor.

I looked into John's brown eyes for a sign of approval. He cracked a smile.

"That's what you really want to do?" John petted my arm. He rested his wine glass on my colorful coffee table. I looked down at the bold, abstract swirls and circles I'd painted on the tabletop during my cross-country romance with Matthew. I felt his memory creep in and grabbed my wine glass.

"No," I replied firmly as John played with a lock of my hair. "I want to graduate from college and work in public relations. But this is a promotion. I'll make more money and work less shifts. I'll be able to take weekdays off to focus on school." My determined eyes fixed on his. Bartender was a coveted position that rarely came open. The bar seemed like a throne, and only four employees got to occupy it. They wore black jeans and black sneakers, a clear differentiation from the all-white server uniforms. I wanted to feel that power. Working while going to college would be much easier behind the bar, where one week of tips would cover a month's rent.

John caressed my hand. "As long as it gets you closer to your dream." His big, brown eyes gazed at me. "I know you will never be a lifer."

I smiled and pecked his cheek, feeling his goatee scratch my face. He'd never seen the picture of me drunk on the floor at Howl at the Moon, pretending to be a dead cockroach. Becoming a lifer had its attractions, and I'd dabbled in that world, *sans* hard drugs. Having a 401K and going to bed before ten seemed more attractive in the long run.

We finished off the first bottle of Riunite, my head resting on John's shoulder. He continued to pet and kiss me like a baby kitten. We talked more shop. The server soap opera had entered its final season. Marco and Gabriela had broken up after a fight during one of their morning surfing sessions. Then Marco had received a forty-percent rating on a Secret Shopper report, and was fired before the ink had dried on the printer paper. Alicia was moving to New York. Karma was doing its bidding.

John pulled a second bottle from the fridge. My motor purred, lubed with affection, alcohol and the sweet taste of fate.

He walked back into the living room. "Can I ask you something, sweetheart?" He stood above me, smiling. I looked up at his perfectly groomed side burns and shiny black goatee. My eyelids batted with curiosity. "Can I stay the night with you?" My heart leapt from his polite surprise.

He pointed to his backpack by the door. "I brought my things." He reached for my hand. "I told my mom I was staying at a friend's house. I hope that's okay."

I grinned, cradling the wine glass in my free hand. "It's about time."

He charged me like a *luchador*. His hands cupped my face as his tongue plunged into my mouth. Wine sloshed all over my chest.

"Hey. No wet T-shirt contests." My lips murmured between kisses.

John looked down at my damp tank top. "Sorry, sweetie." He grabbed my empty wine glass and rested it on the coffee table. "Let me clean that up for you." John dove his tongue into my teeny cleavage.

Ay, dios mio.

We rocked back and forth on the couch, him kissing my lips and neck until my whole body ached. If sex with Marco was soft porn, then sleeping with John was going to be a Danielle Steel novel.

John tugged me into the darkness of my bedroom. He reached for the light switch.

I wagged my finger playfully. "*No me gusta.*" Two glasses of five-percent alcohol bubbly wasn't enough to loosen my inhibitions, and sex was definitely on the menu. After almost a year in Miami, I couldn't help but wonder what sleeping with a purebred Cuban would feel like. My curiosity had been simmering longer than a vat of *ropa vieja*.

A street lamp sprayed slivers of gray light through my closed mini-blinds. John touched my shoulders, guiding me into a seated position on the edge of the bed. He stood over me and kissed my forehead before moving down to my lips. My body shook like a washer on spin cycle. *Ricky Martin's got nothing on you, baby.*

John slipped my wine-soaked tank top over my head, exposing my padded bra. *Ugh.* The Olsen twins had bigger boobs than me, and they hadn't even hit puberty. *He's small. I'm small,* I reminded myself. My eyes followed his as they locked on my chest. He pressed his lips on my shoulder blade, gliding my body back to the center of the bed.

"You're so beautiful," he whispered. "You look like a California girl. I can't believe you're mine."

I blushed, feeling my boobs flattening like pancakes under the weight of his body.

"Those eyes. That hair. That smile." His lips touched my eyebrows.

Relief rippled through me. *Finally!* I wanted to scream with delight. I wrapped my arms around his chest, hugging him tight. His body felt so light and small, I could have bench-pressed him.

"You are too good to me." I squeezed him like a bath sponge. With John, I finally felt beautiful. I felt wanted in my own bed—not a motel room.

He kept pouring on the compliments thicker than suntan oil in August, and my vocal cords iced over like a windshield in winter. No man had been so gentle and intimate, giving compliments while looking into my eyes. My body was officially his; he could mold me like Play-doh. His legs and arms interlocked with mine. We looked like beginners playing a game of Strip Twister.

John pulled away and stood above me. "I want to look at you, baby."

A frown shot across my face. I squirmed a hooked fish, uncomfortable with his bravado. Having a well-mannered guy staring at my half-naked body in silence made me feel like a middle schooler getting my first physical. *What will he do when he sees my scar?* My mind started spinning the web of self-doubt again. John had told me how much he loved my curvy hips, but how long could a Cuban man be satisfied with tiny boobies? Latinas were stacked. I was stacked like a pad of paper. I distracted myself from my insecurities by unzipping his fly. *Calvin Klein boxer briefs!? Rico suave.*

His tongue slid so deep into my mouth, I could hear his heart beating.

He inched his lips to my ear. "You want me to bus your table?"

What?! My back stiffened as my mind reeled. *Is that code for oral sex?* When you only date men at work, sometimes it can be hard for them to see you in a different light.

I pressed my lips to his, hoping to move beyond the shop talk.

He lifted my mini skirt and tugged at my panties, kissing my knees along the way. I arched my back in anticipation of his tongue, which had worked wonders on every inch of my body...except *that one.* My breath quivered with pleasure as I closed my eyes.

John slid up my body faster than a wet Slip 'n Slide. I felt him hard inside me, his small hips thrusting back and forth at warp speed. It felt like a gummy worm was gyrating inside me. John's penis was skinny, short and gooey. *My little man is little everywhere!?* He started moaning, sharp and shrill like a cat trapped in a shower. The shock froze my entire body. He didn't even put on a condom or ask me if I was on the pill.

"*Ey, Mami,*" he whispered in my ear. The hairs of his goatee touched my earlobe, shooting goose bumps down my arms. "Your body drives me crazy." My eyes slammed shut as his lean frame pounded against my skin. I felt like a mechanical bull being ridden by a lemur that had just drunk a case of Red Bull.

My mind raced along with the frantic pace of his hips. *He just called me Mom.* I pictured our Catholic grandmothers hovering over the bed like guardian angels, wagging their fingers. Memories of the ever-polite John flashed through my head. *Could two bottles of fizzy wine turn my Cuban prince into a horny sleaze bag?*

Before I could push the horrid maternal images from my mind, he pushed himself deeper into me. His skinny body arched as he threw back his head and let out a long, screeching wail. John collapsed on top of my half-clothed body—all this in less time than it takes to microwave a bag of popcorn.

Welcome to the world of a Latin lover. The thought scrolled through my head slower than movie credits. Unprotected, primate sex was not on my list of firsts to experience with John! His skin began sticking to mine. I stared at my ceiling in silence, feeling the weight of his body grow heavier. My inner voice began scolding: *You dated him quite a while before you crawled into bed. Why didn't you have the protection talk?* He'd seemed so sweet and harmless—just like Riunite.

At least he's still holding me afterward. Well, sort of. He didn't hop off once he'd reached his goal like a cowboy on a rodeo horse. Every guy is entitled to one quickie after a dry spell, right? I rationalized the situation, trapped under his sweaty body with my skirt crumpled around my waist. Maybe John's manners wouldn't have said *"adiós"* if I would have initiated the heart-to-heart talk. My eyes darted around his body, looking for the best escape route straight to my shower. *Thank God I'm still on the pill.*

While John's limp body covered me, I listened to his breath coast into a relaxed, slow pace. I stared at his thick head of black hair in the darkness. As I raised my fingers to touch his shoulder, he made a sound.

He began to snore.

I squeezed slowly out from underneath him. He yawned and rolled over. His mouth was wide open, his closed eyes, his naked body spread-eagle on my bed. *No, gracias.* I'd just lost my taste for Latin men.

MICHAEL
The Detox Days

I pressed the phone to my chest and stared up at my apartment's pine ceiling. My heart throbbed against the receiver, soaking up his invitation. *He just asked me to have dinner with his parents.*

"Hello? You still there?" Michael's sugary-sweet voice filled the phone line. He always spoke with the exuberant tone of a cruise ship social director.

I lay on my bed, twirling the phone cord. "Yes, sorry. Ummm, well, okay. Sure." My voice sputtered with trepidation and elation. He asked my permission for everything: *Can I take you to dinner? Can I hold your hand? Can I use your bathroom? Would it be okay if I kissed you?* A respectful, polite guy who didn't have a dark side? Too good to be true.

"Are you sure-sure?" Michael's voice fired back to my underwhelming acceptance. I clutched the phone against my cheek like an ice-cold bottle on a beach day, listening eagerly to the phone hum. He'd been driving the bus of our relationship down a very civilized road for two months. No crash. No burn. It felt like real, adult love.

"Sure-sure," I whispered with a grin. After a full year of false starts with men, I'd finally built a little wall of my own. Practicing emotional restraint would help me weed out the Steve Stiflers because those horny toads flocked to me like teens to a kegger. John had only been out of the picture for a few months and had already knocked up his new girlfriend—talk about dodging a bullet!

"Good." The sweet excitement in his voice returned. "I've been wanting to do this for a long time." My mind reeled from the blizzard of bliss. It was the logical progression of a relationship, which had eluded me since leaving the Midwest.

🍺 🍸 🍷 🍹 🍷

THAT WEEK, THE hours crept by. When Sunday finally came, I didn't need his driving directions. Michael's home was located one block off Old Cutler Road, a few miles north of where I'd lived with Chris.

I cruised along the nostalgic road that snaked from Coconut Grove down to Cutler Ridge, watching the mammoth banyan canopies and walled fortresses whiz past my windshield—my daily commute only twelve months before. The fate sign started flashing in my head. Five days had passed since I'd seen Michael—120 hours to think about our mature relationship and my crumbling wall.

The family estate looked more like a compound, covering at least one acre of pine-shrouded land—something I'd never seen before within the Miami city limits. A brown, corral-style fence lined the property, leading me down a driveway as long as a Wal-Mart parking lot. Rows of oak trees flanked the paved drive, and manicured lawns fanned out and disappeared behind a sweeping, ranch-style brick house. It looked like a Kansas City mansion, not the ubiquitous Mediterranean villas of Coral Gables. Even though I'd grown up in a house slightly bigger than their garage, my jitters melted away.

I parked my Chevy Cavalier in the circular drive behind Michael's turquoise Honda Prelude. I let the air conditioning blast my face while readjusting my khaki dress shorts. My pulsed ramped up. I checked my hair and make-up in the rear-view mirror. I needed to bring my A-game, like Julia Roberts in *Pretty Woman* after charm school. Michael was my best catch to date, and those were serious words coming from a girl who grew up bass fishing.

Michael stepped through the double oak doors onto the front steps, his broad shoulders filling the doorway. He stood 6-foot-2 and was the biggest guy I'd ever dated—I'm talking hunky-jock big, not Dunkin'-Donuts-junky big. I still picked up shifts on the floor occasionally, and during that fateful Sunday brunch, the hostess had sat Michael's party of three in my station, in a long booth roomy enough for six people, which would typically piss off any server. But as soon as he'd ordered an Arnold Palmer and his sky-blue eyes met mine, I wanted to know more about him. Michael was Kirk Herbstreit handsome with the body of a linebacker. He had the kind of Cheesecake Factory-savvy to order Crusted Chicken Romano with extra sauce on the side without my upsell. Every time I'd refilled his drink, he'd smiled and said, "Thank you, Lisa." I'd blushed and scurried away to the service bar. Michael had left a twenty-five-percent tip on a $75 tab—passing a critical part of every server's dating litmus test—and he'd circled around the bus station after he'd paid, waiting to ask me out.

Smiles spread across our faces as I walked toward Michael. My heartbeat began sprinting. His rosy cheeks glowed in the late afternoon sun, and his blond hair looked more sun-bleached than usual, making his blue eyes pop. He wore his usual khaki Dockers shorts, a blue-striped Polo and a pair of those leather loafers people wear on yachts. Preppy hot.

I tugged my Limited top from my chest to fan myself. It was a cool, dry day in October, but it suddenly felt as hot and humid as July. My body experienced global warming whenever Michael was around.

"Boy, did I miss you." Michael scooped me up and spun me around in his big arms. I squealed like a child on a merry-go-round, feeling the rush of emotions spiral through my body. His lips darted to mine for a quick kiss then rushed away. My lips parted, yearning for more, as my feet dangled off the ground. I felt like a girl sneaking kisses in a high school hallway.

"Really?" I nuzzled his neck. "Ah, I missed you, too." I inhaled deeply, savoring the familiar scent of his skin—crisp, clean, citrusy. Five days was the longest we'd been apart. It was the honeymoon phase of dating for two full-time students in South Florida, where college campuses almost outnumber shopping malls. I'd begun my first semester at Florida International University's south campus on the Tamiami Trail; Michael was back to school for a physical therapy degree at Florida Atlantic University in Boca Raton, which made my downtown Miami apartment an ideal pit-stop for "alone time" before or after classes.

Michael rested me gently on the concrete step. He pulled my torso closer to his wide chest, engulfing me with one of his soft, bear hugs. I stood on the tippy toes of my chunky leather sandals, drinking in the moment.

I pulled back with a smirk. "Watch it, handsy." My arms stayed wrapped around his waist. "Your parents are inside."

"We have nothing to worry about." He pecked my lips between grins. "My mom and dad aren't stupid." His big arms squeezed me again, making me feel cherished and protected. "We talk about stuff." It seemed so cool to date someone who had conversations about sex with his parents.

The first time he'd made love to me, we'd sat together at the foot of my bed, listening to my Everything but the Girl CD—mellow, estrogen-heavy stuff. He'd held my hands and told me how much he cared for me—how he'd never felt so good about a relationship. He'd asked me if I was ready to take the next step. I'd cradled his rosy cheeks in my palms and kissed his lips softly. There was no alcohol to cloud our judgment. We talked about protection before our clothes were off. No monkey business!

"Still, I want them to like me." I tucked my face into his chest. His crisp cologne filled my nose again. I closed my eyes, relishing his scent.

He breathed into my hair. "They already like you. I like you." I pushed my face deeper into his golf shirt. *This is what love should be like.* My mind twirled from its cloud.

"So this is the house," Michael said cheerfully, as he led me into a grand entryway under a crystal chandelier. The entryway spilled into a formal living room big enough for two fancy couches and a baby grand piano. The centerpiece in my childhood living room was a twelve-gun cabinet.

"How were things on the Gulf?" My mind switched gears. "Felt good to go back?"

Michael tugged at my hand. "Not really. That was my last trip for a long time." For the past three years, Michael had been living in Tampa, working as an athletic trainer for University of South Florida's football team. Even though he had a bachelor's in kinesiology, he'd decided a physical therapy degree would make him more attractive to Division I collegiate football programs, so he'd just moved back home to study at FAU. Yes, I'd stumbled on a "relo"—a recently relocated man—who had no knowledge of my dark dating history. He was twenty-six years old, career-focused and shockingly single.

Michael guided me down the long hallway past three bedrooms and a bathroom. Class pictures of Michael and his brother, from kindergarten to high school graduation, lined each side of the wallpapered hallway. He paused in his bedroom doorway, letting me walk in first. His politeness mirrored John's, and I tried not to let it haunt me. The white boy even cuddled like a Cuban. I didn't have to worry about cultural differences causing tension in our relationship, or him calling me "*Mami*" in bed. He didn't speak Spanish or eat *empanadas*. And he wore condoms.

"See, I told you it wasn't much," Michael said as we stepped into his childhood bedroom. A queen sleigh bed sat in the middle of the spacious room, surrounded by a matching dresser, roll-top desk and bookshelf. Sports memorabilia and old pictures papered the walls.

I poked around his space. "Are you kidding me? This place is huge. And it's free." His bedroom was the same size as the efficiency apartment I'd moved into near Cuban Memorial Boulevard to save money. My eyes scanned Michael's framed high school football and golf team pictures on the walls. All I could afford to hang at my place were colored baskets and a framed poster from the Coconut Grove Arts Festival, but I'd proudly showed Michael my simple home. Living in a shoebox apartment helped me pay all my bills and still have ample time for my studies.

"Yeah, it's just that." Michael paused, his blue eyes cutting through me. He looked away to the football trophies on his dresser. "Being here makes me feel like a kid again, but not in a good way." I watched him walk over to a Miami Hurricanes mascot stuffed animal in the corner and kick it.

I stepped to his bookshelf. "You're really lucky though." I picked up a quarterback figurine and examined its hand-painted detail.

He stuffed his hands in his short pockets. "I guess you're right." His voice bounced each word like a cheerleader. The sound of a football game on television drifted from the other end of the house.

I sat down on the edge of his bed and ran my hands across the red bedspread. It felt plush, expensive. I looked up at Michael watching me survey his surroundings.

Michael stepped toward the bed and leaned over me. My heart shot into my throat like a pinball. I closed my eyes and waited for his lips. His fingers glided down my back. My lungs sucked in air. Sex with Michael was calm and conservative, as I figured it should between two people who truly cared for each other, and were always stone-cold sober.

I threw open my eyes and pulled away. "We shouldn't." My voice had the strength of a respectable college woman, but my hormones were flailing like spring breakers at a rave. We were buttoned-up students who didn't have time for quickies or drinking binges. I now call him my detox boyfriend. It's good for your grades to date one of these boys during college.

His lips brushed my earlobe. "You're probably right."

Michael pulled me down the hall toward the living room, his gigantic hands laced in mine. A Florida room with vaulted ceilings opened to a kitchen-dining room larger than The Cheesecake Factory veranda. A wall of sliding glass doors led to a sparkling pool shaped like a kidney bean. Michael's father stood up from a recliner in the sunken living room. I walked toward him with the confidence of an Ivy League graduate at a job interview. He scooted toward me and smiled as his hand extended to grip mine. He stood as big and broad as Michael with a full head of thick, gray hair and the same piercing, blue eyes.

"Michael tells me you're quite the fisherman," his father said with a laugh, deep lines forming in his cheeks.

I shook his hand firmly, my eyes never leaving his. I knew I'd already scored Brownie points with Michael's dad. For our first date, Michael had taken me fishing off the coast of Key Largo in his family's twenty-eight-foot Boston Whaler. But first, we'd gone swimming at a sandbar hidden beyond a maze of red mangroves. I'd baited my own hook to impress him. We'd caught four yellow-tailed snappers and had cooked them for dinner at his family's waterfront condo overlooking Sunset Cove. We'd eaten on their open-air patio under a palm tree. At sunset, he'd asked me if he could kiss me. It still ranks at the top of my list for best first date of all time. And I did not put out.

I smiled bashfully. "My dad was a good teacher." I decided not to mention the American Legion fishing derby I'd won in third grade. Fishing with Michael had reconnected me to happy memories of my father. I'd learned early on that the only way to get some face time with my dad was to take up his hobbies, so I'd coon hunted and bass fished until my grandma'd bought me Barbie dolls.

I turned to the leather sectional to greet Michael's brother, Jeff, who was sprawled out with one arm pointing a remote control toward the big screen. He was a disheveled, brown-haired version of Michael.

"Did you bring me any Chicken Madeira?" Jeff asked with a sneer.

I shot him a sassy look. "Did you bring me season tickets?" Jeff played football for the University of Miami. I'd waited on him three times with Michael, and his restaurant humor made me feel even more at home.

Over the hum of a mixer, Michael's mother shouted her hellos from the kitchen. Michael ushered me under a doublewide doorway connecting the living room to the kitchen. His mom stood over a white-tiled island circling a hand mixer in a big metal bowl. She was tall and lean with Michael's same button nose, rosy cheeks and big smile.

I walked around the island and reached out my hand as she wiped hers in a dishtowel. Shaking hands was nostalgic after a year of double-cheek kissing strangers—the Latin way to greet someone.

"Nice to see you again," we said in unison. I blushed as we shook hands. She looked like a mid-fifties soccer mom with her diamond stud earrings, a pink golf shirt and a flowery apron.

"Jinx." She laughed.

I suddenly felt like we were long lost girlfriends from middle school. Her lunch order flashed through my mind: Chinese chicken salad, iced tea with no ice, half a slice of White Chocolate Raspberry Truffle cheese-cake—the other half put into a to-go box for Michael's dad.

"Would you like any help?" I asked, my inner waitress working over-time.

"You're our guest, honey." She turned to the sink and flipped on the faucet. "You just make yourself at home." Her hospitality was just enough country to summon my inner Elly May Clampett from eternal exile.

"I haven't had homemade mashed potatoes in years." I looked into the metal bowl with wide eyes. "My mom made them all the time when we were kids. Now I only get them during Thanksgiving dinner."

"When you're the only woman in a house full of men, you have to make them every Sunday." She winked.

I gripped the edge of the kitchen island, nodding. I could feel the bond forming between us and fought back my perma-grin. Their family ties were reeling me in like a marlin. *I could be the daughter she never had. I could be a part of this happy family.*

"I'll put you to work though, mister." She tossed a pair of metal tongs to Michael. He grabbed a ceramic platter off the island and walked over to a casual dining table in front of the sliding glass doors. Then she yelled "Dinner's ready!" over the blaring television just like my mom always did.

Michael pulled out a high-backed oak chair for me then circled the table with a pitcher of iced tea, filling our glasses. The family settled into their usual seats with parents at the heads and sons on the sides. Steaming platters and bowls fanned out along the center of the table. Michael sat down across from me, and we exchanged bashful looks. His mother handed each of us a heavy china plate from the stack in her arms.

I took a long sip of iced tea, feeling the rush of the sugar high I'd traded for tipple years before. Seven years had passed since my family had gathered as a happy unit, eating fried chicken take-out and drinking homemade tea. I'd been so wrapped up in restaurant service that I'd forgotten the true magic of food—it brings loved ones together, even if only for an hour or two.

"Your saw palmettos are beautiful." I nodded toward the trees beyond the backyard pool while dishing potatoes onto my plate. "I've never seen a traveler's palm that big inside the city limits, either."

"Michael told us you study plants." His mom raised a dainty bite of potatoes to her mouth.

I nodded with confidence, trying to fend off a giant grin. "I love how interesting and diverse the ecosystems are down here." I launched into an animated explanation of my scholastic strategy, using my fork as a prop. FIU required more science electives to graduate with a communications degree than KSU, so I'd stocked up on any environmental science class that got me closer to Florida's exotic flora and fauna.

Throughout the conversation, I chewed intentionally slow to avoid warp-speed shoveling, a habit picked up working in restaurants. My elbows were off the table and my back straight. I blabbed on about my father instilling his love of nature in me, but didn't mention the times he never came home from the bar to take me mushroom hunting.

"Your place in the Keys is lovely." My eyes circled the table. "I'm envious that you get to cruise through mangroves anytime you want." I jabbered on about my fascination with the colony of plants and animals living symbiotically in the roots of the red mangrove tree.

"So, what made you want to leave home?" Michael's mother asked.

I stared down at my plate and chewed far longer than necessary. *I knew that one was coming.*

"I had a bad winter." My shoulders shrugged. "I lost my financial aid, and it's easier to make a living and go to school full-time in a big city." My eyes moved from my potatoes to Michael's smile. I'd navigated the anticipated question without making my psychedelic past seem too colorful. Chris—and every mess of a guy I'd cared about since him—were buried in my closet. Forever. I took a long sip of my iced tea, feeling as if my head was finally clear for the first time since the big move.

I cut my steak into tiny bites, feeling all eyes on me. "But my real passion is public relations. I want to work in media relations for the Audubon Society."

His mom sipped her iced tea and glanced at Michael. "Looks like you've finally found someone busier than you."

Michael glanced across the table, his grin growing. Michael's mom told stories about him juggling school, coaching peewee football and volunteering as a trainer at high school games. They never buried their heads in their plates. No one farted or burped. It was nothing like home.

"We've been talking about me so much, maybe we should talk about you." I rested my knife gently on the edge of the plate. "Did you do anything on your trip besides work?" My gaze turned back to Michael's rosy cheeks. He'd spent the previous weekend in Tampa helping out the coaching staff at a USF football game. Michael hadn't told me much about his life back in Tampa—just the gruesome stories about shattered ankles and broken legs he'd helped mend.

Michael grabbed his glass and took a huge gulp. "Ummm, no." His tone was flat. He looked down at his half-eaten tri-tip. "I told you it was my last trip." His voice boomed through the kitchen, filled with guttural frustration. The piece of steak in my mouth felt like a ticking time bomb.

My eyes bounced from Michael to his mother. Everyone buried their heads in their plates. Knives scratched against china. ESPN buzzed from the big screen in the next room. *Okay. What the fuck just happened?* His brother and dad took long sips from their glasses then looked past Michael to the television. I chewed the meat and forced a swallow. My throat felt fiery hot, like I'd just downed a flaming Dr. Pepper. It was as if I'd asked how his grandma was, and she'd just died.

Michael hacked away at his steak as if his knife were a chainsaw. His mother started talking about the latest tropical storm forming off the coast of Africa. Jeff and his dad began reciting highlights from the morning Dolphins' game. My chest pounded with anxiety. I'd flipped some sort of psychological switch and had no idea how to hit rewind.

His mom stood up swiftly, her chair legs scraping the tile floor.

"Can I...uh...help?" My voice cracked. I looked up at Michael's mom, searching for a lifeline. *Let me help clean up this mess. Make whatever just happened disappear.* It was the psychology of a waitress—a clean table wiped away any bad memories of the last meal I'd served. I felt so comfortable washing dishes with Michael in Key Largo. I needed someone to put me to work.

"No, that's all right, honey," she said softly, looking down at us. "I'm sure you and Michael have a lot to talk about." Her blue eyes turned to ice. He lifted his glass and shook the ice cubes loose. My eyes stared at his forehead, waiting for him to look at me. His head flew from left to right. He looked about as comfortable as a straight army sergeant sunbathing on South Beach at 10th and Ocean. I looked down at the remnants of beef on my plate and dropped my napkin on the table.

Michael's face turned beet red. "You want to go outside?"

The front doors closed behind us.

"I'm so sorry." He grabbed my hands on the front steps. "Tonight wasn't supposed to turn out like this." He stared at my fingers as he rubbed them. A wave of relief washed over me. I tucked my bangs behind my ears.

"It's okay. I understand." I wrapped my arms around his waist and squeezed tightly. "Juggling work and school is wearing on you." My chin rested square on his chest. "I get it. I feel the same way." I looked up at him, searching for reassurance. Michael's blue eyes stared down at me. A look of conflict and frustration covered his rosy face. I dropped my arms and stepped back, feeling the steak start to churn in my stomach.

"I think...we...need...to...talk." Michael paused between every word. He scuffed the soles of his shoes on the concrete step. I twirled my hair to keep my hands busy as my frayed emotions dangled in the warm night air. "You remember how we talked about how we weren't going to talk about our past relationships?" His voice trembled the question.

My stomach began twitching with fear. Rather than recite our entire dating history before sleeping together, we'd made a pact not to ask any questions. *Fine by me.* Opening up about my exes would have been as agonizing as playing a game of Truth or Dare sober.

He ran his hands through his blond hair. "Well, I have to talk about it." His somber tone made my nerves feel deep-fried. "I saw my ex-girlfriend last weekend." His emphasis on the word "saw" made my chest hurt. I wrapped my arms around my stomach and squeezed myself. Michael began talking about Shari, a girl he'd dated for a year while on the USF coaching staff. He'd broken it off a few weeks before we'd met. I stuffed my hands in my pockets and stared out at the front lawn.

His blue eyes watered. "I had no intention of doing this." He looked down at me. Words began sputtering from his lips. He'd gone to a post-game party and bumped into her. They'd had a few drinks. His brow furrowed as his head shook. My eyes bounced from his red, sad face to the concrete under our feet.

They did the nasty?! All my dreams of us began to break into pieces.

My mind raced back to the dinner table. "Everyone inside knew about this?" My voice shrieked. Michael was close to his family, which I adored. But the fact that he'd revealed his infidelity to his mom and dad—and decided it would still be a great idea to have me over for dinner—made me feel like the guinea pig in a science experiment.

"How?" My voice shook. "How could she come between this?" Tears pooled in my eyes. "You told me this time was different. You told me I was special." My voice shuddered. I slammed my eyelids shut.

"I'm so sorry." He ran his hands through his hair again. "I don't know what to do. I feel terrible. I'm a complete mess. I'm torn." He grabbed for my hands. I jerked away as if I'd just touched a hot stove. "All I know is that I'm totally in love with you, but I guess I still have feelings for her."

My eyes dashed across his giant front lawn. *Great. Now he tells me he loves me.* My chest felt like the steak Michael had hacked apart. I loved him, too. Part of me wanted to kiss him. The other part wanted to slap him.

I fished for my car keys in my purse. "You can't do this to someone you love." I exhaled deeply, looking at his long driveway. I wanted to tell him that I'd loved him from the minute he'd cleaned my fish on the boat dock, but I bit my lip. "I need to go study." I marched down the front steps and into the familiar world of relationship uncertainty, which never seemed fathomable with Michael.

The bizarre turn of events replayed in my head all the way home. I'd worked too damn hard at not smothering him like a sleeping bag for the relationship to collapse. How can the perfect guy be flipped faster than a house on *Extreme Home Makeover*? Michael was handsome and kind with a bright future. He'd treated me like a queen—until he'd screwed his ex. But, he'd come clean with convincing remorse. *Didn't that score him some forgiveness points?* My mom had forgiven my dad for at least ten major screw-ups before filing for divorce. Michael had a career, manners and a wonderful family. And money. Paying bills and buying groceries would never be an issue in our house. My anger over Michael's betrayal quickly consumed me like a *Seinfeld* marathon on TV. I'd already been burned by the Holy Grail of cheaters—a married man. If there would have never been a Matthew, maybe I could have forgiven Michael.

🍷🍷🍷🍷🍷

AFTER A LONG day of classes, I came home to my dark studio and was greeted by the blinking red light of my answering machine—life before cell phones.

"I just wanted you to know I'm thinking about you." Michael's warm voice filled my tiny apartment. The machine beeped again. "Hey. It's me again. I can't stop thinking about you. I screwed up. I'm sorry. Okay, I should hang up now. Call me." Beep. "Hey. I think my phone cut off, so I just wanted to make sure you got that message."

The final beep hung in the air like a thick cloud of cigarette smoke. It was becoming my daily routine—coming home and listening to Michael's sweet, desperate messages. I collapsed on my bed and looked up at the pine rafters. My emotions were tangled in knots. There weren't any single guys in Miami as great as Michael. I'd dodged enough bullets to know. *How can I start all over again?*

I followed the usual formula to distract myself from the demise of our relationship: a thorough examination at Planned Parenthood. I'd had unprotected sex with Michael once when he'd forgotten to bring a condom. I was vested deeper than a 401K with a boyfriend who had double-dipped, so I needed the kind of solace only a Pap smear and a urine test could provide. The waiting game began.

🍷🍷🍷🍷🍷

THE ANSWERING MACHINE picked up and then the shrill of the dial tone echoed through my apartment for the third time—far too long to keep ignoring. The phone began ringing again. It was a Thursday afternoon in October, and the humidity had loosened its grip on Miami. The changing of the seasons made it easier to accept that Michael and I were probably finished.

"Hello?" The icy greeting passed through my lips.

"It's good to hear your voice." His words cooed through the phone line.

I kept up my guard. "What's going to happen next time you see her again? You know you will."

There was a bloated pause. Michael didn't launch into the canned rebuttal about how she meant nothing to him. I wondered what this Shari girl had to offer that I could not. Big boobs? I didn't hound him with phone calls. I gave him backrubs. I never whined about how our dinner dates involved iced tea and dolphin fingers instead of Sancerre and stone crab—luxuries he could afford.

"I had to tell you. I didn't mean to hurt you." Michael's voice was sincere. I smiled in silence, squeezing the phone receiver. His honesty ripped me apart. We talked about school and work. The normalcy made my nerves relax. "When can I see you again?"

"I don't know," I replied, my voice distant. I stared at the traveler's palm outside my window.

"I appreciate you not yelling at me for what I did."

I twirled the phone cord in my fingers. "I'm not that kind of girl."

"That's why I like you so much."

"You didn't answer my question," I said sternly. The line hummed while I waited.

"I guess...I guess," he paused. "I just need more time." His voice was soft and wispy. My blood began to boil.

"This is not a two-for-one special." My jaw locked. "You have to choose." I felt like I'd just licked a bar of soap. I missed his affection, but the pain was dulling with each passing day. "I'm going to work, and I can do it without cheating on you." I slammed the receiver in its cradle.

🍷🍸🍷🍸🍸

MY PHONE RANG on a Monday afternoon. It had been twelve days since my last conversation with Michael. His voice was warm but distant. He asked how things were at school and work. We talked about midterms. It felt like having a conversation with my stepdad. My hand shook in anger for not ending our fairytale romance on his doorstep.

"I have something I need to talk to you about." The buzz of traffic filled the spaces between his words. "In person. This afternoon." The happy-go-lucky lift in his voice was gone. He sounded like a high school principal. "I can be there in an hour."

"Can't we just talk about it now?" The words seethed from my lips. I glared down at the unopened mail and a pile of homework on my coffee table. "I have a lot of studying to do before work." The lavender OB/GYN postcard atop the pile of mail glowed like a trophy. *I've been cleared. Time to move on.* My body was clean and my mind refocused. I'd started talking to a cute Bolivian boy named David who sat behind me in ecology class and worked at a saltwater aquarium store. He didn't live with his parents or have an ex within driving distance, which were fast becoming prerequisites.

"It's really important," Michael pleaded. "I need to see you face-to-face." The seriousness in his voice forced me to cave and agree to a drive-by. A sliver of excitement sliced through me. *He wants me back. I can be the one who dumps him and ends this mess.* I needed some music with a little venom and turned to my favorite angry musician, Alanis Morissette. My mind raced through the scenarios of why it was so important that he see me. I wanted to magnet the gynecology test to my refrigerator like an A+ report card, but tossed it in the trash can.

I let the music pour through my thin walls into the hallway. When Michael knocked, I casually yelled, "Just a minute," even though I'd been pacing in front of my door. I tugged at my jean shorts and straightened my tank top.

Michael's body filled my doorway. He forced a smile, dressed like he'd just walked off a ritzy golf course. His eyes were buggy and blood-shot. I swept my left arm through the air to usher him in. He ducked under the doorway then stood with his back against the closest wall. His blue eyes looked down to mine, and he glanced away. He looked like a child sent to the corner for a "time out."

The knots in my stomach tugged tighter. I turned off the music.

"Would you like to have a seat?" The words blurted nervously from my mouth. There were two places in my tiny apartment to sit: the cup-shaped couch and the double bed where we'd slept together four times. I didn't know what else to say, so I stood by the entertainment center and twirled my ponytail.

He glanced over at the bed. "I'd rather stand." The room was eerily quiet. I walked to the couch and plopped down. My hardwood floors creaked then silence again. We looked like two strangers making small talk in a doctor's office lobby.

"Soooooo..." I said, watching him shift his body weight back and forth in his leather loafers. "What's going on?" I gripped the edge of the coffee table that separated us. The possibility that he'd come to beg for my forgiveness now seemed as unlikely as Carnie Wilson's weight loss.

He parted his lips. No words came out. He lowered his head and took a deep, loud breath. I could feel his anxiety churning in the air. My nails dug into the tabletop.

Michael ran his hands through his hair. "I'm not sure how to say this." He turned his body toward me. His mouth drooped; his eyes were weighed down with heavy bags. I sat up straight and leaned forward, my nerves frazzled by anticipation.

"Okay." He dropped his hands to his sides. "There's no easy way to say this, so I'm just going to do it." His face flushed a deep red. I held my breath.

"Are you familiar with chlamydia?" His eyes rose to meet mine.

Oh no, he didn't. I slumped back into the couch, nearly kicking the coffee table. Hearing a guy use four-syllable words had always been a turn-on—until that moment. I felt like I'd swallowed a cinder block.

My cheeks ignited. "Yeeessss." I looked at Michael—the guy whom I'd believed had the best husband credentials since Lance. His pretty face was as red as a stop sign. *Wow. Disease does not discriminate.* Michael was a preppy jock who'd be working with doctors in a few years.

I glanced over at the wicker trashcan next to my couch. *Say something, Lisa!* My pulse raged. The silence felt as awkwardly long as the moment after an accidental fart within earshot of a boyfriend.

"Wuh...well...uh." His voice staggered on. "My doctor says I contracted chlamydia, and I've only slept with two girls in the last two years." He took a deep, shaky breath. "And Shari told me she doesn't have it, so I figured that I must have..." He looked at my scowling face, and his lips stopped moving.

I leapt from the couch and threw my hands on my hips. "You see that blue trash can right there?" My arm shot to the floor. "Inside, you'll find the results from a slew of tests I had done because *you* cheated on me." My ponytail whipped around my head. I grabbed the wastebasket, fished out the card and threw it at him. "T-t-t-take that back to Sh-shari!" My mouth stuttered the words faster than Porky Pig on speed.

He kept his eyes locked on the piece of paper. Michael scrunched his nose, and wrinkles formed on his forehead. I stood next to the coffee table and watched his mind do the math.

"I just don't see how this could have happened if..." He rubbed his fingers through his thick, blond hair again.

My hands anchored on my hips. "Go back to Tampa." I shook my head. I wanted to spread his legs like a goal post and kick a football right into his nut sack. I'd promised him complete and total honesty from day one. I'd given him my heart. He'd almost given me the clap.

His shoulders hunched over like a quarterback who'd just lost a big game. I strutted past him to the front door and tugged hard on my doorknob. "Go. Please." My back pressed against the open door. "Just go." I looked up and caught a glimpse of his ashamed, blue eyes and forced myself to look away.

Michael shuffled toward me and paused in the doorway. "I wish we could go back in time." Only a few inches separated us. His citrusy smell nauseated me.

I turned my head and slowly closed the door in his face. My forehead rested against the cool, wooden door, as I listened to him pacing in my hallway before sulking down the stairs. *I never expected an end like this.* I exhaled deeply, letting the shock and anger spill from me. The lesson was so hard to swallow, it would take me ten years to realize what Michael had taught me about love: Even when my relationship wasn't built around sex, it could still be destroyed by sex.

I walked over to the purple card and plucked it off the hardwood floor. *Back to square one.* I let out a thunderous sigh and stepped into the kitchen.

My shaky fingers slid the card under the sand dollar magnet on my freezer. The most important test of my semester didn't happen on a college campus, and I needed a daily reminder.

I also needed a stiff drink.

RAUL
The Craft Beer Days

I leaned forward on the barstool and plucked my Dixie cup off the worn-wood bar. A haze of smoke lingered above two pool tables at the back of the narrow room. It was *our* place—a heterosexual man's haven amid the sea of gay clubs and bars on South Beach—a dark cave with blacked-out windows and a trickle of grunge music fans. No foam parties allowed.

I lifted the clear cup to my lips with a smirk. "So this is the kind of place you bring girls you're courting." The ice-cold, dark lager coated my tongue, flooding my taste buds with layers of rich, bitter yet honeyed flavors—something I'd never experienced in a tap beer before meeting Raul, a fellow college student. His tastes were molded from a lifetime of eating full-throttle Caribbean food, so whatever touched his lips had to be big on flavor.

Two beefy guys with barbed wire tattoos sharpened cues next to the pool table. I glanced down at my blue Express dress shirt and strappy sandals. I must have looked as out of place as Gwyneth Paltrow at a Kentucky truck stop. Raul always took me to Society Hill on South Beach—one of the few places that served pitchers of beer on the beach. It seemed like a foreign country compared to the velvet ropes, thumping sports cars and martini bars lining Washington Avenue just yards away from our barstools.

"I don't need to court you anymore." Raul's full lips spread into a Cheshire Cat grin. "You're my woman." His deep voice emphasized the "wooh" in "woman." Then he burped. I rolled my eyes in disgust.

I ran my fingernails playfully through his wiry, black hair. "You never courted me in the first place, smart ass." He kept his hair buzzed supershort to fend off unruly curls he hated almost as much midterms. But Raul wore a pair of thick-rimmed glasses that made him look like a science geek. He reminded me of the boys in school who always sat in the front row taking copious notes—a constant reminder that looks can be deceiving.

"Come on!" Raul grabbed the edge of my barstool and pulled me closer to him. "You gotta be shitting me. Would you rather go hold hands at some sappy movie, bro?" His biceps flexed tight against the cuffs of his blue-striped T-shirt. Raul always spoke with a half-confident, half-carefree air, and his terms of endearment ranged from "bro" to "baby" to "beeatch." I found it boyishly attractive sometimes, repulsive others.

I shook my head in disbelief as he chugged his Sam Adam's Honey Brown. "Dinner and a movie would be nice once in a while." We'd gone out to dinner just once—Outback Steakhouse on Valentine's Day about four weeks into our relationship—and I'd paid. I cocked my head and glared at him. "You're lucky I'm not a whiny bee-atch." Dating Raul was an exercise in unconventional relationship wisdom that marveled me some days and frustrated me others. I fell into his interests and tastes, like girls often do—favorite music, favorite bars, favorite beers.

His free hand moved to my jeans. I watched my thigh disappear under his gigantic knuckles, hands big enough to palm a basketball. He'd mastered the petting, but nothing else.

An evil smile engulfed his face. "Movie dates are boring." He pulled my leg on his barstool. "Why would you want to go sit in the dark with someone you want to talk to and be quiet for two hours, bro?" I gazed at his baby face, studying his thoughts. *You can't get to know someone if you only go to the movies together.* It was one of the many golden lessons in life that slacker instilled in me, and it took me years to realize it. Raul began rubbing my calf. His touch made my ears muffle the words coming out of his mouth. Raul's affection was a temporary concealer for our problems, just like make-up that covers big zits.

My fingers bridged over the rim of the cup. I nodded my head and propped my right leg onto his hip. *Thank God he doesn't drink Bud Light.*

Raul peered deep into my eyes. "You're the one who wanted this, remember?"

I smiled into our pitcher of beer. "Yeah, yeah, thanks for the intervention." Five months before, I didn't know him. I didn't know that bar. After the unsettling breakup with Michael, my weekly schedule revolved totally around work and school. No television. No dates. No social life. When other Florida International University students were gearing up to party all weekend, I washed my uniforms and prepared for four, back-to-back bar shifts at The Cheesecake Factory. My five-step plan for financial success involved a strict financial budget, an even stricter diet and a relentless drive to graduate with honors—not a full-blown relationship with a Puerto Rican kid from Hialeah who burped in my face.

He raised his beer cup. "Somebody needed to come along and wake you up, woman." Raul grinned between sips. "You needed a man to set you straight." He emphasized the first syllable of every word. Raul had tucked me under his carefree wing the first week of my second semester, and my world immediately had taken a 180-degree turn. The responsible girl had gone to recess. Nearly two years of opportunity for creating epic college memories—my sophomore year at Kansas State and half my junior year at FIU—had passed me by while I'd picked up double shifts and memorized lecture notes. My determination to make lots of money and graduate with honors had bordered on obsession before meeting Raul.

I squealed and play-punched him in the arm. "Whatever, you ass! That's why you kept pursuing me? I needed you, huh?" It was hard to take him seriously; he often reminded me of comedian Paul Rodriguez, with his quirky smirk, big nose and dirty mouth. I'd met Raul on my first day of class at FIU's School of Journalism and Mass Communications. We were the same age with the same major in public relations, so I thought we'd have a lot in common. He'd asked for my number at the end of our first Media Law and Ethics lecture then announced that he'd be dropping the class because he could "put off an elective this boring" for another semester. At the time, no room existed in my focused world for the complications of a relationship. Period. My dating goose was cooked. Hello, cold turkey. My two-year string of humbling breakups had finally spooked me into abstinence. I simply didn't have the strength to carry any more ex-boyfriend baggage. Two months of birth control pills were unnecessarily ingested, which seemed like reason to celebrate. I bought a pet iguana to keep me company and named him "Dax."

Raul pushed my hair from my face. "I kept calling you because you're cool. And you're pretty." He delivered his compliment like a snarky third grader. "You see. I am an emotional guy."

I huffed into my beer. "Whatever." My eyes rolled back. My eyeballs hurt after every barstool conversation with Raul. "You called me because you liked it." I wrapped my lips flirtatiously around the edge of my cup. Raul demanded a life big on flavor and fun, but short on substance.

He pinched my exposed stomach. I batted him away, tugging at the sides of my tight, wide-collared top. He was about as emotional as Arnold

Schwarzenegger in *The Terminator*. On our first date, Raul had sat on his favorite barstool at Society Hill, asking naughty questions that ranged from the craziest place I'd ever had sex to the most erotic spot on my body. We'd made out in the ripped seats of his beat-up Honda like horny teenagers. For an hour, he'd begged and begged me to invite him upstairs, like a kid who wanted his Halloween candy.

While Raul had sucked on my neck and nibbled at my side on our first date—already deploying my shared secrets against me—a bright idea had flown into my tipsy head: I'd use him for sex. Turn the tables. I never expected Raul to call me again.

"You're damn right." He leaned into me, pressing his lips to mine. Raul's kisses were always luscious and sensual, just like John's. I loved the feeling of his mouth engulfing my lips. Raul didn't have the thick goatee, straight hair and square chin like the Cuban guys, but he definitely had the Latino kissing technique mastered. Jedi Master mastered.

He pulled back and looked into my eyes. "But then I got to know you, baby." A big grin spread across my face. Raul always knew when to shut down his smart-ass hydrant and spray on the charm.

I reached for my beer. "I told you I was a nice girl." The fact that a one-night stand had turned into six months of exclusivity gave me a false sense of hope that I could have a long, healthy relationship after years of giving it up too early. Within a week of our first date, those late nights and long afternoons of dissecting court cases about freedom of speech were interrupted by unexpected knocks at my door. Raul would duck under my doorway with a six-pack of quirky beer in hand. The nascent American craft beer movement was gaining steam in big cities. Raul was into trying new things—like Dogfish Head Ale and Midwest girls.

I grabbed his neck and pulled him closer. "Just because we've been together this long doesn't get you off the hook." I threw back my head with a laugh. "You gotta respect your woman." I mimicked him with my best WOOH-man and pressed my lips softly to his.

His luscious lips surrounded mine then he pulled away. "This is the longest I've ever been with one girl." I glanced down at his size eleven tennis shoes hanging over the foot rail. The boy had big everything—and I mean *everything*—except manners.

"I'm not surprised," I replied with a smirk. "Most girls wouldn't put up with your crap for longer than a month." The only way to win with Raul was to play his game—two quick jabs to follow his. I think it felt so good to act like the cocky teenager again because I'd grown up way too fast.

But a relationship can only run so long on great sex and craft beer alone. Before Raul had even ordered the second pitcher on our first date, he'd already ticked way too many boxes in the deal-breaker column: the eleven-inch differential in our heights; his lackadaisical attitude toward college; his constant use of the words "bro" and "dude;" his gushing pride over the fact he still lived at home with his parents and *abuela* and planned to milk that security blanket for as long as he could; his zodiac sign (Sagittarius—the bachelor); his faded, black Honda sedan with the broken AC and missing front bumper; his disdain for Latin dancing; and his lack of a full-time job. He spent every other weekend being a deck hand at the Aventura yacht club, but insisted on working only forty hours *per month* when I clocked forty each week. And there was still that distant fear that he, too, might screw like a monkey.

"Whatever, my ass." Raul raised his beer to his lips. "This works. We fit." His eyes wandered down to my stomach. "We have fun. That's why we're together."

I looked him in the eye. "You can have fun and be responsible at the same time." I remembered those first impromptu visits to my apartment, him sitting on the edge of my bed with a beer while the Beastie Boys blasted in our ears, and a stack of study cue cards weighed heavy in my lap.

"I'll have plenty of time to do grown-up stuff when I'm old." He pushed his thick glasses up his big nose. "The real world isn't going anywhere."

I peered at the liquor bottles on the back bar. "I guess you're right." I rubbed his thigh. Raul constantly put my days of sacrificing happiness today for career success tomorrow into perspective. Most nights, I'd get five hours of sleep, but the lack of rest didn't seem to affect my grades. When I should have crammed for quizzes, I slurped White Russian daiquiris (relapse!) with him at Fat Tuesday. I'd even dropped my International Business class and used the book money to buy Raul dinner. To complete my transformation to a new woman, Jorge chopped off my long, permed curls and sculpted my hair into chunky, straight layers like Jennifer Aniston's on *Friends*.

My palm caressed the pinstripes on his fitted tee. "You know, I would have figured things out with or without you, punk."

🍸🍺🍷🍸🍸

MY EXES COULD always sense when I was taken. How do guys do that? As soon as I'd settled into a somewhat stable relationship, men from my past emerged and circled, like wild dogs hunting for dinner at dusk.

First came the phone call from Matthew—on Valentine's Day night, which pissed me off even more. Raul fished two bottles of Pete's Wicked Ale from the refrigerator while I stood by my nightstand with the phone in my hand, shaking. "Don't...ever...call...me...again." I snipped each word, my voice trembling.

Next up was Chris, who called on a weekday afternoon. He said he'd fallen into a deep depression after our breakup and had been in therapy. He said he was finally a happy person again and living in Philadelphia. I apologized for being immature, for deserting him, for not explaining why I'd left. When I told him a collection agency had been calling for him, he just laughed. It took three years to untangle myself from that pothead's web of finances!

A few weeks later, the phone rang again. That time, Michael's warm voice filled the line. He asked how I'd been and then stuttered through an awkward invitation to dinner. I can't imagine how embarrassing and hard that was after his STD affirmation; I might have given him another chance under different circumstances. He owned a boat and a condo in the Keys, remember?! But my heart was devoted to the skinny Puerto Rican guy whose idea of a perfect date involved the Burger King drive-thru, a six-pack of St. Pauli Girl and a free joint from his buddy, Manny. Raul was always more good than bad, more positive than negative, more party than pooper.

Our pendulum of happiness and frustration swung back and forth every few months. And the swings were as wide as the Golden Glades Interchange. First, Raul went to Disney World with his family the week of my birthday and never so much as called. Raul was notorious for not calling and always being late. He showed up a few days later with a stuffed dolphin and one of his big grins and playful apologies.

The normal boyfriend hibernating deep inside Raul's cave of a brain pounced around the eight-month mark. He massaged my feet after long bartending shifts. He invited me to Sunday dinner at his house with his entire family—all thirteen of them—where we shared a pot of *arroz con pollo* the size of a trashcan. He enrolled in my travel and tourism class, so we could spend more time together then only showed up to bum my notes. It was the kind of yo-yo relationship that kept me holding onto a plantain of hope that he would someday grow into my 100-percent dream guy, not just the thirty percent he was half the time.

🍾🥃🍷🍸🥂

FLORIDA INTERNATIONAL UNIVERSITY required undergraduates without a minor to declare an "area of concentration." These courses had to be outside of my major in mass communications. By the time I started my senior year at FIU in September 1996, I still needed to squeeze sixteen hours about some other topic into my schedule.

My first choice was Environmental Science or French, but those classes were offered on FIU's main campus more than one hour from the communications school campus in North Miami. Spend an hour in traffic on the Palmetto and I-95? I would have rather eaten yucca for a week. And this was back in the golden era of driving in Miami, before u-turn signals and SunPass. The only other school located on the FIU North campus—the Chaplin School of Hospitality & Tourism Management—would have pulled me closer to the business I'd vowed to leave. But when I thumbed through the hospitality curriculum for the first time, I couldn't believe the course names: Wine Technology 101, Advanced Wine Technology, Hotel Marketing, Travel & Tourism. Taking classes that involved wine tasting, studying vineyards and learning about travel destinations seemed like my kind of cakewalk. It was a solid choice for a bartender hell-bent on getting great grades without slaving over books everyday.

During my first Wine Technology 101 lecture, Professor Chip Cassidy told the story of a monk named Dom Pérignon who accidentally created Champagne. He also made us squeeze red grapes in our hands and watch white juice come out to teach us how the pigments in grape skins give wines their color. The revelation hooked me.

I met Raul in the cafeteria after class to brag about my discovery.

"So, when are you going to declare your area of concentration?" I asked, my face one big grin.

He emptied a bag of Doritos into a paper napkin on our table. "At the last possible moment." Raul sneered each word, brushing crumbs from his hands dismissively. "Why are you always crawling up my ass about school?" He wore a Mickey's malt liquor T-shirt and gym shorts, reminding me how little he cared about his appearance.

I stuck out my tongue. "Because we need to graduate, smart ass."

"Next summer? That's like a year away." He mumbled the words through a mouthful of chips.

I threw back my head. "You have nine months. That's only two semesters." I looked down at my sundress then back to his grubby T-shirt.

His face flashed red with frustration. "I might switch majors." He crumpled the empty bag of chips and tossed it across the table. "I don't know if I'm cut out for this shit. You know, there's a lot more writing than I thought."

I nearly coughed up a Dorito. "You're a nut job." My head jerked back in shock. "Don't you want to ever graduate?" I'd dreamed of becoming a writer since sixth grade, and I'd wanted to work in public relations since my first semester in college. I had goals to achieve and a window of time shorter than a pregnancy to get the job done.

"I can always wait until next fall," he mumbled, fondling his Coke bottle.

My eyes practically shot from their sockets. "Are you for real? That's another semester."

"You're doing it again." His voice harped. He reclined in his chair. "You need to chill out."

"I'm doing just fine." I folded my arms across my chest. "I'm not like you." I stared at the unruly whiskers on his unshaven face, feeling us grow farther apart. "I like my classes. I get good grades. I wanna get outta there and have a career."

"And you want to do this by next summer?"

I bit my lip, excited by the thought of having deadlines and goals and over-delivering on both. "If I'm going to work in the wine business, then I need to get moving."

"You wanna drink wine for a living? And you think I'm a slacker?" He shook his head with a scoff. He didn't bring up my father, and I appreciated his rare expression of couth.

"Yes and yes." I folded my arms tighter. "Get used to it." I wanted to spend the rest of my life surrounded by wine—a refined beverage that combines agriculture with alchemy—even though my dad had drinking problems. *What could be more elevating for my lifestyle than working with the world's most cultured beverage?*

"Hey, you're the one who said life should be fun." My head cocked. "Jobs are a big part of life. They should be fun, too." I'd decided that the key to having both career success and job happiness would be applying my skills (communications) in an industry that fascinated me (wine). It sounded way more exciting than writing press releases for a hospital. "Now that I've got my area of concentration locked in, I can work an internship next semester." My voice barked like a CEO. My wine professor hired interns every semester and had a deep network of contacts throughout the South Florida wine community. And because I hailed from a world where the only Justin was a boot maker—not a Paso Robles winery renowned for its red blends—I needed a jump-start on my wine career.

Raul dropped his nose. "You're going to work full-time, go to school full-time and do an internship?"

It was as if he didn't know me...

🍷🍷🍷🍷🍷

RAUL TUGGED BOTH my hands. "Just come with me, baby." It was a Friday night in February, and we were standing right outside Cheesecake in Fat Tuesday's open-air bar. My knees locked at the sight of his cloudy, slit-wide eyes. Whenever he hung around Manny, smoking weed was the *especialidad de la casa*. They wasted most of their nights trying to find the safest place to roll a joint.

My hands pushed his away. "You're a mess." I slung my work apron over my shoulder and loosened my tie. "I'm tired. I'll just stay here." I pulled the scrunchie from my hair and let the straight layers fan around my shoulders. Raul had convinced me to smoke with him on two occasions, and I'd gained five pounds from caving to the chocolate motorboat munchies. With my last semester of college underway, those days were over. I grabbed a barstool and sat down.

"Come on, bro." Raul stared at me, grinning. "Don't leave me hangin'." It was the same thing he'd said that first night in his car after an hour of making out.

"I'm not doing it." I glanced over at Manny on his flip cell phone. "I can't, and even if I could, I don't want to." I crossed my arms and my legs, so he knew I meant business.

After getting the highest grade in my wine class, I'd approached Professor Cassidy about pursuing a career in the wine world. He'd helped me land a part-time gig at The Cellar Club, a members-only wine bar, located at the swanky Biltmore Hotel in Coral Gables. I wrote membership welcome letters, helped track membership dues, fielded phone calls, and helped set up private tastings, and still bartended for Cheesecake at night. I definitely didn't need the money or the extra stress of a second job, but I couldn't pass up the opportunity to get some wine business experience on my résumé before graduation, and to prove Raul wrong.

"You don't have to smoke." His tone was low and hurried. His eyes darted around the bar, scanning the crowd. "I just want to be with you, baby."

His eyes fixed on mine. I looked at him in silence, letting the buzz of bar conversations fill my ears. Raul turned to the bartender to order us two beers.

"No." I snipped. "I told you I'm done with beer."

He rolled his eyes. "They don't serve wine here, baby."

A deep sigh left my chest. "Okay, fine. Close your tab. I'll go."

I peeled myself off the barstool, watching the crush of weekend partiers swallow our empty seats. Raul nibbled on my ear down the escalator then pulled me through a pink metal door into the CocoWalk parking garage.

I stood at the top of the flight of stairs in my black work jeans and button-down shirt, while Raul huddled over Manny in the stairwell landing below. I rested my head against the metal railing and looked down at my wristwatch. Manny fished a Ziploc bag from his jeans' pocket. I scoffed, looking up at the empty stairs above my head. *Hurry up, slackers.* I tapped my black sneakers on the concrete floor.

The heavy metal door between stairwells flew open. Two men in dark uniforms charged in and yelled, "Police! Put your hands up!" My body froze as my worst nightmare unfolded. Adrenaline surged through me.

One officer glanced over his shoulder and spotted me sitting one flight above the drug bust. "You! Get down here!" *Oh, fuck. Not me, too.* I sulked down the stairs, legs wobbling faster than a vibrator. The officer pushed me up against the cinder-block wall and dumped my purse on the concrete floor. Tampons, lipstick, ink pens and spare change rolled around my feet. I looked away, my face flushing red with anger and embarrassment.

The officer pressed my cheek against the cold wall and frisked me. The stairwell smelled of smoke, stale beer and dirty water. Shame spilled over my helpless body. From the corner of my eye, I watched the other cop frisk

Manny then Raul. The disgrace felt sharper and deeper than the time I'd gotten arrested in high school for skinny-dipping. I kept reminding myself of the disclaimer at the beginning of every episode of *Cops*: I was innocent until proven guilty by a court of law.

"She doesn't have anything to do with this," Raul said over his shoulder as the officer kicked his feet apart. "Please, let her go." Raul's hands were laced above his head.

I shot Raul a death stare. *I'm not like him, officer.* Hidden security cameras were probably recording the entire bust. My blood boiled with rage. *If I get fired because of this, I am going to beat you to death with a plantain.*

The cop finished rubbing his hands over my jeans' pockets. I kept my eyes closed and my right cheek pressed against the cold concrete wall. My jaw trembled. I could hear his fingers shuffling through my belongings on the floor.

"She's clean." The man's voice rang out in my left ear. "You can go." His tone was stern and curt like a high school principal.

I turned and watched the other cop pulling Manny out the door in handcuffs.

My eyes locked on Raul's, like lasers burning holes in his head. I took a deep, quivering breath and shook my head.

Raul threw his big hands in the air. "I have to help him, you know." His eyes were wild and pleading. "I can't let him go through this alone. He's my best friend."

My chest thumped wildly as I watched Raul scurry out the door, leaving me alone in the stairwell to pick up my tampons.

Hours later, a fist banged on my front door. I rubbed my eyes and looked at my alarm clock. It was 4:06 a.m. I dragged myself out of bed and peeked through the peephole to see Raul pacing in my hallway. I flipped the dead bolt and opened the door slowly. He blasted past me.

"How could you desert me like that?" His voice wailed; his eyes were buggy and bloodshot. "My best friend is being taken to jail and you run in the other direction. I needed you." My back was pressed against the wall where he'd made love to me a dozen times. I looked down at my silk sleeper shorts and matching top then wrapped my arms around myself. I needed a robe and didn't own one.

"You're turning this on me?" My hands shot from my sides. "You almost got me arrested!" I looked at his bewildered face and rubbed my cold arms. My air-conditioner in the window hummed while we stood in silence, looking at each other. "How could I possibly get a real job with a misdemeanor on my record?"

"All I'm saying is that I needed you to be there for me. You're my girl. You weren't." Raul shoved his hands in his pockets.

"Why is it always one step forward and two steps back with us?" My mind raced from Christmas with his family to the pot bust. "Why can't we just have a normal night out that doesn't involve a fucking tow truck or a cop car?" I'd recently bought a used Honda Civic because my Chevy Cavalier sounded like it had black lung disease, and Raul had convinced me to let him drive it to South Beach the night I'd brought it home. He'd talked me into parking it in a residential neighborhood, which led to the car being towed and me spending two days and $300 to get it out of the impound yard because I only had temporary tags.

"I said I was sorry," he said. "Why can't you let it go?"

"It was your fault, and I had to pay." I turned my back to him and looked at my unmade bed two feet away from us. "I'm always the one that ends up paying." My tiny apartment was never a good place to have an argument with a boyfriend—especially not while wearing lingerie.

"This is me." Raul's voice echoed in my head. "You said you wanted to have more fun."

"This isn't fun anymore," I whispered. My toes circled a plank in my wood floor, as I thought of my new job, my new life, my changing taste.

"Baby." He stepped toward me. "Come on." I could feel his warm breath on my bare shoulders. "I needed you then, I need you now." His warm hands squeezed my cold arms. Tears pooled in my eyes. He spun me around and grabbed my chin. "Look at me," he whispered, wiping a lone tear trailing down my cheek. His brown eyes watered. Seeing Raul's emotional side made me cave. I began to question my actions. *Am I wrong not to be supportive? Did I desert him?* He hugged me long and deep then lifted my chin so our lips would touch.

"Why is it always so damn hard?" I asked, letting the tears pour. Deep down, I knew coasting along with Raul couldn't continue much longer. I just didn't have the energy to find a new boyfriend. And I still thought I needed one so Skin City wouldn't swallow me whole. Starting over from scratch with another guy—fumbling around for weeks to try to figure out if we were compatible or if he was going to turn into a bat and fly away after midnight—seemed like more work than I could handle.

"I didn't mean to hurt you." I watched a tear trickle from his eye for the first time. "You know how much I care about you." Raul wrapped his long arms tight around me. I inhaled his musky cologne, a welcomed scent after the stench of a mall stairwell. My lips began to move, reacting to my need to reciprocate with an "I love you," but I stopped myself. He had yet to tell me he loved me even though I'd said it several times. "I've never said that to anyone but my mom," he'd kept telling me. "It's going to take time." Raul knew how to push my buttons—the good ones and the bad. We'd had passionate, sweaty sex on every piece of furniture in my apartment and against every wall, door and appliance. Raul had the moves—and body—of Mark

Wahlberg in *Boogie Nights*. Not only was it the longest monogamous relationship I'd ever had, it was the first relationship where I'd learned the importance of having sexual chemistry with someone. Too bad we only had the physical part aced.

🍷🍸🍷🍸🍷

MY COLLEGE GRADUATION finally arrived—the day I'd been looking forward to since high school. I sat in the blazing sun of Miami in May, wearing my black cap and gown amidst a sea of fellow classmates and couldn't have been happier. Raul wore dress slacks, a white oxford and a tie. I couldn't help but marvel at his metamorphosis. He sat with my mom and brother in the bleachers on the lawn at FIU's South Campus, whistling, clapping and hollering my name, as I crossed the stage with sweat on my brow and gold honor society ropes around my neck. When the words *"magna cum laude"* echoed through the loud speakers, I raised my chin. My father didn't come to the ceremony, but I hid my hurt under that hideous, tasseled cap. Dad could drive a truck to Canada to fish for a week, but he couldn't get on an airplane to watch his only daughter become the first woman in the family to receive a college diploma. I'd yet to learn the biggest lesson of all in relationships: You can't change a man.

"I'm so proud of you, baby," Raul said afterward, squeezing my hands. That boy could be so good when he needed to be. I wondered if he might like the feeling of that dress shirt and tie so much he'd transform into a devoted career man. It was one of the most rewarding, happy days of my life, and Raul was there by my side. For my graduation present, Raul gave me an iguana that would be "ours." We named him Parker. We'd rocked back to a good place at the eighteen-month mark—my longest relationship in Florida. I began wrestling with the notion that the longer relationships last, the more extremes a girl must endure.

᠙ ᠙ ᠙ ᠙ ᠙

I CAME HOME from an afternoon shift at Cheesecake and found Raul sitting on the futon at my spacious new apartment. A few months before graduation, I'd moved into a one-bedroom apartment in South Miami with a remodeled kitchen, room for a dining room table, a screened-in patio for my lizards and a communal pool in the courtyard. I'd also given him my spare key. Three empty bottles of Samuel Adams Triple Bock were lined up on my coffee table. It was the first week of June and humid as hell.

"I've made a decision about my future," Raul said, swallowing air. I draped my work apron on the back of the futon. He was wearing his usual daytime attire: a beer T-shirt and cotton gym shorts.

He grabbed my hands and pulled me down to the couch. My mind began to gallop. *Has he declared a new major? Will he graduate before the new millennium?* My eyes fixed on his lips, awaiting his next words. I'd made a decision about my future, too. I had a diploma—my gateway to the real world. We'd drifted too far apart.

"I'm sailing to Brazil," he said firmly, rubbing my knuckles. "I'm going to sail on a sixty-foot boat from here to the Rio de Janeiro with a crew of just four." He grabbed a new bottle of beer from a cardboard six-pack next to him. His face had a look of determination I'd never seen. "This is a chance of a lifetime I never thought would happen." I looked into his brown eyes—past the bent rim on his glasses.

I sat on the edge of my futon. "When?"

"I leave this Saturday."

My eyes widened. *Sailors are gypsies of the water*, I thought, mind whizzing back to Matthew. *Who can decide in seven days that they're going to cross the equator by boat and just do it?*

"I'll go to South America, and you'll go to Europe." His big fingers laced into mine. "That sounds like a killer way to spend the summer." I stared down at our entangled hands. I'd won an all-expenses-paid trip to study winemaking in the Burgundy region of France for earning the highest grade in my Wine Technology 101 class.

"My trip is only for six days." My eyes met his. "How long does it take to sail that far?"

He took a deep breath. "I'll be back in September."

I sat in silence on the edge of my futon. I felt like I'd been punched in the throat.

"I know that's a long time to be apart." His eyes locked onto mine. "But will you wait for me?"

The break-up speech I'd already begun practicing flooded my brain. I took a deep breath and collapsed into the cushion. The exit ramp was wider than a Los Angeles freeway.

"Come on, baby," he said. "Don't leave me hanging." His signature line. Raul smiled at me with his brown eyes flashing. He leaned in and started nibbling on my neck.

I pulled away. "Do you think this is the best thing for your future?"

"I've dreamed of doing this since I was a teenager." He peeled the label off a bottle. "If I don't do it now, I may never get the chance."

I admired him for chasing his dreams, no matter how polar opposite they were to mine.

"Ummm, okay," I smiled sheepishly. "I guess I'll wait for you." My teeth clenched as the words crept out of my mouth.

"You will?" A look of pleasant surprise washed over his baby face.

I hopped off the couch. "Three months apart will be good for us." I walked to my refrigerator to grab the chilled bottle of dry rosé.

"That's the only part I'm not cool with," he said. "Guys will be after you."

I poured myself a glass, shaking my head. "I can handle myself." I sipped the strawberry-hued wine from my fancy, Riedel crystal glass. It was crisp, fruity and dry—so much lighter and drinkable than his full-bodied brews, which made me feel bloated. "I'll be just fine." Breaking up before his oceanic adventure—the easy way out—didn't seem fitting after nearly two years of our tumultuous relationship. Call it a moral challenge. A strong woman would choose three months of celibacy over another summer of dating the plethora of immature men who treated their women like cars—lease but never own. Ninety days without the headaches of relationships seemed like a great way to cleanse my soul and say *"adiós"* forever to my college-dating era.

🥂🍶🍷🍸🍾

I STOOD OUTSIDE customs at Miami International Airport, pacing. It was Labor Day weekend: Raul's homecoming. His mother and father stood across the crowded aisle as travelers streamed between us. They never made eye contact or waved, which didn't surprise me. I always felt like a stray dog they didn't want hanging around their house. I was stealing their youngest child, their baby. And I was as white as rice.

A deeply tanned, gangly guy with baggy clothes scuttled into the corridor. Wiry, thick ringlets covered his head. His thin cheeks were covered with scrappy stubble. *Is that my boyfriend or a Bird Road panhandler?* I stood quietly, waiting to see if he'd scan the crowd for me. I watched his eyes move from me to his family on the other side of the barricades. That big grin that had won me over in the first place spread across his face. He waved to his parents then rushed over to me. He dropped his duffle bags and scooped me into his arms. My entire body was a ball of nerves. After two years, I truly cared for him. We'd chalked up so many memories—some quite disturbing then, but laughable now.

"I missed you," he whispered in my ear. His glasses squished my cheeks.

"I missed you, too." I pulled back. I could feel his mother's eyes burning into my head.

"Don't move." He turned to his parents. I watched Raul dart across the aisle and hug each of them. His mother covered his face in kisses. Then Raul walked back to me with his duffle bags slung over his shoulder. "I'm going with you."

An hour later, Raul tugged me up the steps of their beachfront condo. My legs locked just short of the front door.

I looked down at my sundress. "I don't know if this is such a good idea." His family rented a big condo on Hollywood Beach for two weeks every September, and I'd never been invited to join them before. Crashing the treasured family time of thirteen Puerto Rican Americans was something I had not prepared for, and I'm sure his mother had not, either. Raul hadn't made any phone calls the last two months of his journey.

"Come on. It'll be fine," he said with a scoff. "I'm not letting you leave my sight." His tanned fingers squeezed mine. I followed him into the sparkling white great room, which combined living, dining and kitchen into one cozy space. Two of his sisters sat on a tropical-patterned, wicker sofa with their noses buried in *People* and *Cosmopolitan* magazines. "Hi," they said in unison. I looked over to his tall, thick mother, standing over a white kitchen counter.

"*¿Que quieres beber, Raulito?*" she asked. His mom always spoke in Spanish. She began banging cabinet doors and plates in the kitchen. I gripped the straps of my purse, waiting. Sand sprinkled across the white tile floors crunched under my flip-flops. There was no "*¡Hola! ¿Cómo estás?*" for me, and definitely no *bebida*.

"I'll get changed," I said and retreated to the parking lot.

I fished my beach bag from my car. In Miami, bikinis and beach towels were always kept in the trunk in case of emergencies, just like spare tires. And this was an emergency.

We went for a sail to have some alone time.

"I think I should go." I was perched across from him on his Hobe Cat. I wore my new blue-and-green striped bikini. The boat glided parallel to the beach about fifty yards offshore. "I'm not welcome here." My toes and fingers pressed against the fiberglass. I figured his mom wanted him to settle down with a pretty Latina—not spend two years dating a *gringa* transplant who tended bar. My mind zipped back to Alicia telling me Latin men were tethered to their mothers for life.

"Oh, come on." He pulled the ropes on the sail. "Tack!" he shouted coolly, and we ducked our heads as the main sail flew to the other side. "Just give them some time." My ponytail flapped against my neck as I watched his lips. "I've been gone for months, and the first thing I wanted to do was spend time with you. That's hard for my parents." I pushed my sunglasses up my nose and rolled my eyes. Having lived away from home since age eighteen, I could not relate. A fiercely independent woman and a fiercely dependent man make for strange bedfellows.

"I'm never going to be welcome." The wind whipped stray hairs around my face. "I'm a white girl from a broken home who fled to Miami to find a new life where I live alone, don't go to church and want to pimp wine for a living." My hands gripped the top of the fiberglass hull. "I am the devil, *el diablo*." Deep down, I always believed that one of the reasons Raul dated me was because it pissed off his mother.

He rolled his eyes and laughed, brushing off the cultural differences like always.

The fear of confronting him felt like a rusty anchor in my belly, pulling me deeper into the ocean with every passing second. I took a deep breath of salty air. "We can't keep pretending this is going anywhere, you know." I watched the sail above, preparing for the next tack. Tiny turquoise waves patted the bow.

He tugged on the ropes. "Where should it be going?" His bare, tanned chest glistened in the afternoon sun. He looked leaner and more muscular than ever before. I pushed the memories of his sensual touch out of my mind—an easier feat than usual, thanks to his unruly cheek hair and afro.

I looked out into the open ocean, watching the water melt into a deep blue at the horizon. "Nowhere." I took a deep breath of the humid air. "We're in different places in life. We want different things." The imprisoned words flew from my mouth. *I'm a worker; you're a slacker. I want wine; you want beer.* I kept my eyes fixed on my tanned legs against the white fiberglass.

"How do you know that?" he asked. "I've been gone for three months. Spending weeks at sea can change a person." My chest tightened. The wind died down. The jib sail fluttered slowly then collapsed against the pole. The boat stalled twenty yards offshore.

"I'm moving to California." A wave of relief washed over me as soon as the words left my lips.

"You're whaaaaat?" His head crooked as he dropped the rope. The main sail's boom banged against the hull. "When did you decide this?"

"While you were sailing." My eyes stayed fixed on my calves; my heartbeat thrashed. "I started a new job last month working for a wine magazine.

If I want to be successful in winery public relations, I need to live in California wine country." My fingers squeezed my knees. Quality wine grapevines can't grow in the tropics, so most Florida wine jobs were in sales. I'd accepted the fact that the only way to advance my career was to leave Florida, but first, I'd landed one of the few non-sales jobs. *The Wine News*, a well-regarded bi-monthly magazine, had editorial offices located in The Biltmore Hotel. When the publisher learned of my journalism background, she'd offered me a position as editorial assistant. I wrote news blurbs, proofread feature stories, sourced photography and helped inventory all of the wine samples shipped to the editors in hopes of being featured. After gaining a year of experience, I would move to Santa Rosa, California, the largest city in Sonoma County wine country. I would finally be a California girl—just three years after I'd seen the Pacific Ocean for the first time. Maybe I'd meet a winemaker and fall in love.

"One week in France, and you changed, too, I guess." Raul jumped into the water and guided the bow to starboard.

"Nothing has changed." I gripped the edge of the fiberglass boat. "The trip just reinforced my decision." I'd walked on the hallowed ground of grand cru vineyards, such as Clos de Vougeot and Corton-Charlemagne. I'd sipped old Burgundies over candlelight in historic caves, surrounded by the magic mold that clings to stone walls and ceilings, creating ideal conditions for cellaring fine wine. My perspective—and my palate—would never be the same.

"I can't believe you're saying this." He glanced up at my face. "All I thought about on that boat was you." His voice cracked while waves sloshed against his chest. "And how much I missed you. I thought maybe we'd move in together when I graduate." My throat tightened. I felt like I'd swallowed a mango.

"You're finally at the place in our relationship where I wanted you to be a year ago." My toes curled against the fiberglass. I shook my head, glancing out into the still water. We sat in silence, listening to the water slosh against his boat.

Raul exhaled. His head and shoulders bobbed in the water. "Baby, you're the first girl I ever loved." He angled the tiny boat toward the shore with me sitting atop like a princess in a chariot. Hearing the words "girlfriend" and "love" come out of his mouth sounded like a foreign language.

My head cocked sideways. "Oh, now you love me."

"Come on!" His brown eyes pleaded. "You know I love you."

"How many guys spend their entire life with their first love?" My expression was as flat as the water. I glanced from his eyes to my bare feet resting between the hulls. Raul didn't need to scour two states looking for love as I'd done, but he needed to date more girls to be sure which one was The One. I tried to count the number of guys I'd loved since my first and lost count at twenty, and I still wasn't sure how to spot Mr. Right.

"There's someone else, isn't there?" His tiny brown eyes scanned my face from the water.

I looked him straight in the eye. "You think I can't leave you on my own? I can. I am." I'd gone ninety days without a man's touch, and felt like I could conquer the world on my own for the first time. My determination had shifted to focusing on my wine career.

The wind never returned. Raul pulled our boat back to shore as I stared at the blue horizon in silence, envisioning the world that awaited me on the other side.

FERNANDO
The Cheap Red Wine Days

I stood on my balcony and stared down at the courtyard swimming pool, searching for a sign. The patio screens felt like a cage for my runaway thoughts, as my fingers fidgeted with the ink pen. I darted back through the sliding-glass door and grabbed a sheet of paper.

I got lost the other night.

My fingers tingled as I gripped the edges of the paper and reread my words. The cool breeze of a November night brushed my bare shoulders. I walked to the kitchen and poured myself a glass of Elsa Malbec. As the Riedel stem touched my lips, the juicy taste triggered a memory flash. *I should buy a crisp, white. Fernando loves Italian pinot grigio.*

I grabbed the Blockbuster Music bag off my coffee table and ripped open the new jewel cases. The night before, I'd spent an hour thumbing through racks of CDs at Blockbuster CocoWalk, searching for something completely unknown yet comfortably familiar. French National Orchestra. Duke Ellington. Beethoven. Mozart. I'd snapped their plastic cases into my arms like a mother stockpiling hurricane supplies. The unexplainable urge to buy classical music had hit me as soon as he'd driven away in his pick-up truck. And I had no idea why.

The sound of a delicate violin streamed through my apartment. "Violin Sonata No. 5" collided with memories of the past forty-eight hours. The conversation. The dance floor. My dream. I rested my wine glass on the dining room table. When a piano joined the airy strings, I flew onto my tiptoes and extended my arms like a swan. My heels dropped to the floor, landing naturally in "first position." I'd never taken a ballet class in my life.

More violins chanted with the piano. Visions of two horses racing through burning trees flashed in my mind, the same wicked scene from the dream that had woken me the night before. My eyes slammed shut. An endless, shiny wall of white covered my mind like a blizzard.

I rushed back to my desk.

I stood in a crowded room with
bright lights, buzzing conversation
and loud music.
But I couldn't hear a thing.

Two nights. That was all that had passed since *the* moment. My thoughts had strapped themselves into a roller coaster without brakes, but I didn't want the exhilaration to end. I just needed to know why. *Why me? Why him? Why now? Why does the uncertainty of this budding romance feel as if our first date will be followed by a funeral?*

More words hit the paper. My heart bounced with every mental picture reliving Saturday night: squeezing through the crowd at Sloppy Joe's in Coconut Grove, bumping shoulders with him—in the exact same spot—two weekends in a row, and chatting all night about our new careers and recent breakups. I couldn't help but wonder what force was steering my destiny.

The sounds were muffled in my mind.
My eyes were closed, but
I know, even if they'd been open...

I rested the pen on my desk and grabbed my glass of wine. The Argentine Malbec's dark fruits, rustic tannin and spice tasted mysterious to me—the perfect pour to relive our encounter.

"What is it about you, Fernando?" I whispered, gripping the crystal stem. Fernando was no stranger, but I knew him about as well as I knew my dry cleaner. He was Cuban. He'd been dating Alejandra—think Daisy Fuentes with a bigger nose—since high school. She was vivacious, intelligent, driven and my main competition for the highest grade in every public relations class at FIU. She also had grown up in Hialeah on the same street as Raul, and they were as close as cousins.

On that night at Sloppy Joe's, we'd spent two hours talking at a tiny bar in the back corner.

"If Wal-Mart would have sold Camo Barbies, I may have never stopped hunting," I shouted over the music blasting from overhead speakers on the dance floor. My back was arched and my legs crossed at the knee. "The biggest piece of furniture in our living room was my dad's gun cabinet." I pushed the hair off my shoulders, laughing. I wore my favorite button-fly Levi's, a teal tank top that made my blue eyes pop and black slip-on sandals with high heels—comfortable with a touch of class. Fernando's brown eyes widened behind his thin, designer glasses.

He threw back his head. "No way! I have a gun rack in my bedroom." His whole face was one big smile as he leaned into my ear. "I usually don't tell girls about that right away." His goatee was pencil thin; his black hair kept short and sleek.

"Yeah, my experience with loading guns and skinning frogs usually falls into the 'wait-at-least-four-months-before-sharing' category." I sipped a Malibu and pineapple, wishing the bar had a drinkable house red by the glass. I told him how I'd spent many Sunday afternoons as a kid shooting empty beer cans off tree stumps with my dad. While music blasted and the crowd noise hummed, we debated the merits of live bait vs. lures and bait casting vs. spinning reels. The conversation was worthy of a Jeff Foxworthy redneck skit. *This guy can't possibly be Cuban*, I kept telling myself.

My mind continued to race through the memories of that night.

He grabbed the meager wine list from the bar. "So, tell me why I like pinot grigio so much." Fernando loved to drink Santa Margherita Pinot Grigio, which would soon become the most popular Italian wine in America. He had a lean face that reminded me of a young Andy Garcia and wore Banana Republic dress shirts. Yet he drove a black Toyota pick-up truck with a big, metal toolbox spanning the bed—just like my dad.

"Pinot grigio is a good gateway wine for getting started." Our cheeks nearly touched as I chatted over the music. "I think it's because of the combination of fruit, acidity and a touch of sweetness. My first wine love was Riunite D'Oro." It was winter of 1997—more than two years since my summer with John. Between the common interests and the ease of conversation, my heart was doing the "Macarena."

"What wine would pair best with sole *meunière*?" His thin lips looked so cute when he said, "MOON-ee-air." Fernando scooted his barstool closer to mine. "That's my favorite dish at my favorite restaurant." My heartbeat revved like a sports car engine. I'd found a guy who liked to shoot guns and enjoyed fresh fish cooked with a classic French preparation.

Fernando kept asking wine questions like an over-eager bookworm. *Why are white wines so crisp? Why are red wines so dry? Why did cabernet stain his teeth? How can you tell when a wine is corked? What types of stories are in a wine magazine?* It felt so good to have a guy showing interest in my brain before my body.

I looked down at the half-empty bottle of malbec on my patio table, remembering what he said next: "I want to be the guy who thumbs through a wine list with confidence." The guy worked days as a construction foreman. His split personality was utterly fascinating. Throughout the conversation, my mind was swimming in shock. Fernando was the only guy who could relate to the two Lisas: the small-town girl who still liked to go fishing and the career-driven, city woman who wore cocktail dresses to fancy wine tastings.

I got lost the other night.

The poem continued to form in my mind. I jotted down more words then stared into the courtyard below.

"Let's go." Fernando pulled me onto the dance floor. His callused palms cupped my hands, and the feeling of a new touch made my pulse skyrocket. Almost two months had passed since the Raul breakup and more than two years since I'd danced with a man. We started off with bodies farther apart, bouncing to "Hypnotize" by Notorious B.I.G. It was nothing like my *merengue* days, but Fernando had the same fluid hip moves as John, my first Latin lover. My back pressed against his chest as we bounced with the music. Even the drunken college girls sloshing their beers beside us could not knock me off my cloud. Our breakups were a distant memory. We landed on common ground.

The room was dark, almost black.
I had no idea where I was, yet

"Hey!" A voice called out over the music, jolting me from Fernando's trance. My friend Danielle was standing in the middle of the dance floor with her hands on her curvy hips. "We've gotta get outta here." Danielle cocked her head of wavy brown hair toward the door. She had Chelsea Handler's spunk and Nigella Lawson's body—my perfect partner in crime for barhopping. We'd always vowed to use the buddy system, but usually got split within thirty minutes, thanks to our suitors.

I pulled away from him on the crowded dance floor. "I have to go." I tucked my lips behind my teeth, trying to hide my big-ass smile. My body turned away, squeezing between two bouncing girls on the dance floor. The scene moved in slow motion like an instant replay.

My world seemed copacetic even though
I couldn't explain this amazing thing.

Fernando fingers grabbed mine. He spun me around like a bottle. My nose brushed against his hairy chin then our lips touched.

I can only call it electric.
Like nothing I'd ever felt before;
Something so powerful and intoxicating
I got lost when I was most in control.

Even though my eyes were closed, I saw the brightest light. Every nerve in my body prickled. It felt as if a pair of jumper cables was plugged to our chests. I teetered on the edge of numbness and hypersensitivity. There was no music. No bar. No people. Nothing in the world existed except the two of us. I'd never felt such a wicked sensory overload in my life.

It was a rush of uncertainty and nirvana.
I always dreamed it existed, but
Never knew it would be like this.
What a crazy thing—a kiss.

We backed slowly away from each other, our mouths still open. His eyes locked onto mine. We stood two feet apart on the crowded dance floor for what seemed like five minutes—just staring at each other like two frozen statues. I raised my hand to my tingling face. My fingertips felt like lightning rods.

"Holy fuck," Fernando said, his jaw hanging open.

"Holy shit." My eyes stayed locked on his as I backed away, disappearing into the crowd.

I read every scribbled sentence on the paper three times then sat in my swivel desk chair and launched Word Perfect. My fingers flew across the computer keyboard. I desperately needed each line, each word, to be neat and perfect. The clarity would hopefully end the confusion. When the paper fell from my printer, my fingertips caressed the page. I read the poem once more just to relive the sensory rush.

"He is for real," I whispered, looking at my reflection in the patio doors. "You gotta chill out. Pull it together." A single kiss had melted my brain, sucking me dry of rational thoughts. I'd been talking to my reflection in doors, windows, mirrors, my computer screen. Visions of flying horses? I felt more strung out than Fergie from The Black Eyed Peas the night she talked to the clothes hamper. And I'd only had two mixed drinks and two glasses of red wine—over a three-day period.

I grabbed my cell phone and checked for missed calls. Nothing. *Damn.* I poured myself another glass of malbec and took a lengthy sip of the full-bodied, dry wine. The motivation to drink daily went from drinking for sport to drinking for pleasure within days of starting a wine job. Student loans and starting salaries meant fine Burgundies were way above my pay grade, and South American wines were as common as California ones in Miami. I fell hard for the rich, smooth taste of cheap malbec from Argentina. It packed just enough punch. At the time, most big red wines still clocked in under fourteen percent alcohol, and you couldn't get smashed off two glasses of a Napa Valley cabernet like you can today.

My mind replayed the events of Sunday: I spent the morning floating and gloating behind the bar, recommending Santa Margherita to anyone and everyone—then I spotted Fernando, sitting at the other end of the bar, watching me work. He neglected to ask for my number at Sloppy Joe's, and I never offered it. Look where practicing restraint had landed me. We went to a nearby bar after work and watched the Dolphins game...with his best friend. Serious stuff.

After sunset, we sat together in his pick-up truck without the air conditioning on—a late November luxury. He flipped on his CD player and Dave Matthews Band poured into the cab. His lips locked onto mine. The explosion of energy short-circuited my nerves all over again. We both jerked back like we'd been shocked with a cow prod.

He exhaled deeply. "This is insane."

"I know." My voice was breathless. My fingers squeezed both knees of my dirty work jeans. My entire body felt exposed, turned inside and out, every time his skin touched mine.

His forehead rested against my temple, rolling a bolt of desire through me. "What are we going to do?"

My heart pounded as the words crawled across my lips. "I don't know." My forehead stayed pressed to his for minutes, listening to the music and my runaway thoughts.

Fernando gripped my chin. Thirst for his lips poured over me. We kissed over and over while "Crash Into Me" roared from his stereo. Our tongues looped with ease, as if we'd been kissing for months. I could not wait to learn more about the man behind those lips—his hopes and dreams, what he ate for breakfast.

"I'll make you dinner," I whispered as his lips floated across mine. "We'll share a bottle of wine. That's what we'll do."

With the poem out of my head and onto paper, I had less than twenty-four hours to pull myself together and whip up something amazing, and back then, the only chef cooking on my television was an unintelligible Swede on *The Muppet Show.*

🍷🍷🍷🍷🍷

I PREPPED FOR that meal as if it were an Ironman triathlon. The menu, the music, the lighting, the napkins, the wine, the glassware, my hair, my nails, my outfit—everything had to be perfect.

By the time Fernando knocked at my door, all the boxes on my list were checked. The table was set. My apartment spotless. The wine uncorked. My Wonderbra? Strapped on.

I floated to the front door in my short, black skirt and baby-blue rayon top, leaving a pot of boiling penne pasta on my stove. Fernando looked and smelled delicious—black slacks and a crisp dress shirt, all sprinkled with sandalwood. He greeted me with one of his earth-shaking kisses, making me lose myself all over again.

"The pasta!" I rushed back to my galley kitchen. "Make yourself at home! Wine's on the table!"

My mouth drooped. The pot of boiling pasta looked like a tiny swimming pool stuffed with bloated rafts. I dumped the penne into a strainer, launching into triage mode. I tossed in a pre-mixed dressing of minced garlic, olive oil, and salt and pepper. I popped a few tubes into my mouth, chomping and chewing like an old man eating without his dentures. *No!* My heart sank. I added a medley of steamed vegetables and sun-dried tomatoes. It was better—better than eating cardboard. Flatline. Dinner was dead.

I walked sluggishly onto my balcony with two plates in my hands and a frog in my throat.

Fernando raised a Riedel glass filled with Bodega Norton Malbec, another affordable Argentine bottle. "I like this." I flashed a tiny smile while he stared into the glass like a jeweler studying a diamond. He'd said he wanted me to broaden his wine horizons.

I rested an octagon plate in front of him and let out a sigh. "I wish I could say the same for this pasta." Steam drifted above the flickering candle in the middle of the table. I slumped into my chair with a long face.

"What's wrong?" He rubbed my bare knee.

My head shook. "It's terminal." I grabbed the glass of wine he'd poured for me and took a long sip. He lifted a forkful to his lips. I watched his jaws, waiting for his gag reflex to kick in.

Fernando chewed and chewed and chewed. "It's not that bad." He looked like he'd just swallowed raw Brussels sprouts.

My chin dropped. "But I wanted it to be great." I wanted to kick myself for choosing a Cheesecake Factory pasta dish for our first dinner. Employees weren't allowed access to secret recipes, so I'd just tried to wing it after a brief conversation with the pasta chef. "The spice in the sauce was supposed to complement the wine." I poked at a penne tube with my fork. "The pasta isn't soaking up any flavors." For all the years of working in restaurants, I'd failed at my first attempt to pair classy wine and classy food—and for a fellow college graduate who seemed as interested in wine as me.

Fernando laughed and kissed my forehead. "There's always next time." His brown eyes looked black in the candlelight. My clenched jaw loosened.

A grin glinted across my face. "No more talk about food. Tell me about this wine." Fernando lifted his glass.

I smiled with the pride of a teacher. "Malbec is a red grape from France, but it was brought to Argentina in the mid-1800s and has become their flagship red." Fernando nodded along while sniffing the wine. "Malbec packs a lot of flavor for the price. It's the best value I've found." I took a long, satisfying sip. The palate was dry and rich, laced in dark cherries and dusty chocolate. A touch of heat from the alcohol lingered on my tongue, helping unwind my nerves.

I jabbed a broccoli floret. "So what's it feel like to run a job site?" Fernando had a team of twenty employees and contractors working for him. He was twenty-three years old, just like me. The closest I'd come to managing people was new server training.

Fernando's face lit up. "I love getting up every morning." He reached for the wine bottle as he talked. Fernando worked for a small construction company that had landed its first big job building a high-rise in North Miami Beach. He chattered about juggling the time lines and material deliveries. He made sure the carpenters, concrete pourers, plumbers and electricians started their work as soon as the other had finished—the maestro of a construction site. I gazed at his face, following every detail of the conversation and thinking of my dad, the town carpenter. "Dry wall is going up this week." He popped a sun-dried tomato in his mouth.

I rested my fork on the edge of my black plate. "Dry wall? Is that the same thing as sheetrock?" I've never been one to keep quiet when I don't know what someone is talking about. Most of my dad's jobs involved sheetrocking. I'd watched him sheetrock our house in fifth grade. My mom had told Dad the only way she'd get back together was if he remodeled the entire house. So he did.

Fernando cupped both hands around my cheeks. "You're so damn cute." He looked into my eyes. "Yes. It is. I can't believe we're having this conversation. You totally get me." He pressed his lips firmly against my forehead then kissed my nose before finishing with my lips. The energy from his kiss whipped through my body like a tornado. A Cuban guy and a Midwest girl talking carpentry over a bottle of red wine—it was as unlikely as James Bond hooking up with May Day.

"You make me feel alive." His face glowed in the candlelight. "You make me wonder about the world I've never seen. And we've only really known each other for like three days." His tone was soft, yet upbeat. I felt the blood rush to my cheeks.

I smiled, sipping the medium-bodied wine. "I know what you mean." We were putting the "f" in fairytale. *I can't believe this is finally happening. Do not screw it up, Lisa.*

"You left home. You put yourself through college. You follow your dreams. You want to work in wine country." He paused and exhaled. "I have cousins in San Francisco. Now I'm asking myself, 'Why haven't I visited them?' Maybe I should move there."

My heart began to trot. Fernando was born and raised in Kendall, and he still lived at home with his parents, like most Cuban men in their twenties. His father owned a cigar shop on *Calle Ocho*. They seemed like Miamians for life. I couldn't stop the thought of us moving to California wine country from popping into my head.

"You even have pet iguanas." He looked over at Dax and Parker climbing on my potted hibiscus trees. "I love that."

"I love that you have sheetrock." I smirked into my wine glass. Being playful calmed my nerves and took my mind off wondering if he liked me as much as I liked him. We gawked into each other's eyes then began giggling.

He finished a long sip. "Your turn. What's it like to work at a wine magazine?"

I grinned like he'd just handed me a birthday present. "I can't believe I get paid to do this." I stared into my glowing wine glass. "I proofread feature stories once the managing editor is done. I read press releases and decide what news is worth writing about. And then there's the expensive wine I get to drink that I could never afford." A big part of my job was helping organize the magazine's weekly wine tasting, where a "tasting panel" of five men gathered around a table to taste flights of similar wines blind and rate them on a 100-point scale. Their scores appeared in the magazine with tasting notes—a shopping guide of recommended wines for our readers. The panelists always let me taste the remnants of each bottle—the tête de cuvée Champagnes, the Napa Valley cabernets, the grand cru Burgundies—and taught me how to taste wine without swallowing. Proper wine spitting: the first indoctrination into the business.

His eyes perked. "Can you bring me home something amazing?"

Home? I nodded through the shock and tried to change the subject.

I pushed my hair off my shoulders. "What do you think they'll say when they find out?" My eyes drifted to the candle on our table, and intense visions of fire and horses flashed through my mind. I pinched my lips shut.

"I don't really care," Fernando replied, eyes locked on his wine glass. "How could we have known this would happen?" Latins are notorious for their tempers and possessiveness; Raul and Alejandra probably wanted to stuff us in a dumpster behind La Carreta. Learning I'd moved on to another guy was one thing, but Fernando Costas? Now we were talking blood.

I ran my finger around the rim of my glass. "All this time. We were with *them*." I leaned back in my chair, staring into the melting candle. Raul had been calling every two weeks around midnight—his booty call—and some were answered, others ignored. The next time my phone rang, Raul would be calling me way worse than "beeatch."

"I always wondered what you were doing with him." Fernando's voice was soft and controlled. "You two weren't a good match. Just like Ally and me." He explained how Alejandra obsessed about manicures, facials and shopping; she didn't care about the things that were important to him—like fishing, hunting, camping. I could feel the heat of his breath on my shoulder. *I like all those things.*

We sat there silently exchanging grins while bugs buzzed in the courtyard and Natalie Merchant crooned "Jealousy" in my living room. One week before Fernando had kissed me, Raul's full extraction from my life was nearly complete. Danielle had set me up on two disaster dates—one with a thirty-nine-year-old fire fighter and one with the University of Miami Hurricanes mascot, who reeked of Surf detergent and clapped his hands way too much. After swimming in jealousy, Raul had finally moved on.

"I like you." Fernando's head rocked from side to side. "You're different." My heartbeat zipped like bubbles in a Champagne flute. It was so thrilling to have a first date where we talked about our careers and childhood memories, not favorite sexual positions.

Fernando refilled my wine glass and gently rested the empty bottle on the table. We kept one hand locked together and used the other to pick at our plates. The taste of sweet blackberries and spice lingered on my tongue while we talked about our first kiss.

"This may sound totally crazy." His face glowed in the candlelight. My stomach did a triple Lutz as I waited for his next word. "But I want to take this slow." He grabbed my hands and laced his fingers in mine. My heart thrashed in my chest. It was a beautiful declaration—one I'd never heard a man say—almost as beautiful as "I love you." His head tilted toward mine, and our foreheads locked like magnets. I exhaled a quivering breath, feeling our kindred spirits reading each other's minds.

I pulled back to see his brown eyes. "I was hoping you'd say that." His lips glided to mine, and the fireworks exploded again.

"I've never felt anything like this before." His tone was sensitive, yet strong. "I don't want to screw this up." His voice quivered as his fingers locked tighter with mine. My legs began trembling. I'd never seen a man display such tender emotions for anything but his first car. It was my dating palate's first taste of relationship respect and far more refreshing than any glass of wine.

"I feel it, too," I whispered. He kissed the back of my hands while I soaked up our unbelievable conversation. Over a flickering candle, we openly discussed our feelings for one another. The connection between us was special. We owed it to ourselves to enjoy the beginning of something special without leapfrogging into bed.

He leaned back in my chair. "We should set a deadline or something." He paused and laughed into his glass. "Like no sex for at least eight weeks."

I shoved my hand at his chest. "Done." We shook hands, giggling. I looked into my empty wine glass, giddy with glee. All my headaches and heartaches had been worth it. I'd hooked a keeper.

I trotted back from the kitchen with a bottle of Elsa Malbec in one hand and my wine key in the other. My body turned to stone in the doorway. Fernando was standing by my desk, reading a sheet of paper—yes, *that* paper. Fear shot through my brain. I wasn't ready for him to see my sappy, romantic side.

"You wrote this?" Fernando asked, grinning. He sounded like a proud parent who'd stumbled upon his child's A+ paper. "This is about us?"

My head dropped. "You weren't supposed to see that."

"Why not?" His voice screeched. "It's amazing. It's beautiful. It's so freaking true." He held the piece of paper with both hands. "Could you print me a copy? I want to show it to my mom."

That was when I decided Fernando was an alien.

ᛒᛖᛟᛏᛗ

I CALLED MOM on Sunday, eager to hear the test results. Fourteen days had passed since the most insane kiss of my life, and I needed some concrete intel about us—the kind only astrology could provide. Mom had dabbled in reading tarot cards and writing astrological charts for most of my life, and I always asked her to pull every new boyfriend's natal chart and examine it against mine. My relationship with Fernando was surging ahead with electromagnetic kiss marathons continuing to happen in bars, cars and on my futon, but it felt like my brain was possessed by the ghost of Beethoven. My interest in classical music grew stronger. Dreams of fire and horses intensified. Her ephemeris was the only logical place to seek answers.

Fernando's moon was conjunct my sun; his Venus fell in my seventh house of marriage. This is the equivalent of a Super Bowl win in astrological matchmaking, people.

I told her about the dreams. "Maybe he's unlocked a memory from a past life." She suggested I read two books by Dr. Brian Weiss: *Many Lives, Many Masters* and *Only Love is Real: A Story of Soulmates Reunited*.

Once I started reading *Only Love is Real*, I couldn't stop. Before finishing the first chapter, my mind was reeling from the doctor's words:

> *"You are bonded together throughout eternity, and you will never be alone...He may not recognize you, even though you have finally*

met again. You can feel the bond…When you both recognize each other, no volcano could erupt with more passion. The energy released is tremendous."

I finally had an answer, but so much for clarity. It was the kind of secret no woman wants to harbor. *Who should I trust with my freaktastic revelation?* I might as well have told Fernando I dabbled in voodoo and handed him a doll full of stickpins. Fernando's touch had definitely opened a door between our souls. I was experiencing what is known as a past-life recall. One line in the book's preface haunted me: *"A wrong choice or a missed chance can lead to incredible loneliness and suffering."* I read that sentence again and again. *Haven't I suffered enough?* How do you tell the man you love—a man you've dated for three weeks—that your souls are chained for eternity? After he says, "I do" or maybe never. Part of me wanted to leave the book on the top shelf of my desk, so he could find it just like the poem. But I stuffed it into the bottom drawer of my wicker dresser.

🍶🍵🍷🍸🍾

THE THOUGHT OF losing Fernando began to consume me. My hunger to be close to him grew insatiable. The more time we spent together, the larger my appetite. Hectic schedules could only help keep our hormones in check for so long. Fernando worked full-time and took graduate school classes at night. I edited stories about the fledgling organic wine movement between bartending shifts. My head kept telling me to stop fighting the pull. *Let him slip on a condom faster than a pair of Nikes and just do it.*

The periodic table couldn't match our chemistry in bed. Every time we made love, time stood still. I got lost all over again. Sex with Fernando reached a level of euphoria I'd never known existed—long before the endorphin rush. It was my first glimpse into how sex and love can fuse on a higher level—when that love is built on a shared emotional and spiritual connection, and great sex completes the trifecta.

I felt like I could not breathe without him in my presence. I sat in my apartment alone, staring at my cell phone, begging him to call. I talked to my computer screen then cranked up Dave Matthews Band on my stereo and cried through the chorus of "Crash Into Me." I was one drug binge short of a Courtney Love meltdown. I needed professional help. I needed to talk to Dr. Brian Weiss.

Just when I thought life couldn't get any freakier, it did. In Dr. Weiss's book, he mentioned that his practice was located in Miami. I grabbed my phone book and scanned the listings. His office was located on Sunset Drive: the same street as my apartment complex, less than one mile away. *Fate!* I called to make an appointment and learned his fees far exceeded my post-college budget, so I asked his secretary for some suggestions in the $100-$150 range. She suggested a local regressionist. Digging deep into my subconscious through past-life regression could explain my history with Fernando, and what karma we were trying to work out in this lifetime. Cue the crystal balls.

Who needs to spend $3.99 per minute on a Psychic Friends Network phone chat when a girl can get regressed to a past life, in the flesh, for a hundred bucks? I could dedicate an entire chapter to my regression session, but then you'd think I was a complete lunatic rather than a love-struck girl grasping for answers. In a nutshell, a female therapist in her mid-fifties with brown hair and a Princess Leia-sized bun guided me into a sterile, gray office—not so different from a doctor's examination room. She turned off the overhead lights, leaving only a small desk lamp glowing in the back corner. I sat down on this chair thing that was half couch and half doctor's table. My heart began sprinting. I was as tense as a teenager about to get her first pelvic exam.

She talked to me in a soft, calming tone. "Follow the air into your mouth, deep into your lungs. Examine every breath. Deeply." My eyelids were pressed against my eyeballs. My mind looked like this gigantic, dark tunnel. I could feel my breaths relaxing into a slow pace. "Follow the blood flowing through your veins as it moves up to your mind." She continued leading me with her kind voice. "Look for the hallway to life in your mind," she said. "You're going to see a passage way full of doors." It felt like sunshine was blinding me from inside my closed eyes. I saw the doors. The first one was big, black and covered in metal spikes. It was either the doorway to hell, or the entrance to the kinkiest S&M club in the afterworld. My body began to tremble. *Was Robert in there? Marco?* I pushed on, passing the creepy door.

Sunshine poured through the cracks of a weathered-wood door at the end of the hallway. "You'll know which door to open," she whispered.

I saw the brightest light, reminding me of Fernando's first kiss. My hand reached for the doorknob. Suddenly, it felt like a vacuum was sucking me through a hose into another world—like a time warp. Vividly detailed descriptions of the scene poured from my mouth. I could hear the words, but they sounded as if they were coming from the next room. I knew they were my thoughts verbalized, but my brain had never exposed them before.

A thin, dark-skinned woman with long, black hair kneeled over a makeshift crib inside a dirt-floor teepee. Her home was small and bare; there were none of those fancy, animal-hide rugs and fluffy pillows like Arnold had in *Conan the Barbarian*. The woman was in her early twenties. I'd never seen her face before, but I knew her. I was a Pocahontas! *I'm a waitress from Kansas in this lifetime and a Native American living off the land in another?* The gods had a crappier sense of humor than Itchy & Scratchy.

The tribal chief was my husband, but I didn't recognize him. *Definitely not Fernando.* He was much older, maybe late thirties, and he had children from other marriages. Those wives had died. I was raising his children as my own, and I could not get pregnant. The tribe thought I was weak for not giving him a child—an interesting dynamic I wish I'd had time to explore.

"Keep going," she said. "Follow your mind."

The Native American me shuffled through a meadow carrying a big, wooden bucket. The chief's oldest son was walking beside me with another bucket. His son was strong, brave and kind with long, jet-black hair. I guessed he was nineteen. We arrived at a river to fetch water. The son reached to grab my pail, tenderly touching my fingers. My heartbeat gunned like it had at Sloppy Joe's. *Fernando!* He didn't have the same eyes or body, but the touch was unmistakable. My breath fluttered wildly. "Stay in the moment," she said. "Just focus on your breathing." I exhaled deeply. The therapist coached me back to the river. Fernando caressed my arms then pulled me down onto the grass. The sound of water cascading over rocks filled my ears. We made love.

Fucking your husband's son isn't a good idea—not now and not in 1412. I'm not sure how long we'd been trying to keep our forbidden love a secret, but I knew our history just by watching our naked bodies spooning in the meadow. We'd often left the tribe to gather food and didn't come back until dark. I treated him differently than the rest of the children. My mind sped forward to a day when we were off gathering berries in the woods. Fernando wrapped his arms around me and kissed my neck passionately. He pushed me playfully against an oak tree. We heard a twig snap. A tribal yell echoed in the distance.

Busted.

We jumped on our horses and charged into a nearby forest. The sound of hooves smacking against dirt blasted in our ears. I could hear chanting behind us. The chief and his men were closing in. I panted in the therapist's room. "Just breathe. Keep going," she whispered.

Three men on horses darted out in front of us. Our horses reared up and stalled. One man grabbed me by my hair; another lassoed Fernando. They tied us to two pine trees. The men set fire to the brush surrounding our feet. Winds whipped around us, fueling the flames. Our horses paced in circles then dashed through the fire, escaping into the woods. It was exactly the same vision of horses from my dreams. Fernando and I squirmed and screamed, bound to the flaming trees, staring into each other's wild, scared eyes. The chief and his men stood on the other side of the roaring flames, watching us burn.

Afterward, the therapist gave me a cassette tape recording of the 60-minute session. "I think you broke through a big barrier here, and at least you're starting to get some answers." She squeezed my shoulder warmly. "Your newfound interest in classical music might be from another lifetime." She encouraged me to come back for another session.

I hid the tape in my dresser under Dr. Weiss's book.

🍶 🍺 🍷 🍸 🍾

THE HOLIDAY SEASON arrived with its twinkly Christmas palm trees and hordes of tourists wearing Hawaiian shirts and flip-flops. *Should I tell Fernando what is fueling the energy between us?* I'd leave out the teepees and borderline incest parts, of course. *Maybe I should just keep my big mouth shut and enjoy the bliss?* We were young and alive during the golden age of Lycra tops—the miracle fabric—in a city where sweating was unavoidable. We were stocking up on great memories, too. He bought me a necklace for Christmas and took me to a black-tie gala on New Year's Eve. We spent New Year's Day in sweats and T-shirts, curled together on my futon like a human pretzel watching the first *South Park*—the bootleg Brian Boitano-Jesus episode—which, in my book, was as bonding as skydiving together. The following weekend, he snuck me into his bedroom and proudly showed off his guns, fishing poles and camouflage bibs. We made love in his bed, whispering and giggling in the dark. He called me *"Mami,"* and I didn't even flinch.

🍷🍷🍸🍷🍸

THE ANNUAL COCONUT Grove Arts Festival rolled into town in late January, and one of Fernando's cousins was having her *quinceañera* that weekend. After the party, we'd planned to spend a sunny Sunday afternoon, strolling the tent-filled streets, looking at paintings. I told him I'd page him when I got off work. Yes, pagers were still cool in Miami in 1998.

I paged him at five o'clock. No response. I tried again at six. *Nada.* I stared at my Sprint PCS cell phone and begged it to ring, filled with that feeling of helpless desperation. My heart, my whole world, was in his hands. I turned the power off and on then checked again for messages. Nothing. I walked aimlessly through the white tents dotting Peacock Park, squeezing my cell phone like a life preserver, looking blankly at every painting, frame or sculpture.

I called Fernando's private home line. When his answering machine clicked, I quickly hit the "END" button. I called back and listened to his voice then hung up before the beep. *Does he have Caller ID? Does three pages in two hours constitute stalking?* I continued to pace the streets, peeling polish off every nail. My mind raced to Glenn Close boiling a bunny on Michael Douglas' stove in *Fatal Attraction*.

I'm turning into a psycho bitch.

My home phone rang at nine thirty. I hurdled my coffee table and snapped the cordless off the couch before the second ring.

"Hey," he whispered.

"Hi." My pulse galloped. I waited for him to talk. Uncomfortable silence filled the line. Something was wrong. We didn't do wrong. "How was the party?" I forced a chipper tone from my clenched jaw.

"Good." His voice was flat.

"So, do you still want to come over and watch *South Park*?" I asked, grasping for some act of normalcy that would put this bizarre afternoon behind us.

"Uhhh, yeah. But I can't stay." My nerves began to calm. *He is coming over. I can save us.*

I poured myself another glass of Zaca Mesa Z Cuvée, a Rhône blend that packed a lot of fruit flavor for ten bucks. My game plan took shape. We needed to work our way up to the serious stuff—just like my approach to drinking tannic red wine. I would tell him I thought we needed to slow things down. I would tell him we should take some time to really think about how special our connection was. There was no need to rush eternity. This was the lifetime we'd find happily ever after, not be burned at the stake for adultery.

I reached for my doorknob, wearing a tight, sky-blue top and khaki skirt. My hair and make-up were freshly touched up. I opened the door, ready for a big talk.

Fernando stood outside my doorway with his hands stuffed deep in his jean pockets. His eyebrows hid under a baseball cap. Fernando never wore hats outside work. My chest grew tight.

"Aren't you going to come in?" My voice cracked. I forced a smile. My fingers started to shake with fear.

He stepped through the door and pecked me on the cheek. "Hey." He forced a rigid, almost plastic smile, as if he was entering the dentist's office for a root canal. My head throbbed with confusion. I stepped toward him, lifting my chin to his. Kissing was my only defense against the wall forming between us. His lips pressed against mine, and his tongue glided into my mouth. He wrapped his arms around me, pulling me close.

Fernando gripped my shoulders and pushed me away. My eyes shot open, dazed and confused.

"I can't...I can't handle this," he said, shaking his head. My mouth dropped. I reached for his hand. When my fingertips touched his, he jerked his arm away as if he'd just touched a hot skillet. His brown eyes widened. "I'm sorry." Silence filled the room. My chest felt numb as I stared at his glum face, twisted with confusion. "It's...it's just..." He started to move toward me then took a deep, jittery breath and stepped back. He pushed both hands back into his pockets. "You're just." Words staggered from his mouth. "You're just too..." His face flushed pale. I held my breath, squeezing my hands. "This is too good to be true." He stared down at my floor.

His words paralyzed me. I watched his contorted face in shock. My mind screamed, but my lips couldn't move. *Tell him you understand! Tell him something so perfect scares you too! Tell him why he's feeling this way! Tell him your souls have been chained for lifetimes!* I watched him grip my brass door knob. He turned to me. My eyes darted around his face, pleading. *Don't go, please.*

His dark shadow passed outside my living room window. The scent of his spicy-woodsy cologne began to retreat. I inhaled deeply, savoring the remnants of his smell. My mind reeled from the waves of shock and sadness. I listened to his footsteps trail down the three flights of stairs. *Open the door. Stop him.* His truck door opened and slammed shut. My legs didn't move. I could feel my heart splintering into so many pieces not even Ty Pennington could repair me. Our love was worth dying for centuries ago. It was worth fighting for in 1998. *Why aren't you running after him?!* Funny how a girl who'd always chased men in the beginning didn't have the guts to do it in the end. He'd given me his answer. He couldn't handle the power of us. Lines from the Dr. Weiss's book began replaying over and over in my head:

> *"Soul recognition may be subtle and slow…Not everyone is ready to see it right away. There is a timing at work, and patience may be necessary for the one who sees first."*

Patience? I'd been looking for Fernando since my freshman year of college. And he'd just told me I was too good to be true.

I listened to his truck engine rev up. His wheels screeched as he barreled out of my parking lot. I collapsed onto my futon couch and stared at the ceiling. A void filled my chest, the deepest and darkest I'd ever felt.

First came the tears—then the visions of racing horses. Fernando had left me with the haunting memories of our past life, and the sinking feeling that my true love of this lifetime might be lost forever.

TYLER
The Pink Wine Days

I sat on Tyler's twin bed, watching him pull a ball of black socks from his dresser drawer. The morning sun flared behind his muscular torso, giving his tighty-whities a halo. *This guy is full of surprises.* I bit my upper lip as he tousled his damp, blond hair in a towel. His choice in underwear seemed so adult and so, well, white boy—a respite from my former world where all men were Latin, immature or both, and usually wore boxers.

Is he thinking what I'm thinking? I took a deep, perplexed breath while fanning out my new work suit on his bed. Tyler had the body and face of Bart Conner back in his 1984 Summer Olympics heyday, and we'd just taken a serious leap in our relationship. I'd found a nice, handsome gringo—someone who'd never remind me of Fernando when I looked into his icy-blue eyes—the only recipe for healing my wounds.

Tyler caught my stare. I smiled timidly while zipping my XOXO skirt. His cheeks turned bright pink, and he threw both hands over his crotch like a middle schooler dressing in the locker room.

"This is kind of weird." His voice muttered over the grunge music blasting around us. Tyler turned away, looking out the wall of windows across his behemoth bedroom.

My back muscles flinched. I felt like I'd been crane-kicked in the face—Daniel-san style.

I stood up and walked over to the adjacent bay window. "Weird?" I stuffed my shirttails into my tan skirt, looking down at the Intercoastal Waterway during one of its calmest hours. Hearing *that* word describe the morning after our first sleepover made my head spin like a stripper at her first pole dance routine. The night before, he'd insisted we sleep in the guest bedroom and had locked the door behind us. *That* was weird. He'd flipped off the lights and scurried under the bed sheets like a virgin. *That* was strange.

My eyes scanned his rosy cheeks for clues. Tyler's eyes met mine again for a nanosecond and dashed away with his bashful smirk. I buttoned my shimmery blouse and stared blankly at his throbbing stereo speakers in the corner.

"Uh, yeah. I guess I can see that." My tone sounded about as agreeable as a stomach full of habaneros, feeling the vortex of the gutter ball he'd just thrown down my emotional bowling alley. I gnawed a thumbnail to keep from staring at his chiseled chest. Keeping my true feelings bottled inside had gotten easier with 150 days of practice. We'd never slept in the same bed before that night, and we'd been dating for five months. The relationship had moved slower than a barge docking at the Port of Miami, and I'd actually welcomed the change of pace...for a few months.

He turned his back to me and quickly slipped on his gray dress slacks. "Don't watch me like that." His voice was playful, yet snippy. I shook my toweled head in bewilderment, making the turban sway like a coconut palm. After years with Latin lovers, dating a shy guy seemed so refreshing for about four weeks, but had been befuddling ever since. I'd just turned twenty-four and had landed my first full-time job at a wine distributor in Broward County, thanks to a referral from Fernando's sister-in-law. My taste for adult life had been uncorked.

I picked at my acrylic nails. "It's not like we're going to get caught."

"We better not." He fished a white T-shirt from his dresser. "My mom would never speak to me again." I glanced over at the stereo to hide my rolling eyes. Sneaking around felt as out of style as wearing Jordache jeans. After graduating from Florida State University, Tyler had moved back to his parents' house to save money for his own apartment. Despite fierce independence, I still found myself drawn to guys who lived with their parents—a psychology study for another time.

"Come on," I replied. "It's not like they don't know what's going on." His parents were vacationing in Antigua, which had prompted Tyler's sweet invitation to sleep over—two nights in a row.

"I'm their angel." Tyler pulled on his T-shirt. "Cody is the one who gets in trouble." Tyler had an identical twin who lived in northern Florida and was just as cute and athletic. Dating a twin always intrigued me, as my dad had a twin.

"What time will you get off, uh, work?" I stopped myself short of saying "home" and disappeared into a daydream. Sleeping in a house in the same bed with Tyler was the closest I'd gotten to cohabitation since Chris. We both had college degrees and full-time jobs with benefits; he worked as an accountant for a small financial firm. We both liked to run and had practiced karate in middle school. We both had blond hair and sky-blue eyes; my friends called us Ken and Barbie. Our conversations revolved around *South Park* episodes. We were the epitome of compatibility. It had taken me four months to feel repaired enough to put my heart out there again. I'd almost accepted the fact that Fernando would never want me back. Almost.

With Tyler, our kisses had enough spark, our conversations had enough substance and our worlds had enough common ground.

His voice pulled me back into the moment. "Don't forget to park where I told you, and don't get here until after five thirty." I squeezed my tan dress jacket with both hands to suppress my anger. Tyler sat down on the matching bed across the room. The thought of Tyler and his identical twin brother sleeping in their identical twin beds wearing matching Superman Underoos brought a sliver of a smile to my face.

"Don't worry." My voice sassed through his room. "I won't park in the driveway." His masterful plan to hide my overnight stay? Parking across the street. Sleeping at Tyler's cut thirty minutes off my commute and thirty pounds of frustration off my chest. I'd recently moved out of my apartment in South Miami to share a house in North Miami Beach with Scott and Diane, former coworkers who fell in love not long after they'd met at Cheesecake Factory. Sharing a house with a newly engaged couple felt about as comfortable as peeing in the woods.

"I'll call you when I get home," Tyler said.

I glanced down the hallway. "I've got plenty of work to do." My voice was cool and crisp. "If I don't answer, I'll call you when I'm free." I'd decided to get serious about my dating strategy—i.e. actually having a strategy. Learning to be as patient as a Penfolds Grange collector did not come easy, but losing Fernando was the relationship wake-up call I'd needed since high school. I'd always told myself to just put my heart out there from the beginning and the right guy would fall for me—at a time when their hormones were running on Hawaiian Tropic bikini contests. So, the time had finally arrived to set some ground rules to overcome the double standards of dating. No more offering my phone number. No more calling a guy before he called me. No more invitations for drinks, dinner and sleepovers within the first month. Ditching my cling-on habit required professional help—i.e. the Bible of dating books, *The Rules™: Time-Tested Secrets for Capturing the Heart of Mr. Right.* I'd broken every rule in it. Don't accept a date for Saturday night after Wednesday? I'd said "yes" to Raul on Saturdays at 9:48 that night, and had offered to drive—and pick up the bar tab.

"I'll be hungry before dark," he said.

I turned my back to him. "I'll get here when I can." Following *The Rules* with Tyler had worked wonders. Boundaries became my best friends. I'd declined his first date invitation (Rule #7). I'd never called him first (Rule #5). Face-to-face meet-ups occurred once or twice a week at restaurants or ballparks, contingent upon my schedule as much as his. When Tyler wasn't auditing financial records, he played baseball for the West Palm Beach Expos, minor league affiliates of the Montreal Expos. I'd perched myself on aluminum bleachers in the grand stand, cheering as he'd dove to catch line drives at third base. We'd exchanged soft, sweet kisses in the parking lot next to our cars before going our separate ways home. But, the only diamond on his mind involved a baseball field.

"What should we make for dinner?" I asked, walking toward the adjoining bathroom. His fancy, thick carpet felt warm and soft under my bare feet. I plucked a brush from my toiletry bag and eagerly awaited his answer. Sitting down with Tyler to share a home-cooked meal and a bottle of wine was a moment I'd anticipated more than the release of the Cabbage Patch Kids in fifth grade.

"I'm not really big on dinner." Tyler kept his nose in his closet, thumbing through dress shirts. "I usually eat a bagel and a banana." Tyler tugged a crisp, white shirt off a hanger. "A bowl of oatmeal with skim milk, and I'm good to go." His rigorous training schedule included a strict, minimalistic dietary plan—not what you'd expect from someone who worked out harder than trainer Bob on *The Biggest Loser.*

I stared at my damp hair in the mirror and gritted my teeth. *Why can't he play along?*

"But, hon, I'll make you cookies." My voice chirped like Eric Cartman's mom from *South Park*. Tyler cracked a giggle. Conversations with Tyler were rarely serious. I should have expected nothing more from someone who called my vagina a "cha-cha."

"How about some Cheesy Poofs?" Tyler replied in his Cartman voice. I laughed until my eyes met the mirror and caught a glimpse of the horrific laugh lines creasing my cheeks. I grabbed my hairdryer in a huff. The motor's buzz drifted through the second floor while I wrapped layers of hair around the sculpting brush. It was September 1998. I'd graduated from college sixteen months prior and had lived alone for more than three years. Most of my friends back home were engaged or married. Several had babies. Me? I had a part-time boyfriend who dreamed of being called up to the majors.

Tyler stepped into the bathroom doorway. "Hey, we could go for a run tonight." His tone was soft, warm. He looked like a Kenneth Cole model in his freshly pressed slacks. All that eye candy helped distract me from our idling relationship.

"I don't know if I can keep up with you." I fluffed the layers of my hair. My lips twisted with a smirk. We'd never gone running together before.

"I'll go slow. I promise." His blue eyes sparkled as he buttoned his oxford. My cheeks plumped from smiling wide. *Isn't this what I'd always wanted?* A man who'd ease slowly into my life—not parachute into my apartment wielding a box of condoms? I didn't have much free time for Tyler anyway, working two jobs in two counties. Even though I spent weekdays running the distributor's desktop publishing department, I kept working weekends as news editor of *The Wine News* in Coral Gables. Writing wine news blurbs and editing feature stories was keeping my dream of moving to California alive—a dream that I'd moved to the backburner once feelings for Tyler had developed. Falling in love meant making compromises, and I only had a few years left in the optimal age window to find my husband.

I moved toward Tyler and kissed his lips softly. My chest flushed with happiness. Kissing him always felt like returning to the playground. Tyler's lips lingered over mine, gentle and sweet. Our fireworks were more like sparklers than Fernando's Saturn missiles, but it was a start.

"You can take one of my bagels for breakfast." He pecked me again on the lips. I closed my eyes, relishing his sweet taste.

My lips chased his, sneaking another peck. "No way." I scrunched my face. "Carbs are my worst enemy." To keep my mind off Fernando, I'd thrown myself into an intense workout regime that included running five days a week. My thighs were the thinnest since my senior year of high school—thin enough to attract a hottie who knew his way around a bank and a ball field.

🍷🍸🍷🍸🍷

WORKING AT A wine distributor for the first time felt like visiting a tribal village in Africa. Everyone dressed the same, people spoke in tongues and men held all the power. The guys wore golf shirts, khaki Dockers and penny loafers with two accessories: sunglasses and an insulated bag filled with chilled wine bottles. Restaurants were accounts. Wines were SKUs. The word "VIA" was spoken as often as chardonnay—code for a same-day order personally delivered to the account by a sales rep. Blitzes were no longer puff pastries in my world. Supplier ride-withs—days sales reps spent driving a winery's sales manager to accounts to taste wines and get wine list placements—sent the reps rushing into my office in search of winery brochures and the latest tasting notes. My days were spent running the distributor's publishing department, which designed and printed wine lists, cocktail lists, and food menus for restaurants, hotels and bars. (The things distributors did in South Florida in the 1990s to get accounts to sell their alcohol—I could write an entire book just on that.) There were only a handful of women in wine and spirits sales at the distributor back then, but numbers were increasing. The idea of selling wine to strangers made my stomach spin, so I stuck to the de facto female role: marketing.

Dating Tyler was a world apart from my daily life in distribution. Driving to see him after hours of wine tasting with suppliers at the general sales meeting, I wondered if the cavernous difference in our careers was good or bad for our relationship.

The evening after our first sleepover, I zoomed into Tyler's cul-de-sac in my silver Volkswagen Golf and yanked the parking break. *Welcome back to your designated spot.* Sneaking around made me feel like a stashed case of beer on prom night. I sat in my car in my work suit with the air conditioning blasting, admiring his swanky Lauderdale-by-the-Sea home. It reminded me of Tara from *Gone with the Wind*, painted bright white with as many windows as the White House and six massive columns stretching from a brick terrace to the roofline of the second story. My hometown only had one mansion like that.

I stepped out of my chilly car onto the warm pavement and walked swiftly up his brick sidewalk, my sling-back heels clicking along the way. Sweat began to form on my chest from the sticky, summer air. Rows of palm trees and sculpted bushes jetted out from a circular drive, which looked like a golf club entrance. A sparkling white yacht glided by on the Intracoastal behind their colonial mansion. Tyler's house belonged on a postcard. My dad's backyard had a decaying barn and a pigeon coop. His parents played tennis at a country club. Mine played pool at the American

Legion. But Dorothy had outgrown Kansas. I could identify merlot's plummy nuances in a blind tasting. I owned a sequined gown and had worn it twice. I'd shed as much of my stereotype as possible and believed I could win the heart of a rich boy and the approval of his parents. When Tyler had invited me over to meet his parents for the first time, he'd made me swear that I'd say we met at a Third Eye Blind concert in Coconut Grove. Our first lie.

My knuckles tapped on his glass side door. Tyler trotted through the long, galley kitchen in gym shorts and a Kappa Alpha T-shirt. He tugged me quickly in the door.

"Hi," he said in his boyish tone and kissed me softly on the lips.

"Now this feels weird." I pulled away from his lips playfully, still clutching my purse and jacket. "Should we go launch AOL Instant Messenger?" I'd met Tyler on Yahoo! Personals—the new online forum for buying and selling used crap...and finding the love of your life. At the time, dial-up Internet was taking the country by storm, but meeting men online was considered too taboo and risky, especially in a metropolitan city with a robust homicide rate. Enter *You've Got Mail*. Meg Ryan and Tom Hanks had inspired me to take a chance at Internet love and look at my results. I'd loved the excitement of rushing home after work to flirt with Tyler on the computer for hours.

"Hey, I can talk to girls without a keyboard." He flashed a bashful grin. We'd chatted online for two weeks before Tyler had asked me out on a face-to-face date to the Third Eye Blind concert. His outgoing alter ego had sent me hours of flirtatious IMs filled with lots of "hehehes," "LOLs," "*grins*" and smiley faces.

"You're late. You need to suit up." He plucked a half-eaten bagel from the kitchen counter and took a bite. "I need to enjoy my freedom while I have it." He chewed with a smile.

I could feel my face turning to stone and sulked into the den. Tyler had four months to prepare for his CPA Exam and often dive-bombed those little reminders into our conversations. His use of the word "my" added another layer to my mounting disappointment.

"Your upper body is too stiff," he said as we jogged up his cul-de-sac, past rows of electric gates, stucco walls and coconut palms. The fiery sun sank into the horizon as we turned onto Federal Highway and headed north toward Lighthouse Point.

"Really?" A gentle breeze helped keep us comfortable in the evening heat. "What am I doing wrong?" My eyes bounced from the pavement to my Coconut Grove Arts Festival tank top.

"Let your arms flow with your body movement. Don't think about your legs. Your arms should propel you. My coach always told me to pretend that I had bananas in my hands." I watched his arm movements and mimicked him, feeling my lung capacity increase and my body relax into the cadence. It was the first time Tyler had been my teacher, which endeared him to me even more.

The warm air filled my lungs. My heart hummed, in sync with our pace. I felt strong, in control and on top of the world, like I always do while running. The thought of spending every evening jogging with Tyler bounced in my head. Shoulder to shoulder, we glided down the sidewalk.

"I got a call from a headhunter today," he said between breaths. "Deloitte & Touche has an opening for a financial analyst in West Palm." The words danced off his tongue.

My arms tightened again. *West Palm? Hell, why not New York?* My ponytail slapped the back of my head. West Palm Beach was forty-five minutes north of his house. If he took that job, we'd be right back where we'd started, geographically speaking. And he was gushing the news like a lottery winner.

I stared blankly at the Nike sneakers flying underneath me. "Did you send in your résumé?"

"I have an interview next week."

"That's...uh...great." The words panted from my lips. I surged forward, bananas in my hands. My little voice began throwing her own fastballs: *He's supposed to be asking you to share an apartment! You're going the wrong way.*

We showered together after our run. *I like this routine*, I thought as I covered my torso in soapsuds. Tyler's blue eyes floated over my kidney surgery scars as if they were invisible. Guys never really cared about any of my scars. I'd been self-conscious all those years when I should have been owning my flaws like tribal tattoos.

I rubbed my pouf sponge on his washboard stomach. His face turned red, and we both giggled. Tyler was more conservative than *Fox News* on Monday morning—the kind of guy that made me feel wholesome despite my string of exes.

We walked downstairs to the kitchen, wearing fresh sets of T-shirts and gym shorts like two workout buddies. The kitchen was almost as long and wide as my apartment. Two walls of floor-to-ceiling white cabinets opened to a wide den with French doors and magnificent views of the Intracoastal. The room always smelled like Bath & Body Works.

"Don't you have anything we could cook?" I asked, peeking over his shoulder. The first and only time I'd cooked for him at my place, we'd had *salade chevre chaud* and a bottle of Mercurey *rouge*—my favorite food and wine pairing from the graduation trip to France. Tyler opened the refrigerator door and closed it quickly.

"Let's just order pizza." His suggestion was spontaneous and un-healthy—two traits I didn't think existed in Tyler's world. My mood instantly lightened. I professed my love for Pizza Hut Pepperoni Lovers Thin 'N Crispy—they hooked me forever with the Care Bear glassware series in 1984—but Tyler replied, "I don't like their crust."

We returned an hour later with a bottle of Tavel Rosé, a lovely blush wine from France's Rhône Valley, and two lukewarm Papa John's pizzas: a Hawaiian for him and a double pepperoni for me.

I stacked the pizza boxes on the kitchen counter. "Can we eat in the formal dining room?" Their dining room looked like a fancy hotel banquet room with satin wallpaper and ornate wainscoting. I envisioned us sipping our glasses of pink wine under the sparkling chandelier at the cherry table in hand-carved, high-backed chairs. I looked down at my frumpy gym clothes and frowned.

Tyler grabbed the pizza boxes and marched them over to the round oak table in the den. "Let's just eat in here. It's easier." He bounced back to the kitchen and returned with a roll of paper towels and two paper plates. Tacky.

Their den was four shades of brown, which always struck me funny, considering how pristine and bright the home looked from the outside. The dark paneled walls were sprinkled with colorful pictures of the boys and family portraits over the years. A thick, almost shaggy, brown carpet covered the floor. Two sets of French doors with waterway views made the room feel relaxingly cozy.

I pulled a corkscrew from my purse—wine pros never leave home without it—and opened the tall, skinny bottle. I plucked two crystal glasses from his mom's china cabinet.

"We can't break those," Tyler said as I poured the salmon-hued wine.

I set the bottle firmly on the table. "I think we'll manage." My voice held an edge. *I was a waitress for eight years, remember?*

Tyler took a baby sip. "It's just as sharp as the red one." Tyler's first fine wine tasting experience was that bottle of Mercurey, and I'd been schooling him ever since.

I stuffed my nose in the glass and inhaled deeply. Subtle aromas of strawberry, cherry, minerals and spice flirted with my olfactory nerve. I sipped the pale wine, feeling its crisp acidity and hint of citrus tickle my tongue. There is always something innocent about a glass of dry rosé—the simplicity of how it heightens all the senses with just a whisper of color, bouquet and fruit. No other wine spoke to me like rosé in the summer of 1998.

"Sharp is just acidity." I swirled my glass by the stem with ease. "You'll get used to it." Weekends writing for *The Wine News* often required attending wine festivals and black-tie galas. I eagerly awaited the night I could strut into a ballroom in a evening gown, holding his hand. Tyler still didn't know the difference between pinot noir and pinot blanc, so that was going to take some time.

"I feel gay drinking pink wine." He tried swirling the glass at the base of the stem as I'd taught him. America was still eons away from the brosé movement.

"Get over yourself." I sniffed with a scoff. "Real men drink pink—except white zinfandel—the cheap stuff." Tyler asked about the difference between white zinfandel and a red zinfandel, like all wine newbies do. I explained, with enthusiasm, how fermenting red grapes on their skins gives the wine its color.

He raised the glass to his lips and took another sip. "It tastes." He paused, studying the wine glass. "I don't know. Like rocks. Like dirt."

"It does have a little minerality on the finish." I sipped to reaffirm. "French wines, more than any other, express the characteristics of the soil they are grown in. The ground is a critical element to the wine's *terroir*." I coolly explained the French concept of *terroir*—the many factors in a natural environment that contribute to a wine's taste, including the soil, topography and climate.

He pushed his glass away. "I don't think I like earthy wine." Tyler scrunched his nose and picked up a piece of pizza with his fingers.

My eyebrows caved. "Come on. It's fruity and easy to drink." I shoved his wine glass back toward him. "Tavel is a good value. And rosé tastes great with pizza." *Ugh. Newbies.* The wine was crisp and precise, like those dress shirts he wore to work.

My knife sliced hard through a piece of pepperoni. "What would you do if your mom walked in right now?" I poked my knife at the door. I looked over at the designer sofa with scalloped edges and remembered his mother waiting there to meet me for the first time. She had dark-blond hair with a classy, bob haircut. Her legs were gracefully crossed at an angle with Cole Hahn loafers on her feet. A copy of *Architectural Digest* was pressed between her manicured fingertips. She looked like a cross between Linda Evans from *Dynasty* and Chris Evert, with her mint-collared shirt and matching gold bracelet and necklace.

Tyler chewed his crust and swallowed. "I'd poo in my pants." He couldn't even say the word "shit" in my presence, which I found cute sometimes, immature others. "She'd kill me."

"Parents aren't stupid." I took a lingering sip. "You're twenty-three years old." I recalled her swan-like motions, rising from the couch and extending her dainty hand. She'd spoken with the conviction and confidence of a queen. She'd congratulated me on graduating top of my class from FIU and asked questions about what I loved most about writing for a wine magazine. Meanwhile, my mind was sifting through all my baggage I'd been hiding from Tyler—my father's drinking problem, Robert the coke user, Michael's STD or my string of Latin lovers. I wondered if seeing her son date a girl from Podunk got her tennis skirt in a bunch. I'd show his family that I had some class. Someday I would bring over a bottle of cabernet sauvignon—something elegant and timeless, such as Jordan or Shafer—if Tyler ever invited me to Sunday dinner with his family.

Tyler put his nose over the glass and sniffed deeply, following my lead. He still cupped the bowl of the glass with his hand, but I didn't correct his technique. Tyler's tasting skills and palate would come around with practice. I'd moved him quickly past the sugary-sweet flavors of starter wines like white zin and Riunite D'Oro. "Trust me. The taste of good wine will grow on you," I'd told him multiple times.

He rested the glass on his oak table. "It seems so strange to drink wine after going running. And it's a weeknight." He pulled another piece of pizza from the box.

My head cocked sideways. "A glass of wine with dinner is good for you." I looked into my glass while swirling it. "It's good for your heart, and it enhances the flavors in your food." It was that time when wine consumption was climbing, thanks to the aforementioned *60 Minutes* segment about the French paradox—how French people drank more wine and ate fatter foods but were healthier than Americans.

"I should switch to water." He pushed his glass away again. "I need to study tonight." I looked down at my half-eaten piece of pizza and chewed slowly.

I poured myself another glass, wondering if we'd ever get on the same page.

🍷🍷🍷🍷🍷

TYLER POKED AT my stereo's remote control, clicking through songs. I sat on the edge of my futon, nervously swirling my wine glass. My roommates pushed around moving boxes in the dining room. I had two weeks to find a roommate or be evicted, and a week had passed since Tyler and I had played house.

"What should I do?" I asked, voice cracking. I wore a short tunic dress and black sandals—something that would get his attention.

"I don't know." His tone was flat; he reached for his wine glass. I tapped my foot, watching his muscular arms flex. He wore a Florida Marlins T-shirt and gym shorts—his usual after-work look. Third Eye Blind's "Semi-Charmed Life" bopped in the air around us.

My body sunk into my futon couch. "An eviction notice? I feel so dirty." My roommates had abruptly decided to move back to Atlanta. I sipped a healthy pour of Glen Carlou South African Chardonnay. Flavors of vanilla and ripe apple danced across my tongue—so sweet despite the sour moment. "What's next? An application for food stamps?"

"Stop it. You'll be fine. You have a great job, and you're the most responsible, normal girl I've ever dated." He leaned back, his shoulder resting against mine. "That's why I like you." I sniffed my wine, startled by his unexpected compliment.

"That's all I've ever wanted." I stared into the golden-hued glass of wine. "For a nice guy to realize I'm normal." A normal girl was supposed to be the jackpot in South Florida—no hair extensions, no plastic surgery, no jealous ex-boyfriends, no nagging, no overuse of the word "irregardless" and no addiction to expensive jewelry. I kept telling myself that being normal was the key to landing a nice man.

Tyler began jabbering about his interview, which took place over lunch at Ruth's Chris in West Palm Beach's new CityPlace complex.

"They offered me the job before the waiter presented the check," he said with a smirk, all pleased with himself.

"That's great news." My voice croaked. I kept glaring into my half-empty glass.

He turned his knees toward me. "There's something I need to ask you." His usual bashful tone turned sincere.

My stomach began knitting itself into a crochet scarf. I squeezed the stem of my wine glass. *Finally. The proposal I've been waiting for.* "Okay. Shoot." My eyelashes fluttered.

"Well, I'll finally be getting my own apartment." He sat down his wine glass. "And I was wondering if you'd be willing to take Rocky." His blue eyes locked on my face.

I looked at his beautiful head of blond hair, feeling like I'd just been hit in the chest with a line drive. Rocky was his pet bearded dragon. "Take? Like take for a weekend?" I needed a lifeline. I grabbed the wine bottle off my coffee table and poured myself another glass of chardonnay.

"Like an adoption." He rubbed his palms together. "Think of it as joint custody. You love lizards, and I don't think I'm going to have time for him with the new job and everything else."

Holy shit. I want to move in together, and he just wants me to raise his fucking lizard. I straightened my back, feeling the anger rage through me. My dreams began to crack like a thin sheet of ice on a pond. I swirled my glass to calm my nerves.

"I could take him on weekends or something." Tyler bumped his knee against mine and smiled, waiting for my response.

I squared my shoulders to him. "In case you didn't notice, I'm a little busy with my own 'everything else' right now."

His back fell hard against my futon. "Okay...I'll take that as a 'no.'" He grabbed his wine off the coffee table and took a long drink. "This is really sharp." He peered into the wine glass.

I folded my arms. "Tell me about it." My voice could have cut right through him—sharp and crisp like a sauvignon blanc, not a chardonnay. But, I was too emotionally exhausted to teach him the difference.

🍷🍷🍷🍷🍷

I FOUND A classified ad on Yahoo!—not the dating section—from someone in Hallandale Beach looking for a roommate to share a three-bedroom house in a gated community. I quickly moved in with Brandon, the homeowner, who was tall with short black hair, round glasses and always wore a tie. He worked for a paper manufacturer located in the same business park as the wine distributor. My new place in Broward County cut twenty minutes off my commute to Tyler's new apartment in Palm Beach County. We continued to chat online at least three or four nights a week. When the weekend rolled around, he usually fit me into his schedule.

wanna come up 4 a sleepover? he asked on instant message with a smiley face, *wink* and *grin*. I took the bait.

Driving to Palm Beach County from Broward for the first time felt like crossing over into a different country. The grassy marshes flanking I-95 north of Boca Raton morphed into strip malls and business parks the farther I drove.

I climbed Tyler's open-air stairway with heavy legs, admiring the tropical gardens surrounding his building. When I found his unit on the third floor, I paused in the humid air and tugged on the edges of my cotton dress. My fingers fluffed my flat hair before knocking on the door.

The door openly slowly, and Tyler peeked around the edge. He smiled sweetly and pecked my lips. I rested my duffle bag on the floor. His kitchen was the size of a walk-in closet and opened to a skinny living room with a sliding-glass door and small terrace overlooking a courtyard. Tyler proudly showed me around his mismatched living room—a mix of freebie furniture from relatives.

"Now we both have our own places." He stood in the center of his living room, grinning. His need for a life independent from mine baffled me. *If he doesn't want to be with me, why is he keeping me around?* I stood with my arms laced, waiting for him to be hospitable.

I looked into his bedroom. There was only a twin bed and one night-stand. My teeth began grinding. *Does he expect me to sleep on the couch? As if!*

He tilted his head. "What's wrong?"

I planted both hands on my hips. "I'm your guest. You haven't offered me anything to drink."

"I'm sorry," he replied. "But I only have milk and water." He flashed a bashful smile, hoping to squelch my disappointment. I glanced over at my duffle bag, wondering if I should leave.

We drove to CityPlace, ten minutes east of his apartment. The open-air entertainment complex had three stories of bustling bars and restaurants. Things were looking up.

"What do you want to eat?" I asked, hopping out of his Honda Civic in the parking garage. "I heard there are some great restaurants here with really progressive wine lists." My eyes bopped around his handsome face, waiting for an answer that would make my mood go from okay to great.

"I don't really care," Tyler replied. "I haven't been anywhere but Ruth's Chris." My chin dropped in defeat.

We walked into the shopping center's piazza. "Do you wanna try something new?" I waited for him to grab my hand, like always.

"Let's start with a martini." I spotted a Blue Martini bar and guided Tyler to the terrace.

I ordered a cosmopolitan; he ordered a Kalik, the beer of The Bahamas. I sighed and looked sheepishly around at the other tables. *Did people with real jobs drink cheap beer? I no longer did.* The high-top tables were filled with young men and women in designer suits sipping from their inverted pyramids. I picked at my fingernails, unsure of what to say. Tyler raved about his office in the fancy high-rise off Worth Avenue and how awesome it was to walk to the bars after work and have a beer with his new colleagues. I sipped on my pink martini, feeling more perturbed with each swallow. Once we finished our drinks, Tyler said he wanted to take me to his favorite local dinner spot as a surprise.

Within minutes, we pulled into a Blimpie on Okeechobee Boulevard. A freakin' sub shop.

We squeezed awkwardly into his twin bed that night and had our usual, sweet, conservative, missionary sex. We slept on our sides so I wouldn't fall off the bed.

🍷🍸🍸🍸🍸

I WOKE UP the next morning, cramped and disoriented. *Where am I? Oh, yeah.* Tyler breathed deeply on my shoulder, still fast asleep. I slipped quietly out of his tiny bed and tiptoed to the doorway in my tank top and panties. I turned back and watched him sleeping peacefully. *Will there ever be enough room for me in his life?* Nearly half a decade of prime honeymooning years had evaporated. Moving forward with the CPA Exam was his goal. Moving forward with our relationship was mine.

I grabbed my clothes and gingerly pulled them on. We'd spent a half-year dating, and the topic of "our future" had never come up once. He'd told me he liked me, and there was one "I missed you" when he'd picked me up at the airport. He'd stayed consistent all these months—bashful, bright and full of potential—just like a French rosé on a summer night.

I walked over to his sliding glass doors. The high rises of downtown West Palm glistened in the distance, lit by a pink sunrise. "What am I doing here?" I muttered to myself, resting my head against the warm glass. My palate had evolved from beer to vodka to sweet white wines to dry rosés and silky reds. My taste in men was maturing, too.

My fingers pressed against the cool glass doors as despair raked through my chest. For months, I'd kept telling myself Tyler was worth waiting for—worth putting off my dream of moving to Sonoma wine country. *He wants a girl like me—he just isn't ready for a serious relationship. Fine dining and wine tasting will grow on him.* I'd been brainwashing myself with affirmations as bitter as cheap box wine. It was time for my inner wino to spit or swallow—go or stay. *Will he ever be ready? Will he ever love wine?* The questions rolled through me as rays of sunshine sprayed into his living room. My eyes stayed fixed on the horizon. *You have to do this. Put your needs first for once.* Our relationship wasn't built on sex, so a part of me didn't want to give up on one of the few relationships that had started out right.

My days of working overtime to win a guy's heart were long gone. I was listening to my own heart and using my head for the first time. I wanted to spend my life with someone who shared my passions and made me his number one priority.

This time, I would not run away. I would not leave a note. I would tell him it was over and why to his face—like all adults should.

And for the first time in my life, more than anything, I hoped we could just be friends.

PAUL
The Napa Wine Days

It can't be good luck if you tell a guy you love him for the first time while you're puking your brains out. I suppressed the urge to blurt that declaration back at the gray-haired woman. A vise of embarrassment clamped tighter around my throat while she sat primly in her armchair, awaiting my answer. My eyes scanned the blank faces of the other couples in the circle, crowded around her accent rug as if it was a campfire.

I sat on the edge of my folding chair, squeezing its seat to keep my hands from shaking. "What I love most about Paul..." I took a long, deep breath like a drag on a fancy cigarette. "We'll, it's hard to pick just one thing. He's devoted to me. He's always there for me when I need advice about work. He helps me do all the things guys usually don't, like cooking, cleaning and running errands. He'd rather spend weekends with me than with a bunch of guys. He's dependable. He's strong. He takes charge of situations. He's smart." I spouted the words until my lungs ran out of breath.

Our rosy-cheeked host smiled in approval. My stomach swirled with anxiety as I turned to Paul in his matching chair. His strong face flashed pale white.

Did I say something wrong again? My heartbeat ran wild under my taupe turtleneck. The last thing he'd wanted to do on Valentine's Day was attend a couples' workshop with a life coach named Ziggy. For what seemed like the first time in years, he'd agreed to a weekend activity that didn't involve us cleaning the house, weeding the yard, balancing our checkbooks or shopping for groceries.

Ziggy readjusted her reading glasses. "What do you love about Lisa, Paul?" The words trickled from her mouth with a warming grace. Then silence. Flames crackled in a fancy marble fireplace across the room. It felt more like a parlor in a Victorian home than an office for holistic healing and life coaching.

My fingers rubbed my Gap jeans, anticipating the compliments I'd been craving. I stuffed my hands deep between my clamped thighs before looking over at Paul's profile. A long, wide nose and full brow line dominated his features. He wore Hugo Boss jeans and a cashmere designer sweater. Paul always dressed classy, among the many things that attracted me to him.

He pressed his fingertips together. "She...uhhh...ummm..." I stared at his face, waiting for his lips to move. I'd never known Paul to be at a loss for words. "Well, uhhh, she's a great support tool for my career."

My eyes zoomed from his face to the wide eyes in the circle. I felt like two jackrabbits were humping in my chest. Coach Ziggy cleared her throat and smiled. *That's the first thing he thinks of?! What about pretty? Affectionate? Caring?* My mind screamed the rebuttal. My mouth felt drier than a young cabernet aged in new oak.

"And?" Ziggy asked, baiting him to continue. I watched his lips move, but the words were muffled inside my racing head. Smart. Dedicated. Affectionate. *Why hasn't he said pretty?*

She shuffled her hands in her lap. "Before we move onto the next couple, why don't you tell me how you met?"

"Through work," we said in unison, our tone flatter than cheap bubbly. I turned to Paul, waiting for a scowl to flare over his disapproving face. He rubbed his shaved head. Paul had the same wide nose and ass-kicking look as Frank Martin, *The Transporter*—minus the BMW.

"We carpooled to a trade show about five years ago, and we've been together ever since," I said with a timid smile. Paul had worked as a sales manager for a corporate wine company, handling their business in grocery stores and wine shops throughout South Florida. He was one of my "suppliers" as we say in the wine trade.

Our fate had been sealed in November 1998, about a month after I'd broken up with Tyler, when Paul had invited me to share a ride to the distributor's annual trade show in Key West. A fatality accident had closed Seven Mile Bridge on Highway 1, so we'd spent eight hours in Paul's sparkling Ford sedan, talking about work, relationships and life. He too had grown up in a tiny farming town and had paid his way through college by waiting tables. We'd covered more ground in one car ride than most people do in five dates. I'd known little about Paul before that night, except that he was separated from his wife, had a dog, wore expensive ties and was the only supplier who stopped by my office every week with an armload of brochures and tasting notes for his wine brands.

I raised my eyes to Ziggy. "He was always my favorite customer." I smiled, remembering our start. Paul had possessions that screamed maturity: tasseled leather loafers, a company car, an expense account and a black Day Planner (i.e. life before smartphones), which he clutched under his arm like a priest carrying the Bible. And he could stick his nose in a glass of red wine and guess the varietal with ninety percent accuracy. My kind of guy.

"It's the easiest relationship I've ever had," I continued. "Paul never played games." After we'd returned from Key West, he'd called me every night. He'd picked up every tab for lunch, dinner or drinks. He'd chose nights and weekends with me versus drinking beer in a bar or playing a round on the golf course. No boyfriend had really made me his top priority before. Within a month, he'd asked me to move into his apartment. We'd just spent a Saturday night drinking Kristone Rosé sparkling wine at a Kendall-Jackson employee's house party, and I'd told him I loved him while puking on the bumper of his car. Kristone became *our* wine until it was discontinued—just one year later. Talk about a sign.

Ziggy chuckled. "Relationships are never easy."

"It was easy." I gnawed on my pinky nail. "I thought it was." I paused, feeling my chest tighten. "He was such a great boyfriend, unlike any I'd dated before." I watched the side of Paul's rigid face. His jaw locked as the word "was" left my throat. In the beginning, Paul didn't seem to care about the South Beach hotel manager or the Bacardi sales rep I'd slept with. I'd made the classic mistakes young women often do in this business: go to a "work" event on an empty stomach, forget to follow the one-glass-of-water-for-every-glass-of-wine rule, get tipsy and accept a ride home from a coworker, account or supplier. There was no Uber to the rescue.

Living with Paul had immediately brought a sense of order to my jumbled life. Before meeting Paul, I'd learned how to blend a Rumrunner, organize a wine festival, write a wine auction news article and make homemade chardonnay, but the bare necessities had fallen to the wayside. Paul had taught me chapters in the book of chores my parents had skipped over, from making the bed daily and folding towels hotel-style to grocery shopping with a list (every Sunday afternoon at three o'clock and he pushed the cart!). Our life had more structure than U.S. Army boot camp.

Ziggy shifted her body toward Paul. "Did you find the relationship easy from the beginning as well, Paul?"

"Yes." His flat tone sliced through my heart. "But I thought it was just fine two months ago." His eyes never met mine. I inhaled, feeling the exasperation filling my chest. For the first two years, we were as inseparable as three-year-old twins. We'd go to the gym together at six every morning. We'd shower together every day before work. We ate the same cereal side by side at our dining room table. Paul was my best friend and co-pilot in the world of wine. When it came to the wine business, we made one hell of a team. He was the salesman; I was the marketer.

"Lisa, you said on the phone you wanted to improve how the two of you communicate." Ziggy patted out the creases in her long skirt, waiting patiently for my reply. My stomach squished with angst. I felt like I'd eaten a gallon of ice cream.

"Well, it seems like every time we talk, the conversation turns *adversarial*." I stared down at my laced fingers. "I've been reading some books, and I think that's what has happened, and I know it's not healthy." I could feel Paul's brown eyes staring at me. My insides churned. He exhaled a deep, frustrated breath, the kind I'd come to expect at least once a week. Life had gotten to the point where we argued about whether or not the creamed spinach had enough parmesan cheese, or if the dog had been fed at the right time of day: 6 a.m. and 6 p.m., sharp.

"Do you agree with her, Paul?" Ziggy asked, sitting on the edge of her chair.

He squirmed like a kid in a dentist's chair. "Yeah, I suppose there's some truth to that. I'm just not sure if changing how we talk will make her happy." His eyes locked on the woman while my teeth hacked away at my fingernails.

"When did the arguing start?"

Paul folded his arms across his thick, muscular chest and looked at me.

My shoulders dropped with a shrug.

"When we moved to California." His sharp tone cut through me. It always did.

My eyes fixed on my fingers while Paul described our big cross-country move. Moving from Florida to California had made me feel as emotionally drained as a full-time funeral singer. I'd received a job offer in July 2001 to run the events department at E&J Gallo Winery, the largest family wine company in the world. Paul didn't want to leave South Florida. His high-paying sales job had had many perks—the company car, the unlimited expense account, the quarterly bonus. When he'd asked me if I would go to California without him, I'd lain in his queen-sized bed like a corpse and couldn't say a word.

"The job market out here hasn't been as easy for him as it has been for me." My chest tightened as I talked about our jobs. In California, my career had soared and his had sputtered. I'd traveled around the country to major cities, decorating wine tasting stations at wine festivals and pouring samples for consumers. Paul had worked at the corporate offices of a wine retail chain in the East Bay. His expense account had been hacked down faster than a redwood in a Pacific Northwest lumberyard.

I fidgeted with the remnants of nail polish left on my fingers. "I think, ummm, his job put a lot of stress on our relationship." My guilt had helped me endure the arguing for nearly two years. He'd shot down my first four selections on fabric designs for our den window valence. He'd complained when I'd bought new clothes without consulting him first. He'd scolded me when I'd bought a blue collar for his dog because she'd been wearing red ones her entire life. Paul had finally taken an operations job with an online wine retailer in San Francisco, and we'd relocated from the Central Valley to Sonoma County—my college dream—but the bickering didn't stop.

"My job?" Paul huffed, squaring his broad shoulders. "I think it was your job."

I recoiled into the back of my chair. *Here we go again.* During my work trips, I'd call him from a hotel room (where I spent a third of my time), and he'd snap at me about how he had to clean up dog puke and take out the trash while I'd been nibbling on sautéed fish at white-table cloth restaurants. He'd made big sacrifices for my career; I'd deserved to take some heat for it.

"Your job is the only issue we've ever had." The words shot from his mouth. Paul always had grip and a long finish...just like his favorite wine: Napa cabernets from Howell Mountain.

My chin fell in defeat. "I guess he's right." Trying to argue with Paul sucked the energy out of me.

Our coach moved along to questioning the next couple. We were the youngest in the circle, which made my guilt grow.

My mind drifted while two retired teachers talked about losing their sex drives. *Great. More to look forward to.* Our troubles probably began in 1999 when I'd moved to a competitor wine distributor to be director of public relations and special events. We could no longer sit together at black-tie wine auction galas. Paul would nip at my heels during wine tastings, telling me that my work was done and it was time to go home. I'd always wanted to stay until the end of each tasting and remove empty wine bottles, tasting note cards and tablecloths from the stations. I'd wanted the wine suppliers—my clients—to see my strong work ethic. I'd wanted to enjoy my well-deserved break during the tasting, strolling through the ballroom with a wine glass in hand, sampling the latest vintages from every table.

A woman in her fifties started sobbing into a tissue while her graying spouse squeezed her hand. They'd just diagnosed themselves with empty nest syndrome.

Paul turned to me. "You see? Marriage is hard."

My head oscillated like an electric fan. "I thought things would get easier once we moved to California." The words blurted from my shaking jaw. Paul and I had been engaged for almost a year before I'd felt ready to set a wedding date in 2000. Once the engagement ring was finally on my finger, marriage had scared me more than a life's supply of white zinfandel. I didn't want to end up divorced. I didn't want my kids to have the same childhood as me. Paul knew how to run a household and manage finances. He knew why marriages fall apart. Paul had more life experiences than me. He'd already learned from his mistakes. This might be a great strategy for choosing a Wii bowling partner, but not a husband.

"Did you go to premarital counseling?" Ziggy asked, her reading glasses clutched between her bony fingers.

I bit my upper lip. "No." Tears began to pool in the corners of my eyes. I took a deep breath to fight them off. *How could I possibly tell Paul my darkest secret?* The hurdles I'd needed to cross before our wedding even seemed too big for Lolo Jones. I'd always yearned to feel the exhilaration of spiritual chemistry with Paul, even a half of kilowatt of what I'd felt with Fernando. Every kiss was a search for a hidden switch I'd hopefully find and flip, unleashing that undiscovered passion between us. Five months before the wedding, I'd secretly begun seeing a therapist. I'd told her about my childhood with an alcoholic father, my reservations about Paul and my feelings for Fernando. The psychologist had asked me questions that made conversations go in circles, which always looped back to my father's alcoholism and my career choice. I couldn't comprehend her logic. Wine is about the memories that are unlocked when you open a bottle, the triumphs of each vintage, the hands that helped craft it and how the perfect wine can elevate the flavors of a simple meal. The alcohol is just an afterthought to me. Those therapy sessions weren't giving me answers, so I'd decided to take the advice of a relative: "Marry your best friend because all the magic fades away." Within a year, our moving van was headed to California.

Paul looked at the sobbing woman. "Our nest may always be empty." His brusque voice shot into my ears. "She has issues with having children." The other couples' eyes bounced from him to me like cats chasing a laser pointer.

I took a deep breath and pushed up the sleeves on my turtleneck sweater. *Not the dreaded "C" word again.* "Maybe, umm, I do have issues with motherhood." I struggled to find words that wouldn't send Paul into a tizzy while the faces of empathy looked at me. Most women my age had baby fever; I had baby malaria. As soon as I'd turned twenty-nine, the high-speed train of life I'd been riding for nearly a decade—get diploma, start career, find husband, buy house, get pregnant—began to travel in slow motion. The big 3-0 meant far more than another layer of cellulite on my thighs, crow's feet scratching away at my eyes and my biological clock counting down like Jack Bauer's timer on *24*.

"My friend said a switch would flip inside me someday, and I'd want to get pregnant." My eyes locked with the empty nesters. "It hasn't happened." I'd feared getting older and having babies more than a date night with Jason Voorhees from *Friday the 13th*. Diapers and diarrhea and snot and screams were so not my rodeo. But, I'd been married to a devoted husband and fellow wine guru for more than three years, and something was missing. Maybe it was a baby. Maternity was, after all, expected of me.

"So, you've never talked about your feelings before?" Ziggy's eyes scanned his face then mine. She plucked a notepad from the arm of her chair and jotted some notes. I felt like a science project.

Paul folded his arms across his thick chest. "She's been going to therapy since last summer." I glared at the floor, feeling my cheeks get hot. I'd been forcing changes in our life for two years, hoping to find marriage utopia. New houses. New paint. New furniture. When it came to work, I felt like a skilled rock climber cruising up a mountain. At home, I felt like a klutz who couldn't walk two feet without falling on my face. I'd finally broken down and found a psychologist.

"I have a lot of things to work out." I stared at my clenched fists. "I thought it would be better for me to talk to someone alone." After almost two years in California, we were talking openly about our relationship with others for the first time—even if it was with a Marin County grandma who dabbled in life coaching and massage therapy.

"She didn't have a great relationship with her dad. He committed suicide." His tone was as firm as a CEO giving a keynote speech. My lungs sucked in air and froze, feeling my heart break all over again. Paul looked at my face before turning to Ziggy. "I think that might have something to do with her unhappiness."

My eyes dropped to the floor, searching for a deep crack to crawl into.

Ziggy's face flashed from curiosity to sympathy. "Do you want to talk about him?"

My fingers began to tremble.

Did I want to talk about how they found his body in a truck in the middle the woods baking in the summer sun?

Did I want to talk about cleaning out his home after his death, only to find that he never even opened my wedding invitation?

"No, this isn't about my dad." My teeth snipped the words. I took a shaky breath. "He has nothing to do with this." My fingers barreled through my straight hair. I exhaled until my lungs hurt. Talking to him, talking about him—neither were ever easy.

Dad had become really depressed, swimming in a life full of regrets. He'd stopped working, showering, cleaning his house or paying bills. He'd upgraded from beer to cigarettes and crystal meth, supposedly. Trying to wrap my melon around how my father became a drug addict was about as easy as telling the difference between a Volnay and a Pommard in a blind tasting. The man I knew only drank root beer on Sunday because it was the Lord's Day—and it nursed his hangover. The only stick hanging from his mouth was a Slim Jim. But mental illness can derail life faster than a freight train when untreated.

Two months before our wedding day, a sheriff had found his body in his beat-up truck, parked in a deserted field with a sock stuffed in the back muffler. My family had just begun discussing an intervention plan.

Amid all that pain and shock, I'd made peace with his death. I'd accepted the fact long ago that I couldn't control other people's actions. I'd also accepted the hand that was dealt to me—a frail family bond that had weakened further with time and distance. The tragedy had brought Paul and I closer during that time when I'd questioned our future. His father had died of lung cancer when he was a baby.

"This day is about all of you." Ziggy's gray bun bounced with her bobbing head. "We can talk about whatever you wish."

I slipped my palms between my knees. "I would rather we spend this time talking about how to bring passion to our marriage." My voice croaked. My growing willingness to be open about my feelings in Paul's presence made me feel as strong as a baby ox. My response to any argument had always been to retreat faster than the finish on a glass of Two Buck Chuck. In my mid-twenties, I'd never possessed the courage to say, "We need to have a talk." Confronting Paul made me feel as if the weight of Shaquille O'Neal had been lifted off my shoulders.

"You're happy with your life?" Ziggy asked Paul, her brown eyes sparkling.

"Yes," Paul replied with a hiss. "We have a great life." She turned her knees toward me. I squirmed in my seat.

"I know our life could be far worse." I looked down at my ankle boots. "I have a lot to be thankful for." It was the same pep talk I'd been giving myself for the last twelve months on my morning run in our neighborhood. We owned a home on a hill with views of Sonoma's Hood Mountain. We had good jobs. We drove nice cars. There were women in Africa living in huts with no clean water and five hungry children. I needed to suck it up and be happy.

The coach asked the sexless couple where they saw themselves in five years. For the last twelve months, one ominous thought had been circling in my head like a buzzard hunting mice: *If I live another thirty years like this, will I look back on my life with regret?*

I sat up on the edge of my seat with all eyes on me. "Romance is important to me." I took a deep breath. "I want to feel adored. I want a little magic now and then. An unexpected candlelight dinner or flowers would be nice, too." My head whipped around toward Paul. At home, I'd begun suggesting to Paul how we could kiss, touch, talk and make love to improve our connection. He'd flipped his shiny lid.

Paul fanned out his chest. "I don't know why she can't just be happy." He opened his hand. "I cook dinner almost every night. I pay the bills. I help clean the house and shop for groceries. I wash her car. I sit in the chair with her at night while we watch TV with my arm around her. I tell her I love her every day." Each fingertip counted another way he showed his love. "Nothing is ever enough." His voice boomed like always, laced with a southern drawl that gave his arguments a warm sweetness. The man could debate better than Tom Cruise in *A Few Good Men*.

250

I stared at my knees. "He is a great husband." Paul did do most of the chores. I'd cooked for him a couple of times when we'd first started dating then he took over. The former waitress who'd whip out pots and pans on the second date didn't even boil water once married. If the way to a man's heart was through his stomach, Paul should have starved to death after week four. *Why did I lose my desire to cook? Why are all the things he does for me not enough?*

My mind drifted to our nightly routine. We'd often sit at our dining room table with a row of half-empty bottles between us—usually samples of pricey Napa Valley reds left over from Paul's workday. We'd sniff, swirl and sip, analyzing each wine's aromas and flavors, the structure of the palate and the grip of the tannins on the finish. We'd try to guess the type of barrels used for aging and if other grape varietals were used in the blend, like sommeliers taking a certification exam. We'd talk about the daily wine news headlines. *Isn't that what I've always wanted?*

Paul squared his broad shoulders again. "You've been traveling forty percent of the time for more than two years. I handle everything here. Even when you're home, your head is still at work." My eyes moved from his red face to my wedding ring. Three months earlier, Paul had landed a high-level corporate job with a wine supplier who specialized in California and Italian wines. Their offices were headquartered outside New York City, so he'd been traveling, too.

Paul turned back to Ziggy. "She cares more about her job than she does our marriage."

My body sunk into the chair, stunned. "How can you say that?"

"Honey, please," Paul scoffed, folding his arms across his chest.

I stared at the rug. "We're here, aren't we?" My shoulders caved. I did travel too much and worked too many hours. I'd dry my hair in the car just to get to work early. When he'd called me at my desk around five thirty to ask me when I was coming home, I'd say, "In about fifteen minutes." We'd have the same conversation two more times, him calling back after thirty minutes and yelling, "Honey!" as soon as I'd pick up the phone at my desk, still typing away on email. Whenever I'd call him on my way home and he'd start to talk about his day, my mind immediately raced back to the office and another to-do list item for tomorrow.

I took a deep breath. "We both need to try harder." My voice quivered. I wore baggy clothes to cover my thick hips. I didn't fix my hair or wear makeup on weekends. I thought I'd never be able to be thin again after age thirty. My sex drive had shifted into reverse; I no longer felt physically attracted to him.

I turned toward Paul, and more hidden feelings leapt into my throat. "You never tell me I'm pretty. I know you said you're working on it, but it seems so, well, forced." My eyes fixed on his, as the lingering taste of confidence filled me. I'd gained fifteen pounds within a month of dating Paul, eating his favorite foods: Toaster Strudels, fried sausage, Totino's frozen pizza, creamed spinach, macaroni and cheese and Phish Food ice cream. I'd brainwashed myself into believing that sex pretty much stopped after marriage and would disappear once we had kids. I was actually looking forward to life without sex.

Ziggy crooked her neck at Paul. He popped his knuckles.

I shot him a death stare and shivered. "Why are you doing that?"

Paul glared back. "I'll stop cracking my knuckles when you stop biting your fingernails."

Well, this is going about as smoothly as a Rebel Wilson pole dance.

ROGER STACKED THE Louis Martini Cabernet Sauvignon bottles on the banquet table like bowling pins, as concessionaires wandered from booth to booth on the convention center floor, handing exhibitors bus tubs of ice.

"Don't place more than two bottles of each varietal on display," I said, moving the bottles into an elegant V. "This is too much. It reinforces the big brand image. We want the consumers to think we're boutique." My hair bounced along with my authoritative tone. I wore an INC pants suit and black flats—all business.

Roger, a coworker who'd just relocated with the winery to California from Canada, was new to the marketing department at Gallo, and his boss had sent him to spend a weekend with me at the Cincinnati International Wine Festival, learning the corporate brand standards for wine pouring events. We were setting up for the grand tastings—the standard format our industry employs for most events—where dozens of white-skirted banquet tables line a ballroom or convention center hall, and each winery gets its own station to pour from. Boring. I tried to dress things up with pretty tablecloths, tasting note cards and flowers—elegant touches to help our brands stand out in the sea of sameness.

Roger returned the extra bottles to the wine cases under the table. "Okay. Makes sense." He wore a dark gray suit and striped tie and had the debonair look of Hugh Grant. "What's next on your list?" His voice had a serious yet warm tone.

"Well, whites are on ice." I looked down at my laminated check-off list. "Our par is three bottles. Never open more than that to start." We began uncorking the reds, stiffing each bottle, tasting and spitting into the wax-covered bucket—making sure each was fully expressive and not cork-tainted or muted in flavor—for the hundreds of consumers who were going to descend on us within thirty minutes.

Working for Gallo was my first winery job, and it did so much more than teach me how make a wine tasting table look pretty or how to talk to consumers about wine. I learned how to write creative brief, lead presentations and understand wine marketing from concept to execution. I learned how to navigate the hierarchy of a corporation and get shit done. It allowed me to see new places, taste thousands of wines and learn the power of conversations that occur during business travel.

That evening, I hopped onto a cherry barstool at the bank-turned-bar hotspot in downtown Cincinnati. The stately brick building had been transformed into a cocktail lounge with live jazz and a Speakeasy vibe. Huge vaults along one wall had been converted to wine, spirits and cigar cellars. It seemed like the perfect place to unwind after a long day on my feet, pouring wine.

A man in a tuxedo played a piano in the corner. I swayed to the music and ordered a Duckhorn Merlot from the leather-bound menu, thrilled to be back on the road, awakening my internal compass with a new adventure in a new time zone.

Roger joined me at a high-top table and loosened his tie. A young woman who worked for our local wine distributor stopped by the table to thank us for flying in to support their state's largest wine tasting. Roger immediately stepped off his barstool and pulled out a chair for her. *Do guys still do that, or did hell just freeze over?* The woman said she couldn't stay and buzzed toward the door.

I swirled my glass of Napa wine on the marble tabletop. "I wish my husband did that." I thought of all the times Paul had entered restaurants before me. Two weeks had crept by since the couple's workshop.

"I was raised to treat all women like that," he replied matter-of-factly in his fancy suit. "Women should be respected. Put on a pedestal." My blue eyes flew to his. He drank Dewars on the rocks. The man had class from brain to toe.

I shook my head and swirled my wine glass. "Wait until you get married someday. Relationships aren't that easy." I took a long sip, letting the juicy flavors of dark cherries and chocolate coat my mouth. Napa merlot had strength and finesse that made me believe the adage, "You are what you drink." I gripped the stem of my glass firmly, admiring the inky wine. "It's not a fairytale like we want it to be when we're young. It's friendship, partnership, working together, compromising." I took a deep breath, channeling my inner Dr. Phil. "It's a lot of work." My straight hair brushed across the shoulders of my INC suit jacket. I'd recently cut my hair the shortest it had been since my senior year of school—without consulting with Paul in advance—and he was furious.

Roger's finger rounded the rim of his rocks glass. "Marriage should be the easiest thing in your life, not the hardest."

I grabbed my wine glass and took a long sip, soaking in every word. *Easiest? Pass this man a crack pipe.*

He took a deep breath. "What about romance, passion and fun?" You didn't mention any of those things." My eyes met his and rushed back to my wine glass. I felt as exposed as a lingerie model at a photo shoot.

"I just wish he'd tell me I'm beautiful." I gazed into the dark hue of my merlot. The beat of my heart rang out in my ears. Ideas sprinted through my head faster than Usain Bolt. I felt so alive, having an unfiltered conversation about relationships with a guy.

Roger sat back and pressed both palms on the table. "You've got to be kidding me." His eyes fixed on my face. "Your husband doesn't tell you you're beautiful?" He laced his hands around the back of his head.

My head nodded over the wine glass. "Would you excuse me?" I darted into the bathroom.

I stood over the sink, staring at my face in the mirror. His every word echoed in my head. My entire body felt hooked up to jumper cables. *Maybe I am not asking for too much.* I let the enlightenment of Roger's little talk flush through me. My eyes looked brighter, my chin stronger. The forehead scar that had bugged me since grade school didn't seem so noticeable. I fished my raisin lipstick from my purse and smoothed it on, listening to the muffled jazz outside the door. Acting on my new therapist's advice—verbalize versus internalize—had opened a floodgate of feelings inside me. Pieces of the puzzle were fusing in my head. Roger and I were having this conversation for a reason, and the reason was *not* because I was stupid and made bad decisions.

When I returned to our table, Roger hopped up and pulled out my chair. I blushed. A fresh bottle of Evian and another glass of red wine were sitting in front of my seat. "They were out of merlot, so I ordered you a malbec from Argentina." He helped me into my chair. "I hope that's okay." I flashed him a big grin. Roger knew nothing of my life in Miami or my love of malbec.

I lifted the glass and inhaled. The bouquet of earthy plums and blackberries filled my nose. "Paul wouldn't be able to guess what this is." A smirk crossed my lips.

A saxophone began wailing along with the dancing piano melody. The crowded tables around us began to empty. A votive candle flickered on the table, making our huddled faces glow.

"It is wrong that I don't want to go home?" I stared into the flame between us, feeling my chest constrict. Traveling was the sensorial lifeline of my marriage. On the road, I'd eat Thai, Indian or Japanese food, rebelling against Paul's meat-and-potatoes diet. I'd visit bustling bars and chat with strangers. My world view expanded. My wanderlust thrived.

Roger shook his head.

"I've only traveled with Paul once for work this year, and it was a disaster." Two months before, one of my biannual business trips to New York had aligned with Paul's schedule. When Paul had walked into our hotel room at the Grand Hyatt Central Station, I'd rushed to the door and pressed my lips against his. He'd pulled away quickly, leaving me with that abandoned feeling of his fleeting kiss.

"I told him I don't think that I'm asking for too much." The tightness in my chest released through the entire confession. Paul had picked the restaurant, as always—a steakhouse where he could order a loaded baked potato and a rib eye. On our walk to dinner, he'd cut me off in a crosswalk, nearly knocking me into a mound of muddy snow. At Morton's, he'd ordered a bottle of Mount Veeder cabernet and a wedge salad to share without consulting me. I'd asked if we could remodel our 1970s master bathroom, which he'd quickly vetoed, so I'd suggested the smaller guest bathroom. Denied again. We'd just received pay raises. The man was tighter with money than a Bernie Madoff victim.

"I told him he treated me like I was invisible." My voice shook as I relived our big fight back in the hotel room. "I told him nothing in the relationship was mine. I told him he had to win me back."

Roger's fingers bridged the rim of his glass. "How do your parents feel about him?"

"He's never really gotten along with anyone from my family," I replied. "Honestly, that's one of the things that attracted me to him. He's totally different from them. He's confident. He takes charge. He speaks his mind. I've always been trying to become a stronger person than I was ten years ago."

"It honestly didn't bother you that he didn't get along with your family?" Roger leaned back on his barstool. "That would be so hard for me. We're really tight." He looked down into his Dewars.

I wish I could say the same. I sipped my wine slowly, letting the ripe berry flavors and dusty tannins linger on my palate. "It didn't bother me at first. I wanted to escape the Midwestern lifestyle." Whenever I'd report back on the latest gossip from home—shotgun weddings, births, welfare checks, DUI arrests—Paul would shoot off a round of digs. "I'm tired of the jokes and put-downs." I raised my eyes to meet Roger's. "My upbringing is part of who I am. It helped me grow into the person I've become. I wouldn't trade my childhood with anyone." I lifted my glass with strength and confidence—a small-town girl who once dabbled in hunting *and* needlepoint now traveled the country, promoting fine wines for a living. *So much for becoming a crochet queen.*

Roger nodded and took a long sip of Dewars. I continued revealing my life story, from childhood and cross-country moves to my father's suicide and the therapy sessions. He rocked back and forth in his chair, inhaling and exhaling.

"He seemed like he'd be a great husband when I was twenty-four." I recounted Paul's attributes and our comfortable wine life together. "I married my best friend because all the magic fades away." I stared deep into my wine glass and saw clarity for the first time in years.

Roger shook his head. "You settled." His blue eyes anchored to mine. "I'm sorry to be so frank with you, but you settled for less than you deserve. Life is too short to be with someone who doesn't make you so happy, you can't wait to see him every day."

My knees began shaking under the table. My eyes darted from his face to the piano player across the room. Dive-bomber. Direct hit. His words triggered a flashback. Until that moment, I'd forgotten that I'd called my old friend Danielle three months before my wedding, freaked out about the roller coaster of emotions. "You're settling," she'd said in her curtly way. "Trust me. I've been engaged before and got out before it was too late. Call it off." She was the only person who'd been straight up with me about my decision to marry Paul. I'd buried her statement in the deepest corner of my mind like a bad secret.

"I want to tell you a story," Roger said, filling the uncomfortable silence. "I was an expert at the art of settling for years." He loosened his necktie. "It all started with one girl." His index finger wagged above his rocks glass. Roger proceeded to tell me about a girl he'd met at University of California at San Diego. His face lit up as he talked about meeting her at a college bar, their first kiss, the amazing sex, the way they could read each other's minds. My head nodded until my neck hurt. My mind flew to the dance floor with Fernando.

"I felt that once," I interrupted, my fingers gripping the edge of the marble table. "God, I miss that feeling." Roger smiled then continued. Their relationship had lasted four years. The passion never stopped. She dreamed of working in Thailand; he wanted to live in California near his family. "We just found ourselves at a crossroads, and we couldn't go down the same path." He ran his fingers through his light-brown hair. I looked into his sad eyes and wanted to hug him until he smiled again.

"I was devastated," he said. "A part of me died. But now I know I cannot get involved with a woman unless I feel that same level of connection." His shook his rocks glass until the ice cubes jingled. "My soulmate is out there somewhere. We'll find each other someday." He stared into the votive.

I leaned closer to the flame. "How did you move on?"

His firm face flickered in the candlelight. "The benchmark has been set for the kind of woman I want to spend the rest of my life with. End of story." He threw back a gulp of Dewars. My eyes swelled with astonishment. *A dating benchmark? I could have used one of those about forty times.* I collapsed against the back of my chair and sipped the smooth wine.

"I called Fernando the first week of January." The words blurted from my lips. "I haven't been able to stop thinking about him for seven years." My confession spilled across the table like a shattered bottle of booze. I told Roger about the phone call I'd made to Fernando's office six weeks prior. Getting closure with Fernando was supposed to unclog my heart valves, unclutter my brain. If I could close the door on our love, I could finally unlock the hidden passion between Paul and me. But deep down, I'd always wondered if Fernando might be thinking about me and regretting our breakup. I'd felt like a telemarketer making my first cold call. The small talk was so small, I'd needed a microscope. Fernando and Alessandra were expecting their first child, a boy, in just eight weeks. He'd hardly remembered the abrupt end to our relationship! "Oh, yeah. We were crazy kids back then," he'd said with a smug laugh.

I looked Roger in the eye. "When I hung up the phone, I didn't have the urge to smack him upside the head with a bottle of pinot grigio. I was happy. I was hopeful." I gripped my wine glass. Speaking to Fernando had given me a newfound hope that my heart was no longer chained to his, and my life could truly move on. But I still felt like there was a rock in my stomach every time I walked into my house after work and kissed Paul.

"You have to find your balance. You are the only one who truly knows what happiness means to you." Roger's deep eyes anchored to mine. "Everyone has a different definition of happiness. Stop listening to other people and follow your heart." I sat quietly, nodding, letting his words sink in. *There are billions of people on this planet. How could I think there was only one guy who was perfect for me—and that guy didn't want to be with me?* Roger waved over the cocktail waitress and ordered me another bottle of Evian. My cheeks flushed.

I looked around the near-empty bar. The foggy confusion that had consumed me for the past few years began to lift, freeing my mind. The room felt as serene as a day spa. After months of banging my head against the wall, searching for answers, the puzzle pieces had snapped together. I'd spent thousands of dollars on therapists and all I'd really needed was a heart-to-heart talk with a stranger at a Midwest bar. The source of my problems became as clear as Fernando's glass of Santa Margherita: I settled. I could no longer live without the magic of soul love—not for another month, not for another thirty years.

"You build your house on sand, and it cannot stand." I chanted the words of my yoga instructor, Baron Baptiste. "Your emotional house should be like a rock." I caressed the marble tabletop, nodding my head. My nickname in grade school was loud-mouth Lisa. Why did it take me five years to open up? Paul had made so many sacrifices for my career, and our move to California had ultimately helped him land his dream job, too. *Time to say goodbye to my guilt.*

"Being alone isn't easy, you know," Roger said, signing the bill.

My chin dropped. "I know. I remember." I sipped the last of my silky malbec, remembering the self-conscious girl who'd stayed in unhealthy relationships because she was scared of being alone. A life filled with wine had changed me. I glanced down at my wedding ring. It always felt as if I was looking at someone else's hand.

We walked back to our hotel. It was a chilly, dry night in early March with remnants of a recent snowstorm piled along the street curbs. Roger put his heavy coat and wool scarf around my shoulders. I tucked my arm under his the old-fashioned way, as if we were strolling down the sidewalk in 1944, not 2004. We stood in silence at the elevator doors in our hotel lobby, looking at each other.

"Are you ready to go to sleep?" he asked.

I shook my head.

We ambled into the lobby café next to the front desk. It was two in the morning. Napkins fanned like peacock tails on top of white plates, waiting for guests who'd arrive for breakfast in a few hours. We sat in a horseshoe-shaped booth side by side in front of two preset place settings. He reached for my hand. My heartbeat shot up like a cork popping from a Champagne bottle. I had not felt that much excitement since Fernando. We'd bared our souls to each other. We had a bond, and I must admit, I found him very attractive. We're talking Hugh-Grant-before-the-hooker-snafu attractive. I stared at our interlocked hands. My trembling fingers caressed his knuckles.

I looked into his kind eyes. "Everything in life happens for a reason, you know?" He pulled my hand to his face and kissed it softly. It was thirty-five degrees outside, and I wanted to crank the AC. My entire body tingled from the spark of his touch. Part of me wanted to invite Roger up to my room, to have one chance to feel the wave of passion pour over me that I'd given up on years before, to have a physical barrier placed between my husband and me.

I squeezed Roger's hand and rested it on the table. My fists slid into my coat pockets. "I'm not a cheater." I looked down at the untouched place setting in front of me. Tears swelled in my eyes. "I never want to hurt anyone like that." Construction of my emotional house had already begun.

Roger cocked his head. "Me neither."

I gazed at his oblong face. "I'm so glad I came to Cincinnati." I thought of a chain email my mom had sent me—the kind where you forward it to five people and will have good luck for ten years or something like that. It had said: *Every person we meet in life is not a coincidence but a destiny. Every person we meet in life is either a student or a teacher.* I've always lived by the belief that no person, place or thing in my life is here by accident. Fate guided me to spend that long evening in that city in that bar with that man.

"Thank you for tonight," he said softly, touching my hand one last time. I watched as he climbed out of the vinyl booth and disappeared into the elevator.

🍺🍸🍷🍸🍸

PAUL DROPPED HIS keys on the kitchen counter and strolled into the living room, surprised to find me sitting rigidly on our Ethan Allen couch. Three weeks had slinked by since my Cincinnati awakening, and Paul had been on a business trip for five days, giving me plenty of time to sort out a plan.

"We need to talk." My jaw quivered. I watched him walk around the coffee table and plop down, leaving a cushion of space between us. Anxiety whipped around my queasy stomach. My mind's eye could see the speech I'd been rehearsing for three days, which was now a wrinkled piece of paper crammed into the front of my packed suitcase, hidden in our guest room closet.

"I'm very sorry for the way I've been acting." My voice and hands shook. He sat on the edge of his cushion, thick arms folded across his broad chest. He didn't say a word. I'd spent a week Googling tips on communications tactics: start with the acknowledgment of fault to soften any defensive reaction. The advice sounded pretty damn good for the most important conversation in my life with the most aggressive communicator I'd ever known.

"It's just that I've been thinking a lot about our discussions about communication, affection, things I want us to improve on." My mouth felt cotton-ball dry. I'd strategically selected the words "discussions" and "improve on" versus "fights" and "change." He nodded his head. We both sat in silence, staring at each other. I looked down at my sweaty palms, clasped atop my Jones New York dress slacks.

"It's not fair to you that I keep asking you to do things that don't come naturally to you." I paused to swallow. "Your relationship should be the easy thing in your life, not the hardest." As I recited Roger's mantra, my voice grew stronger, more confident. "If you truly love and cherish someone, your actions toward that person should be effortless." My chin lifted with conviction.

"But I do love you, honey." His sharp tone chipped away at my heart. For the last six years, that type of response would have made me withdraw from the conversation—retreating to a falsely peaceful silence where my isolated thoughts and confused feelings ran circles in my mind.

"I know you love me. And I love you, too." I paused to regain my focus. "But you don't adore me. You don't cherish me. The intimacy I'm starving for would come naturally if you adored me." I looked out the sliding glass doors across the room to our deck. "I finally realized we have to face the truth. We're not soulmates." My chest fluttered under my blue silk shirt. I felt like I'd crossed mile twenty-four of a marathon.

He looked me in the eye. "You don't think we're soulmates?" His tone made it sound more like a cocky statement. I'd told Paul about Fernando when he took me to Islamorada for our first Christmas together. He'd said he thought we had lots of soulmates in each lifetime. It took me almost six years to finally believe him.

My eyes watered. A downpour of sadness flooded my chest. "I've been thinking about the past and the future a lot." My voice trembled. "I have regrets." My shoulders felt like I'd been lifting weights for two days. "I'm regretful of how our relationship started. How could you really ever respect me and love me the way I want you to anyway?" I looked down at the carpet. "I had no respect for myself." My heart bashed against my rib cage. The first night in Key West, we'd skipped dinner and headed straight to Sloppy Joe's for three rounds of Mind Erasers—a decision my mind could never erase. We'd had a sloppy make-out session at the bar, and then Paul had followed me back to my hotel. He was still legally married, and we'd screwed in my room like two college kids on spring break. I'd spent the next morning in a steaming hot shower scrubbing my skin as voraciously as Meryl Streep during the contamination scene in *Silkwood*.

"We were separated," he said in an annoyed tone whipped out whenever I brought up his first marriage.

"That is not the point." My jaw locked in frustration. "I just know I can't live another thirty years and look back on my life with regret." Tears streamed down my face. "I have a hole in my heart. It's been there since before we met. I know what it's like to feel an electric connection with someone, something so powerful on a spiritual, emotional and physical level." I took a deep breath. "I had it. I lost it. I thought I could live the rest of my life without it, but I know in my heart of hearts that it wouldn't be fair to either of us. Your soulmate is out there, too." My voice boomed with determination. Any worries about being judged were buried in a decade of failing at finding true love—a decade that was officially over.

Paul's palms rubbed his khaki slacks. His somber face turned to mine. "If you felt like this before we got married, why did you go through with it?" His sad eyes pleaded with me for the first time since our New York trip.

My fingers trembled in my lap. I looked down at our fancy Ethan Allen coffee table. "I figured it was just wedding jitters. That's what most women said when I asked for advice." Then I recited those reckless words: *Marry your best friend. All the magic fades away.*

Paul sat on the couch in silence, looking out the sliding glass doors across the room. I stared at the little wrinkle in the side of his blank face.

"Do you have anything you want to say?" My voice cracked. I anxiously watched him for at least a minute. I couldn't tell if he was going to fly from his cushion in a fit of rage or grab the remote and flip on the evening news.

"I'm scared. I'm sad," he said, matter-of-factly. "You know me. I show no emotion." He leaned back on the couch and continued looking blankly out the doors to our deck. I stared at his shaved head. Paul never minced words. We'd lasted longer than most NFL head coach contracts, and his response to the end of our marriage was as muted as a cabernet with cork taint.

I shook my head, feeling a half-smile spread across my face. *Yep. I knew him.* And I finally knew myself, too. The girl who craved affection and romance had married the responsible, wound-tight guy who couldn't show emotions. I never would have stopped wanting more.

My eyes scanned the wine rack across the room filled with expensive bottles we'd been saving for a special occasion—1992 Caymus Special Selection Cabernet, 1995 Swanson Alexis, 1999 Groth Reserve Cabernet. I sat quietly on the couch, listening to Paul's breath. My chest felt as if a grape gondola full of stress had been removed. It took me ten years to truly overcome my fear of confrontation, but part of me still felt rotten for leaving him. We'd built a life together that would have to be dismantled piece by piece. The other part of me wanted to grab that bottle of Swanson Alexis, pour a glass and toast to the most empowering feeling in the world. I'd faced my fears. I'd taken back control of my destiny. My mind began to sprint through the possibilities of a new life that was about to begin.

"You're still going to edit my presentations for work, aren't you?" Paul's voice rang in my ears.

A gasp zoomed from my mouth. "Are you serious?" I glared at the side of his face. Any remaining ounce of guilt or fear leapt from my body and flew out the window. My exorcism was complete—minus the holy water and spinning head.

My eyes drifted back to our wine rack. A feeling swept over my body I'd never felt during a breakup: total validation.

CHANCE
The Sonoma Wine Days

Chance's Jeep bounced along a rocky path snaking up the eastern ridge of Moon Mountain. It was a crisp, sunny evening, and Northern California wine country was awakening from its winter slumber—fruit trees blossoming, red clovers sprouting between vineyard rows, grapevines bursting new buds. Chance cranked the truck's parking brake mid-slope below a forest of Manzanita and pine trees. I hopped out of the cab and into nature's cradle of life, feeling reborn and ready to raise a toast to Mother Earth—and to Hammurabi, the inventor of divorce.

My eyes floated across his Sonoma vineyard. "Wow. What a view." Rolling hills carpeted with wildflowers and grapevines fanned out around a cluster of boulders bigger than minivans. Vineyards that gorgeous deserved two-page spreads in *Wine Enthusiast*. Scents of mustard and chamomile drifted in the breeze. Chance grabbed my hand, pulling me toward the rock formation. My chest fluttered beneath my DKNY top.

"We've divided the vineyard into thirty parcels, according to sun exposure, soil type, incline and elevation." Chance waved his arm toward the patchwork quilt of vineyard blocks. "This cabernet block here is five-hundred feet below that zinfandel block up there." He pointed to the top of the mountain, chattering like a second grader on Show and Tell Day. I nodded, captivated by the intricacies of mountain farming, which stresses the grapevines, resulting in smaller berries and thus more concentrated flavors in the wine. But Chance didn't look like your typical winegrower. He stood 5-foot-11 and probably weighed 190 pounds. He kept his short, light-blond hair tousled with thick gel and had striking, light-blue eyes, like Tom Scavo from *Desperate Housewives*. He wore faded Lucky Brand jeans and a sage paisley-print shirt—a gentleman farmer in every way.

His ears glowed reddish pink from the evening sun at his back. "We're on our fifth leaf. The vines have taken well to the soils here." My heart throbbed with rapture. Winemakers count the age of young vines by leaf, not year. It turned me on when Chance talked viticulture. I was one smitten wine kitten.

I gazed at the endless rows of grapevines with tiny, pink-edged leaves sprouting from skinny trunks. "Any problems with frost this season?" My voice was firm, yet cool like a cop at a routine traffic stop. It was early April, and the vines had just emerged from their winter sleep and pushed their first buds of the season—the beginning of the grapevine's growth cycle known as "bud break." Spring frost can damage baby buds and significantly decrease the size of the crop.

"So far, so good." Chance kicked the dirt as he walked. "But we've got another month before we're out of the woods." He stopped short of a cluster of car-sized rocks at the edge of the vineyard and pointed. "You gotta check out the view from up there."

Chance climbed onto one of the boulders and extended his hands to me. I dug my Via Spiga boots into the red, rocky dirt to get some traction. "You should be bringing journalists up here," I said, grabbing his hands, "not just the girls you're courting." I smirked as he pulled me up. "You have a real story, and a picture of this place would be worth ten thousand words in my book."

"I suppose." Chance reached for my hand; my pulse surged. "I'm new to this wine marketing stuff." His hands were smoother and smaller than Paul's, and I liked that about him.

We stood side by side on a moss-covered rock in our fancy blue jeans and designer boots. I cupped my right hand above my eyes to block the sun. San Pablo Bay glistened on the hazy blue horizon.

"It's even better here." Chance pulled my body in front of his. He wrapped his big arms around me. My heart leapt into my mouth. The guy had so much promise, and our bodies had never been that close.

"What clones did you plant?" I asked with authority, hoping to calm my nerves. Birds chirped in the nearby forest.

"Clone seven, Clone two and some Martini." I could feel his lips near my ear as he spoke. "They all do well in these volcanic soils."

"You're so lucky to be able to start a winery right now," I said, feeling the warmth of his chest against my back. "Land prices are going through the roof." I took a deep breath and closed my eyes. Thank God, getting a divorce wasn't as expensive as buying real estate. Three weeks had passed since I'd told Paul our marriage was over. After years of struggling with internal turmoil over my marriage, I wanted to juggle men like bowling pins and perfect the art of dating without a deadline.

Chance laced his hands around my waist. "Dad and I have been holding onto this piece of land for ten years." My stomach tingled. *A man with patience when it comes to his dreams—just like the new me.*

I kept my back straight and didn't lean into him.

"I'm glad you wanted to come here." He whispered in my ear.

I pulled out of his hug, keeping one hand locked with his. "I'm a sucker for good tacos." We were deep into our second date, after two hours of eating tacos and sipping Negra Modelos at Chance's favorite taqueria in Sonoma. Our first "blind" date was more like a myopia date. I'd seen plenty of pictures of "KingofCabernet" on his Match.com profile, but everything else about this wine guy was a little blurry.

"You're a cheap date." He sat down on the rock and tugged me to join him. Chance's profile picture showed him toasting with a fishbowl-sized wine glass of Cabernet Sauvignon; his biography was riddled with *South Park*-worthy jokes. He seemed like just the right amount of wrong.

I sat Indian-style in front of him on the bumpy rock, letting the evening sun warm my face. *First a damn fine baseball player and now a winemaker. The online dating Gods have been good to me.*

Chance wrapped his arms around me. "What are you thinking?"

"I'm thinking we should've had a bottle of sparkling wine with dinner instead of beer." I felt grossly bloated but refrained from bringing up my stalled digestion. Talk about dating buzz kill.

I looked down at his arms covering my cozy fleece jacket. There was a tenderness to his touch—so different from the rigidity of Paul's thick biceps and broad chest. I gazed out at his baby grapevines and savored the moment of the new.

His head rested on the crown of my head. "Next time. It's a date."

We sat on top of what seemed like the wine world and just gazed at his magnificent mountainside view. My heart and mind were sprinting. It was way too soon to meet The One—that dashing winemaker I'd daydreamed about after breaking up with Raul in Miami. I took another deep breath and forced the ridiculous thoughts from my head.

I looked over my shoulder to Chance. "What was it like growing up here?" A lot of women in the wine business who aren't born into a winemaking family dream of finding a single guy like Chance. He grew up in Napa Valley wine country, owned a few rental properties in Sonoma and Napa with his father, and planned to launch his own wine label making zinfandel and cabernet sauvignon from his estate-grown grapes. He was an entrepreneur who spent his days managing two of the most prized assets in wine country: vineyards and real estate.

"It was...well...umm...interesting," Chance said. "There's a lot of wealth. There's a lot of poverty. I had an interesting mix of friends. It taught me a lot about having money, but not so much money that it changes you." His profound statement lingered in my head. I sat in silence, thinking about my upbringing and the reality of my new life in wine country.

"I've always wanted more than I had." I wrapped my arms around my knees. "But it's only changed me for the good." I peered out at the rolling hills blending into the horizon. Pink, orange and lavender began mixing in the sky, signaling the finale of a wine country sunset.

"I can't wait for you to meet my friends," Chance said excitedly. "My real friends. Not just all the people around town who have known me since I had braces." He laughed. Dating Chance was a social rebirth as much as it was a wine dream. He'd already introduced me to tons of people from the Sonoma wine community—Napa's more laid-back neighbor—and had my calendar booked solid with parties, dinners and wine tastings for the next three weeks. My desire to date a man who could provide the mental stimulation of deep conversation, as well as a fun night on the town, had been realized after years of living with a homebody.

"Hey, you wanna meet Darth next?" Chance spoke in a bellowing voice with a smirk. Chance named his dog Darth Vader, a *Star Wars* tribute any child of the 1970s would appreciate.

Chance hopped down from the huge rock and extended his arms to me. My body glided down his. I looked up into his eyes, as blue as an afternoon sky. The silence was uncomfortable but sweet. He leaned down to me, and my eyes instinctively closed. His lips felt soft, wet and lustful. *Finally, a kiss I can get lost in.* I listened to the birds chirping with eyes wide shut. My mind danced with the magic of the moment: a vintner and a wine marketer, kissing in the middle of his vineyard.

Chance closed the front door of his house behind me. "Do you want anything to drink?" He owned a ranch-style home with an attached apartment near the Sonoma town square, not far from his vineyard. As I stepped under the vaulted ceiling of his living room, Chance darted behind the accent wall that led to his kitchen. "Make yourself at home!"

A tiny ball of fur rocketed from the hallway toward me, his collar ringing faster than the New York Stock Exchange bell. Darth was a toy Pomeranian—more Chewbacca than Vader—and so dainty Paris Hilton's chihuahua could have kicked its ass.

I scooped the fluffy puppy into my hands, lowering my left cheek to his tiny nose. *I miss our dog, but she belongs with Paul.* I sat down on Chance's cushy couch, laughing and nuzzling Darth. I glanced around the room. Every white wall was bare, except for a dartboard next to the fireplace. Sliding glass doors off the living room opened to a flagstone terrace with a gas grill, a white plastic table and four chairs, shaded by a redwood pergola. I smiled at the discovery of a forgotten relic: the bachelor pad.

Chance buzzed out of the kitchen. "Sure you don't want some wine?" He handed me a glass of water without dropping cadence and trotted over to an old stereo tower next to a tiny, dusty television. He was a ball of energy—just like his dog and kind of like Robert in a haunting way.

"I'm pacing myself." I watched while he zipped through CD cases stacked on the speakers. James Taylor's greatest hits drifted through the room—a warm, calming baritone to offset the erratic Chance.

He flew through the house, tugging my arms through the animated tour of his personal world. Chance busted into each room waving his arms like Kramer from *Seinfeld*, before rattling off declarations about his home improvement plans for the backyard hot tub, office and guest bathroom. His endless energy rejuvenated my hope that most men in their thirties didn't spend four hours a day in a recliner with a remote control in hand.

Chance pulled me into the kitchen. "I'm still hungry." He tugged open the refrigerator door. "We should snack."

"Why? We just ate dinner like two hours ago." Mexican food was not my idea of a light meal. After a plate of tacos, I wouldn't be hungry for a day, and I'd need to run six miles the following morning.

"We need to keep our metabolism up." He stuffed his head deeper into the fridge.

I peeked over his shoulder, discreetly scanning his inventory. A dozen cans of Slim Fast shakes lined the door's shelves, and Weight Watchers chilled-and-ready meal boxes filled the bottom drawer. Two-liter bottles of caffeine-free Diet Coke dotted the top rack. My mind began cycling like a dishwasher. *Danger! Danger!* My dating radar hit code red.

Chance grabbed a plastic to-go box packed with wilted romaine then scrunched his nose and shoved it back in. "Do you like popcorn? I know I've got popcorn." He whipped around and hunted through the cupboards.

I leaned against his kitchen counter, letting his true colors sink in.

Chance pulled a Diet Coke from the refrigerator then looked at the glass in my hand. "I should just drink water, shouldn't I?" His eyes darted from my glass to the plastic bottle in his hands. I shrugged, hoping my indifference would make him change the subject. He sat the bottle down on the countertop. "I'm really getting into a new work-out routine." Chance grinned with pride.

I smiled, gripping the glass in my hands. "Oh, really. Tell me more." I did a lot of listening to Chance's stories back in the beginning, and I didn't mind a bit. He never talked about the evening news or reality TV. Chance had started running four days a week at Jack London State Park. I liked the idea of dating an exercise buddy.

His eyes danced around my forehead. "I'm eating take-out salads from Sonoma Market." His voice chirped. "I got my BMI done a few weeks ago. I need to lose ten pounds."

I stared inquisitively as he untucked his shirt and pinched his capacious love handles. *I suppose I'll take enthusiasm for body mass over Sunday mass any day.*

"My jeans are way too tight. Look!" Chance shrieked, tossing a hip thrust like one of the Fly Girls on *In Living Color.* I felt like I was talking to my teenage self.

I coughed down a gulp of water. "You're a guy. You look fine." I rested the glass on his counter. "How long have you owned this place?" *Divert, divert! The last thing I need is for this date to turn into a gym rat wannabe show and tell.*

Chance jabbered on, standing over his kitchen sink. "You know, body mass index doesn't lie, right? The numbers are always right." I looked deep into my water glass and thought of Paul. *Hang in there. This is way more interesting than watching Tucker Carlson garble the news.*

"Just cut back on the carbs and sugar." I rapped my fingernails impatiently on the counter. "Burn off more calories than you take in." I looked down at the Gap jeans I hadn't worn since college. Fat and married—I thought the two went together like Asian massage parlors and happy endings. Once I'd gotten off the Paul diet, the pounds had melted away.

"You're going to be so good for me." Chance grabbed the soda bottle from the counter and poured it down the sink. "I shouldn't drink this crap anyway, right? It has Equal in it. It's unnatural. I'm going to drink water from now on, just like you." I watched his hand gripping the upside-down bottle. My mind began ticking off boxes—the bad ones. The man had more quirks than the cast of *Pee-wee's Playhouse*. His eyes darted back to the fridge. "I'm thinking about becoming a vegetarian or maybe a vegan." He tossed the plastic bottle in the recycling bin and clapped his hands with a sense of accomplishment.

I watched the tiny wrinkles crease across his forehead. I wanted to study his mind like mechanics do car engines. Chance was a fascinating creature.

Chance opened a bottle of Gundlach Bundschu Merlot, a supple wine from one of the oldest family wineries in all of California. We moved to the couch, and he popped his favorite CD into the stereo: Kenny Chesney's "When the Sun Goes Down." I'd despised country music since college, blaming it all on my roots. The dating emergency sirens were now blaring in my head.

I sniffed my glass of purple-hued wine, letting scents of blackberries and plums fill my nose. My heart rapped in my chest. Not liking a man's music choices was one thing, but seeing a month's supply of Slim Fast in a single guy's fridge was a whole different enchilada.

Maybe I should bring up the bloating now...put a fork in this date.

"Sonoma Valley makes the best Merlots." Chance took a deep whiff of his glass and turned to me.

Oh, crap.

He leaned in and kissed me softly. I felt the air from his lungs enter my mouth. His tongue looped slowly around mine then quickened. *What moves!* My ears throbbed from the acrobatics unfolding in my mouth, silencing all the questions in my head. His stubble brushed my chin. Tiny tremors of excitement rippled through me—not the shockwaves of Fernando, but just enough chemistry to remember the thrilling surge. We kissed for what seemed like an hour while his dog whined at our feet.

I pulled away from him. "I should go home." I smiled and felt a tinge of pain. My chin was raw, my lips puffy and sore. My face hadn't felt that beat up from a make-out session since high school. I hopped off the couch and moved toward the door, with Chance and his tiny dog chasing behind me.

🍺🍸🍷🍸🍸

CHANCE SLID INTO a green vinyl booth at Amigo's, another one of his favorite Mexican restaurants. "You'll love this place. Everything is fresh."

I scanned the plastic-covered menu with purpose. *We're going running later. Resist the nachos.* Chance always called me right after work to invite me on a date—for that night. I loved the spontaneity of it all. The memory of Paul's tight leash on my life made me want to accept every one of Chance's invitations.

He leaned across the speckled tabletop. "Why don't you get the vegetarian burrito, and I'll get a chicken chimichanga."

I glanced up from the menu. "I thought you wanted to eat light?" "La Bamba" drifted from the cantina's surround sound system.

"I'm really hungry," Chance replied in his ever-hyper tone, his torso hidden behind the giant menu. "We'll work out later. We can just drink water instead of margaritas to make up for the calories."

I rolled my eyes and returned to studying the menu. "Eat whatever you want. I'm not the boss of you." My mocking tone sounded like a sister sassing a sibling.

The waitress arrived with a plastic basket of tortilla chips and two ramekins of salsa. Chance lunged at one ramekin like a football lineman trying to recover a fumble. My mouth dropped. He speed-scooped mounds of *pico de gallo* onto the chips, never taking his eyes off the bowl.

The entire basket of chips was gone in less than two minutes.

My stomach began churning. I looked around the half-empty restaurant in embarrassment. The waitress returned with our waters.

Chance shoved the empty basket toward her. "We want more chips and salsa." The words grunted from his mouth. I shot him a mean stare and gritted my teeth.

I looked up at our annoyed waitress. "Please and thank you very much." *How many strikes is that against him? I've lost count.*

"I'm serious about you sleeping at my place." Chance popped another tortilla into his mouth. "You are welcome any night. It might be easier on both of you."

I shook my head, keeping my nose buried in the menu. My chest got tight every time Chance brought up my living situation. I'd moved into one of the guest bedrooms of my house, and Paul had kept the master. We'd stuck a for-sale-by-owner sign in the front yard and got full asking price from our neighbors within twenty-four hours. Welcome to real estate in wine country. Some nights Paul and I ate dinner together in the living room while watching the news. We barked about work like military sergeants from neighboring platoons. I edited his presentations like a good "support tool" would. I walked the dog. The only real difference between marriage and divorce was we didn't sleep in the same bed. It was beyond weird.

"Thanks." I smiled sweetly into my menu. "I'll think about it." I dunked a chip into the salsa and chewed slowly. Staying at Chance's house on a weeknight would add thirty-five minutes to my commute, which was the only excuse I felt comfortable giving him. My days of getting too close too fast were so 1994. I wanted to live a life being comfortable alone. Fit a boyfriend into my space, on my own terms, once my wine cellar was restocked. I'd purchased a bright, airy townhouse in northwest Santa Rosa, and the sale would close as soon as my old house cleared home inspections with the new buyers. Until then, Paul was still a part of my life.

I felt Chance staring at my forehead and looked up at him. The waitress buzzed in and dropped off two ginormous plates, distracting us from the conversation.

While Chance inhaled his jumbo chimichanga—and two sides of sour cream—I poked at my taco salad like a picky child. Whenever I shared a table with Chance, I chewed like a turtle, while visions of Kirstie Alley's Jenny Craig commercials danced in my head.

Chance pushed his empty plate to the center of the table. "I feel bloated." He rubbed his hand on his belly. The logo on his Sonoma Valley Harvest Auction T-shirt moved in a circle. "Why did you let me eat all that food, gorgeous?" His eyes bounced around my face. Chance was the moscato of boyfriends: unrefined, overhyped and cloyingly sweet.

The red peppers in my mouth suddenly felt like spears. I wanted to spit them out and harpoon his "bloated" belly. "You know you sound crazy, right?" I pointed my knife at him then sliced my taco shell.

Chance slouched in the booth. "We should have shared that taco salad."

I pressed my back against the booth, shaking my head. I felt as if I was watching Gas-X commercial try-outs. The tortillas started churning in my stomach. *Wait for it...he's about to tell you he's been seeing a therapist.*

We didn't go running that night.

🍸🍶🍹🍷🍸

CHANCE SHARED HIS happy-go-lucky world with me well into summer, and we left a trail of smiles, good times and great stories in our wake around the Sonoma square. The social butterfly in him made up for the food freak. Chance didn't even have cable television, and his idea of weekly chores was surfing ads on Craigslist. I even shrugged off his zodiac sign—Virgo—my polar opposite. Sure, Chance marched to the beat of a different drum only his Pomeranian could hear, but we were just having fun. His kisses made my stomach tingle. His compliments made me smile. The Sonoma County wines we shared were approachable, yet complex and refined with layers of flavors that continued to unfold—tastes that suited the first chapter in my new life.

For the first time since starting my job as a wine events manager, I yearned to travel less. Packing my bag, settling into that window seat and making myself at home in a hotel room weren't as exciting as they'd been during my marriage. I wanted to spend my free time exploring Sonoma County's winding back roads, mountaintops, restaurant patios and hidden tasting rooms. Every weekend felt like a vacation—one of the greatest gifts of living in a wine paradise.

🍷🍷🍸🍹🍸

CONVERSATIONS WITH CHANCE often revolved around the marketing strategy for his new wine brand. While he'd grown up in wine country and had majored in business at Chico State, the business of wine was still as foreign to him as the art of willpower. Nurturing a vineyard throughout the growing season and marketing a wine brand are two different animals. And he'd found a girl who could fill his holes.

Chance pulled me into his office. "You really think I need to benchmark against other wines before choosing a brand name?" He wanted to call his wine label Chance Gannon Vineyards. Eponymous labeling had been employed successfully by grape growers since the 1970s, but it was spring 2004, and competition in the wine business was exploding as fast as the real estate market.

My hands cradled the wine bottle with a mock-up label taped to the front. "Have you considered dropping the word 'vineyards' or making it singular? Or maybe a little smaller?" The label was black matte with double-gold foil squares around his name.

"Why would I do that?" His voice shrieked with shock as he stood over me in his dusty jeans and boots. A look of horror shot from his blue eyes. "Winemaking starts in the vineyard. The wine comes from my vineyards."

"Yes, but you own one vineyard. Plurals equal size. You don't want consumers thinking you are big." I spoke with the confidence of a college professor, wearing my late spring office attire: dressy capris and a short-sleeved top. "You want to be boutique. Artisan. You have a singular, amazing site just over the hill from a historic vineyard. Your marketing should milk that for all it's worth." My voice was stern. His vineyard might have been divided into thirty parcels, but it was a singular estate vineyard, and he owned it. Chance had untapped equity he needed to exploit from day one. The word "estate" remains a powerful quality cue in wine marketing.

I looked up at Chance's face. He stared at the bottle with a puzzled look then nodded approvingly. I smiled, feeling the heavy stroke to my ego. Being involved in the decision-making process of a new brand gave me a power charge. My position as events manager kept me too low on the marketing totem pole to engage in new product development, and Gallo cranked out new wine labels almost as fast as Wal-Mart opens stores.

"If you want to get a strong reputation as a grower, do what Gary Pisoni did." I leaned against his desk. "Sell your grapes to the high-profile winemakers. Ask them to vineyard-designate the wine they make from your vineyard with your name. Then when you start your own label, you already have name recognition and credibility."

280

He continued nodding. "Do you know how smart you are?" His face beamed with pride. I glanced down at the full glass of sauvignon blanc he'd poured me and grinned. It felt nice to be appreciated for my creativity and strategic instincts, and not be called a "tool."

"Have you ever thought about going with a one-word brand name?" I asked, swirling the wine in my glass. I tried to offer my advice in small doses, but he'd opened a floodgate in my wine marketing psyche.

His eyebrows scrunched.

"Single words convey strength, power, confidence. Plus they are easy to recall." I grabbed the Bordeaux-style sample bottle from his desk. "Think about it. You know the names. Ridge, Bond, Harlan, Colgin." I paused, looking at his eyes fixed on my lips. "You could be Chance Gannon Vineyards, or you could be CHANCE with bold, elegant, all caps and the estate-vineyard designate stacked in smaller letters underneath: 'Chance Gannon Estate Vineyard, Moon Mountain.'" I moved my fingers across the label to demonstrate my idea. "Your first name has such great meaning and strong imagery in people's minds. You want consumers to take a chance. Try your wines." I sat the bottle back down on his desk. "You should play that up."

He walked around the desk, cupped my chin with both hands and kissed me. "You're so good for me." He pulled back and looked deep into my eyes. "I'm so lucky." My body felt warm—my spirits rewarded, wanted and appreciated—all of which are important in relationships. His eyes darted to the computer on his desk. "Would you mind looking at my website?" His hand flew to his mouse. A big grin draped across my face.

I sat down at the desk and watched him launch Internet Explorer. My eyes scanned his home page.

"Will you consider other options on the font?" I asked from his office chair. "Times New Roman is pedestrian. You want something readable but more distinctive and elegant." I looked up at him standing over me. He shrugged. I reached for a cup filled with ink pens. "Can I print these pages?" Chance nodded and scurried over to the printer spitting out his website copy. As my eyes scanned the sentences of every page—Vineyards, History, People, Wines, Contact Us—I scribbled grammar edits and questions where key newsworthy information was lacking. I smiled, letting the gratification of improving his marketing materials wash over me. My penchant for copyediting had been neglected since leaving *The Wine News*.

Chance leaned over my shoulder. "You could help me with my long-term strategy. There's so much to launching a wine beyond the packaging and the website, right?"

My head bobbed the response.

"You have lots of things to think about once your label is done," I said. "What kind of wine club are you going to launch, if and how your vineyard is featured on the appellation maps, which winery associations you should join, which wine festivals and seminars you should pour at, which distributors you hire to represent you, whether or not you want to open a tasting room." My tongue rolled until I reached for my wine glass. I sipped the crisp wine, letting its bright acidity raise my spirits higher.

"I've never been so pumped." His ears moved up and down as he grinned. "This is our chance of a lifetime." He emphasized the word "chance." Both of his hands squeezed my shoulders. I looked at the mock-up homepage on the computer screen. A big knot formed in my throat, gliding quickly down to my stomach. I felt like I'd been punched with a double magnum. He'd hit a button. We couldn't rewind.

My hands gripped his tidy Formica desk. My face was as pale as a pinot gris.

"What's wrong?" Chance stepped in front of the desk. "Was it the pun?" His eyes buzzed about my face.

I stared at the paper for what seemed like five minutes. "Umm, something doesn't feel right." My eyes fixed on the splashes of blue ink. My throat tightened. "This is starting to move really fast."

Chance fired back. "I'll give you space. Just ask. Just tell me what I need to do. I'm new at all this." Chance had asked me countless times if I was ready to have a boyfriend again. I'd responded with a bottomless "yes." He was four years older than me and had never been engaged. Long-term commitments didn't seem to be his thing. Hanging out with Chance felt like being in a sorority-fraternity clique again, except we all had important jobs, owned homes and dabbled in the stock market. Suddenly, he was talking "we" and "lifetime." It wasn't very Virgo.

I stood up from the desk. "I think it's, ummm, it's more than that." I took a deep breath and exhaled. "Maybe I'm just not cut out for a life of wine all day and all night." The words echoed in my head. *I can handle his Slim Fast but not his wine?* My lips tingled from the shock of my realization.

I squeezed the pen in my hand, staring down at my sandals. That pen was like a kite, ready to help me fly in a new direction. "I think this is just too comfortable. It's too familiar." My book was unwritten. I could go anywhere, date anyone, find my way to true love—and maybe that journey needed to be with someone who wasn't married to the wine business like me. Even though I'd dreamed of marrying a vintner, living a life of wine 24-7 suddenly seemed as boring as drinking pinot noir every day to me. Sorry, Miles from *Sideways*. My soul craved diversity—a "wine light" romance to pair with Sonoma County's bounty of wine regions. I didn't think Chance could ever contribute to my dreams that existed beyond the bottle.

I PAINTED THE bedrooms in my townhouse sky blue and butter-scotch—colors Paul had vetoed at our house. The first night at my new home, I didn't invite Chance over for a drink or dinner. I wanted to be alone, enjoying my safe haven for personal time, space and reflection. Paul had started dating a college senior, and she'd moved into his new house the day after the moving truck had left. Maybe she was The One. Maybe he would give her everything she wanted.

I marinated a chicken breast in Jamaican spices and tossed it on my new George Foreman, then heated a pot of black beans mixed with *pico de gallo*, Pickapepper sauce and a spritz of fresh lime juice—healthy, Caribbean comfort food I'd enjoyed for years in Florida and had abandoned when I'd started living with Paul. I lit the candles on the dinner table and poured myself a glass of Gallo's MacMurray Ranch Pinot Gris from the Russian River Valley. *Crisp, bright, refreshing.* Putting myself first and appreciating all the strength that can come from such selfishness was a new concept. Being alone never felt or tasted so good.

🍶🍷🍸🍹🍾

"WE'RE GETTING SALADS, right?" Chance asked in his ever-hurried pace as we sat down at Mary's Pizza on the Sonoma square. Six weeks had blown by since my first date with the frantic foodie. Nights on the town with Chance felt more like Young Professionals' mixers, so I wasn't ready to give up all the opportunities to meet interesting people.

I settled into my seat. "Yes, and nothing fattening like a Caesar." I'd told him I'd eat at Mary's only if we didn't order pizza. Carbs were an occasional splurge, not a weekly staple. And I didn't want to hear Chance complain about his bloated gut for the next two days.

He ordered the margherita pizza and drummed his hands on the ging-ham-checkered tablecloth. I shook my head. He bounced around in his spindled chair, singing along with Madonna's "Die Another Day" drifting through the loud dining room. When the server asked us if we'd like fresh bread, Chance fired back, "Yes, please." My eyes flew across the table. He knew I didn't like the temptation of bread with meals. Chance gobbled three pieces of bread from the wicker basket before I organized my thoughts.

"Why are you eating that?" I shoved my straw around my plastic water glass. "You keep on saying you want to eat healthy." My voice was sharp and exasperated. I leaned back in my spindled chair.

He doused another slice of bread with olive oil. "EVOO is healthy. This bread is made fresh daily. Isn't that healthy?"

My cheeks flushed hot with frustration. The waiter returned with our glasses of Benziger Syrah. I took a long sip and hoped the silky red from a great family winery would lighten my mood.

"Listen." I sat the wine glass on the table. "You can eat whatever you want. I don't care. I'm not your mom." I folded my arms. Chance stared at me, stunned. "I just hate hearing you complain about what you eat after you've already eaten it." I wouldn't have been surprised if the guy mastur-bated to Richard Simmons *Sweatin' to the Oldies*. The buzz of the busy restaurant filled my ears. Standing up to Paul had given me the confidence to confront Chance. Being good for him meant telling the truth, even when it hurt.

He pushed the breadbasket into the center of the table. "You're right." His hand waved in the air, motioning our waiter to return. "Please take this away." Chance lifted his bread plate and the basket in the air.

"Are you going to come to my parents' barbecue for Mother's Day?" he asked, setting a packet of Equal on his fork and launching it like a catapult. I covered my mortified face.

"Don't you think it's a little early for me to be meeting your family?" My eyes stayed focused on the stem of my wine glass.

His mouth dropped open. "We've been dating for more than a month."

I swirled my purple-hued wine. "That's not a very long time." My eyes drifted to the window while I lingered over the Syrah's pepper and plum notes, its smooth body and spice undertones. A bold grape that had been rightly tamed by its winemaker. Chance had spice and spunk; maybe he could rein in his potential, too.

"Let's change the subject." Chance rapped his palms on the tabletop. "I can't wait for our trip." He started dancing in his chair. I forced a smile; I wanted to crawl under the table and get swept away with the bread crumbs. Blinded by the bliss of a new romance, I'd made the classic dating mistake of a woman in her thirties: I'd invited him to travel, by airplane, with me—before I'd seen his true chimichanga. Chance and I would soon be jetting off to the New Orleans Wine & Food Experience, held each year over Memorial Day weekend. NOWFE—as wine people call it—had always been my favorite business trip of the year, but I was dreading it like a college calculus final. I'd prayed for an act of fate to sideline his trip: a canceled flight, a bottling problem with his cabernet, an unexpected press check on his new labels.

Once Chance finished his pizza, he collapsed against the spindles of the wooden chair. "I shouldn't have—" He stopped mid-sentence as his eyes met mine. "Uhhh, never mind. That was my last pizza anyway. I'm going to drink Slim Fast for a week now." I looked down at my half-eaten garden salad and pushed it aside. *Maybe I should ask if he needs to borrow a tampon.*

OUR NEW ORLEANS weekend nosedived faster than premium Australian wine sales after the critter brand invasion. Chance descended on the culinary mecca with magnum force, scarfing down po' boys and beignets all day. Then he lay in our hotel bed at one o'clock in the morning, whining his regrets and rubbing his belly. He asked me to go to the hotel gift shop and buy Pepto. He wore his favorite wrinkled shirt and Lucky jeans to our winemaker dinner at Galatoire's. I wore an INC suit.

"Why can't you come taste with me?" He asked with a pout, standing in front of my winery table at the convention center's grand tasting.

"I'm busy working." I poured two tipsy cougars another sample of Rancho Zabaco Zinfandel. "Go have fun." I shooed him away to the Commander's Palace station for a bowl of turtle soup.

After the grand tasting, I strolled in front of Saint Louis Cathedral without Chance. I indulged in another tarot card reading from the Willie Nelson look-a-like who had told me—one year before—that my house was going to crumble. Within twenty-four hours, a small earthquake had hit Santa Rosa. Within twelve months, the house was sold, and my divorce papers filed. This time, he said I'd fall madly in love with a tall, thin man with dark hair and blue eyes.

On that brisk night in May, I walked the bustling streets of the French Quarter by myself, remembering the last few years, as well as the zany days of my first and only Mardi Gras. My path in life had zigzagged more times than a *Top Gun* fighter pilot. Back in Kansas, if you would have told me I'd be living in California by age thirty, working for the largest wine company in the world, I would have replied, "Yeah right, and chickens have nipples."

In just one decade, I'd gone from eating Salisbury steak boil-in-bags to sipping Dry Creek zinfandels. Cue the Virginia Slims ads.

🍷🥂🍸🍹

CHANCE INSTALLED A new motor in his hot tub, also courtesy of Craigslist. Dating a guy with a hot tub was on my bucket list, so I accepted the invitation to what he said would be the first of many "bikini and bubbly under the stars" parties—even though I knew deep down that it might be my last.

"As long as it's just a few people," I said then suggested he invite only Karl and Melanie, who'd just started dating. Melanie was a good friend of mine who worked for the Sonoma County Wineries Association (now Sonoma County Vintners) and lived in the town of Napa. I didn't want to be alone with Chance, but I didn't want to bounce around his house forcing smiles with a bunch of half-naked people either. I needed a wing woman.

Sitting in a hot tub drinking sparkling wine in the moonlight wasn't so relaxing while getting the stink eye. Chance sat alone on the other side of the six-person hot tub. A small patio light glowed in the darkness, dimly lighting Chance's knotted face. I claimed my spot in the corner farthest from his reach. I wore a long-lost bikini—the one my butt was never supposed to fit into after getting married—giving my confidence an extra boost. We all sat in the dark, sipping our glasses of Domaine Carneros Brut, making small talk about recent crappy weather, which had affected the blooming phase of the grapevines. Melanie pulled Karl inside the house to make some popcorn. All part of the plan.

"The tart green apples on the palate are really nice." I lifted a half-empty glass to my lips. Chance and I had not seen each other since New Orleans.

The sparkling wine's yeasty citrus aromas filled my nose. I was already daydreaming of sitting on Domaine Carneros's sweeping, stone terrace—with a guy who didn't drink Pepto for breakfast.

"Yeah," he replied flatly. "I guess so." Chance glared at me through the rising steam.

I watched the warm water bubble around us. "How are things going with your label printing?"

"Good."

Awkward.

My chest tightened with anticipation. "I think we should talk." I rested the flute on the wooden frame surrounding his hot tub. The tension in the air was as thick as the steam. My back arched. A girl calling the shots? I didn't see that growing up in Kansas. Confrontation took practice, and after one divorce, I felt like a breakup Jedi.

"Okay," he muttered.

We looked at each other in silence, wavy water bouncing between us.

"You know, we've had a lot of fun together." My hands skimmed the water's surface. Jets pulsated on my lower back and calves. The deep massage relaxed my edgy nerves.

Chance chugged his Champagne flute. "So what's the problem?"

"Yes, we have fun." My voice began to shake. "I just want to make sure, umm, that we're on the same page about where this is heading." I readjusted my wet ponytail, feeling my heartbeat throbbing in my ears. I grabbed my Champagne flute and took a long sip, letting the zippy bubbly reenergize me.

His icy-blue eyes blinked repeatedly. I couldn't tell if he was crying or just sweating too much. He looked like he'd just watched the end of the movie, *Beaches.*

"I like you." My voice trembled as I pressed on. I sipped the sparkling wine, letting the lively bubbles lift my mood. "You're a great kisser. You're ambitious and a whole lotta fun." I inhaled then exhaled. A medicine ball of nerves weighed heavy inside my chest.

Steam rolled off the bubbling hot tub between us. Chance's jaw bobbed silently. He looked like Beaker the Muppet.

"I just don't think," I forced my eyes to stay focused on his, "getting any more serious than this is the right thing for me." With the truth spilled into the steamy air, the wine glass in my hand stopped shaking. "I want to make sure you're okay with that."

I took another long sip, letting the tiny bubbles coat my throat. Chance stared at me and said nothing. I felt as uncomfortable as a cabernet collector at a pink wine tasting.

"I'm sorry," I said, finally. "I know it's weird having this conversation." I looked up to the dark sky and searched for the Big Dipper. The night I'd made out with Fernando in his truck crossed my mind. I'd find that thrill again—in another place, with another man.

"I just don't understand what's wrong." Chance's eyes pierced through me. "I think you're awesome. We have all the things you mentioned." He paused. "We're great together. We both love the wine business." His eyes searched my face for a sign.

"I already have enough wine in my life." I raised my flute to my lips.

His head dropped. "If you need more space, I understand."

"This isn't about my divorce." My mouth fired back faster than a rifle. I brushed my free arm through the water.

Chance stared down at the bubbles, letting my words soak in. "I...I just...I can't..." He threw his hands in the air. "I can't just have a casual relationship with you."

Our silent stare-off picked up again. I took another sip. My mouth filled with flavors of apples and custard, my mind with empathy.

"I want more." His sorrow seeped through the warm air around my sweaty face. The tables were turned. I was seated in the chair of so many men I'd dated.

"I'm sorry, Chance." I climbed out of the hot tub. "That's not what I want." My heart ached for hurting him, but I still wanted to flip off the author of *Men are from Mars, Women are from Venus* in celebration of my victory against social norms. If I could have learned sooner how confident taking control of my dating life would make me feel, I'd probably had started dumping guys as a teenager.

I wrapped a towel around my waist. Chance's eyes met mine one last time. As the steam rose, I watched my dream of marrying a winemaker disappear into the night.

KEVIN
The Champagne Days

I'd never been to Arizona before, but the experience felt eerily familiar. My eyes bounced from the road to the scribbled paper pinched against the steering wheel. I took a deep, chilled breath of vented air, a welcome recess after a long day under the desert sun with my mystery man. Following his driving directions was almost as easy as following my heart.

Within minutes, I spotted the exit number he'd jotted on my hotel notepad and pulled off the freeway. Giant cacti flanked the entrance to his neighborhood. I almost expected one of them to turn into Gumby and stick me in the ass for being so—well, so Lisa—chasing the dream of finding my dream guy, any place, any time. Pueblo-style houses painted vibrant Southwest colors lined the streets, each with its identical, thimble-sized lot. It reminded me of tract-home communities back in California's Central Valley.

I parked my Toyota Camry rental on a cul-de-sac and primped in the visor mirror. My eyes darted back and forth between the piece of paper and a line of streetside mailboxes. I counted the numbers on the houses, moving farther and farther down the street. When I found number 1972 at the end of the circle, my heart took a long drink of adrenaline. There were only three cars on the entire street, and one was mine. He'd invited me to a barbecue. I'd expected a street full of cars and a trail of dance music and laughter spilling from the backyard. I glanced down at the car key, dangling from the ignition.

Twelve hours had passed since my flight had landed in Phoenix. I'd just finished the roughest and longest work trip of my event planning career—four days each at *Food & Wine Magazine*'s Classic at Aspen, the first-ever VinExpo Americas, and the Telluride Wine Festival in Colorado—and still had three days in Arizona before returning home to Sonoma County. My muscles were sore from carrying cases of wine all day and sleeping on firm hotel mattresses all night, but I didn't mind. I was living life by my rules, flying around the country popping corks for strangers who shared my love of wine. In the business, we call them friends. Gallo's national sales meeting had kicked off that morning at the swanky Phoenician resort, perched at the foot of Camelback Mountain.

Eight hours later, I found myself sitting in a rental car in the suburbs of Scottsdale about to enter the house of a man I'd just met. My white knuckles clutched the steering wheel. I exhaled, pushing my apprehension out into the painted sky of the sweltering desert. Kevin had been partially vetted. He subscribed to *Wine Spectator* and knew the difference between merlot and malbec, so he'd passed the first test. *Time for number two.*

I walked slowly toward the front of his terra cotta-colored house, feeling the heat radiate into my Franco Sarto sandals. It was eight o'clock and still ninety-five degrees. My backless Bebe top stuck to my stomach. I fluffed the long layers of my hair then tugged at my cream capris. I wanted to look fresh and fabulous—not sweaty and oily like the first time. We'd met that morning at The Phoenician's Olympic-sized pool, after he'd interrupted my in-depth read of *Wine Spectator's* 2002 Burgundy vintage report. Kevin had seen me in an old, faded bikini with no make-up and a messy ponytail sprouting atop my head like a palm tree, and he'd *still* invited me over.

Kevin opened the rustic, wood front door. The butterflies buzzed in my stomach. He wore a light-blue golf shirt and cargo shorts, and his tanned skin glowed under the front porch light.

He smiled warmly. "Hey, you. Welcome to the burbs." His perfect teeth looked even whiter when his sunburned cheeks plumped. Kevin had hazel eyes and fuzzy, light-brown hair. He was boyishly handsome like Eric Brady from *Days of our Lives*.

I looked past him in the doorway. "What happened to the party?" I could only hear the hum of his central air conditioning. The bottle of wine in my hand suddenly felt like a dumbbell.

"Well, Maya got a tummy ache on the way home from the pool." His toned body leaned against the door. "I think she ate too many french fries." He winked and grinned.

I smiled back, twirling the bottle in my hands. "We did eat a lot today, didn't we?" Kevin was a professional golfer who taught private lessons at The Phoenician; as a perk, the clubhouse manager gave Kevin access to all hotel amenities. Maya was his five-year-old daughter. I'd spent the entire afternoon with Maya and her Dora the Explorer arm floats, playing Jaws and Marco Polo under the grotto waterfall. We'd shared two orders of fries inside their cabana.

Kevin leaned in closer to me. "We talked a lot, too." I felt my sunburned cheeks getting warmer and looked down at my freshly painted toenails. We'd talked about life and relationships for at least three hours. We were both starting all over again in our thirties, so I'd wanted to learn more about him, but cautiously. Kevin split his time between San Diego, his primary residence where most of his wealthy clients lived, and Scottsdale, where his only child resided with her mom. Kevin had looked so adorable wrapping a towel around Maya's tiny body before lifting a Capri Sun juice pouch to her lips. He was unlike any man I'd ever dated.

"I should go." I held out the bottle of Gallo cabernet sauvignon as a peace offering. After noticing three copies of *Wine Spectator* on my lounge chair that day, Kevin had started up a conversation about his favorite wines. He loved cabernets, especially those from Napa Valley and Bordeaux. I wanted to show him that Sonoma County cabs were just as good, but not if we'd be drinking alone inside his house.

"Don't be silly." He rolled his eyes with a scoff. "She's in bed, fast asleep." Kevin waved his arms, motioning me into the entryway. I stood on the step, looking at his hazel eyes. My mind raced. *He has a daughter. He's a good guy.* I stepped through the door hesitantly and felt it close behind me. Kevin and his ex were amidst a complicated divorce due to joint-custody negotiations. It had been dragging out for a year. She also lived in Scottsdale, not far from Kevin's house—the house they used to share. All of this didn't faze me for some reason. Their situation made me realize how lucky I was to experience a divorce as swift and smooth as an eBay auction. All I had left to do was watch the clock countdown until our divorce was final in September. But that didn't mean I was ready to meet Kevin's wife.

"I'm glad you came." Kevin cradled the bottle of wine with both hands. "I was worried you wouldn't."

"Why?" I looked down at the Mexican tiles fanning out around my sandals. "Because I hardly know you?" I stuffed my hands into my pockets. We stood in the entryway, smiling through the awkwardness.

"Well, there's that, and I have baggage." Kevin chuckled, his laughter spilling down the hallway. The tension in my chest released as I giggled. When we weren't playing with his daughter at the pool, we'd commiserated about our marriages and how great it felt to be starting over. Common

ground had fueled our conversation all afternoon. I wanted to learn more
about the guy who spent his mornings surfing La Jolla Shores before being
whisked away on a private jet to play eighteen holes in Cabo San Lucas. He
seemed like The Most Interesting Man in the World—minus the pet tiger
and gray beard.

I fidgeted with my purse, smirking. "We all have baggage. Men just carry
theirs better."

"Very funny." Kevin extended his arm like a nightclub doorman and
ushered me toward the great room. The hallway opened to a gigantic room
with vaulted ceilings and rustic beams. An L-shaped tan sectional covered
one side of the living room with a big screen TV and a kid's toy chest spanning the adjacent wall.

Kevin sat the bottle of wine on a granite island in the modern kitchen.
Kenny G drifted from a small Bose stereo near the kitchen sink. My mind
kept ticking off the good, and the bad, boxes. *What man under the age of
fifty listens to Kenny G?*

"Can I open this?" Kevin gripped the bottle's capsule. "I haven't drunk
Gallo in years." He stood in front of his refrigerator, which was covered
with crayon drawings. My nerves began to relax.

"It's no Screaming Eagle." I pushed my hair off my face. "But I think
you'll like it." When I'd asked Kevin what his favorite wine was, he'd said
Screaming Eagle—a Grand Canyon-sized sign that the man had great taste
and money. Kevin was the type of guy who knew how to get on the mailing
lists of Screaming Eagle and Harlan, something I'm still not capable of after
twenty years in the wine business. I looked around his bare home and its
smattering of furniture. No pictures. No knickknacks. My guard flew back
up.

"I know. I really need to decorate." He shook his head. "It's hard living
in two places." He grabbed a corkscrew from the island drawer and opened

the bottle effortlessly. As quickly as he'd lose a Brownie point, he'd score one. "When I'm here, I want to spend all my time playing with Maya—not hanging pictures."

I nervously picked at my fingernails while he poured the inky red wine into two glasses.

He handed me a half-full glass, the perfect amount for allowing a wine to breathe. *Bonus.* Kevin motioned for me to follow him over to the sectional couch. He sat on the long leg of the L, so I claimed the short one, putting two cushions of space between us. I kept my back straight and legs crossed at the knee. My heartbeat was humming like a sewing machine.

Kevin pointed at the glass's crystal base anchored between my thumb and index finger. "Isn't this the proper way to hold a wine glass?"

"Yes." I moved my hands to palm the bowl of the glass. "And this is a great trick if your white wine is too cold. The body heat from your hands will increase the temperature of the wine, releasing the bouquet." My hair bounced around my face. The average restaurant typically serves white wines at thirty-five degrees—the temperature of a bar cooler. "When wines are too cold, their scents are muted, but you don't want to warm up a wine if it's already the right temperature. That will accentuate the alcohol."

Kevin studied his glass and perfected his grip on the stem. "You are so interesting." He looked over at me with his big eyes and long lashes. I stuck my nose in the glass, ignoring his compliment.

"I should probably shut up." I inhaled the wine's aromas of black cherry and cigar box. "I promise I'm not a wine snob."

"I'm so glad we met today." His words filled my ears. I took a long sip of the Gallo wine, feeling his compliments seep deep into my chest. My sunburned cheeks got even warmer. I smiled and looked down at the ruby-red wine in my glass.

I rested the wine glass on the coffee table. "It sure is interesting how our paths in life take unexpected detours." I sat down and neatly placed my palms on my knees. "But it all happens for a reason. You just have to ride the wave. See where it takes you." I shrugged and looked at the bottle of Gallo resting on the coffee table. While Maya had taken turns jumping off the pool's edge into Kevin's arms and mine, I'd told him about my move to Florida and how that journey had led me to a wine class in college and then a career working for the Gallos—an amazing wine family with a tenacious work ethic. Kevin had grown up in Indiana and shared at least one of my philosophies in life: live where other people vacation.

"Everything in life happens for a reason," Kevin murmured, nodding. My head flew to his lips. *My mantra!* I took a long sip of the silky cabernet, wondering if it was a sign. "We hadn't been to The Phoenician in two months. But for some reason, I woke up this morning and asked Maya if she wanted to go." His hazel eyes pierced mine.

I peered into my glass and nosed the black-fruit bouquet. The fate train had pulled into my station once again.

"You're strong." Kevin rested his glass on the coffee table. "I like that about you." A magnum-sized grin plastered across my face. That boy could pour it on thicker than Texas chili.

"Strength comes from defeating weakness." I took a long sip. Flavors of cherry and cassis lingered on my palate while I recounted my doubts about Paul. "I chalked it up to jitters." I shook my head. "Marrying him was easier than breaking it off." I swirled my glass in reflection.

Kevin grabbed the wine bottle and tilted it toward my glass. Like a trained sommelier, he carefully spun the bottle counter-clockwise at the end of the pour, ensuring no wine dripped on the table. *Impressive. If he offers me a wine charm, I'm going to faint.*

"I made a list of the most important things in our relationship." My head whipped toward him. "The first three things that popped into my head were the house, the dog and the finances." I counted with my fingers while the strength in my voice grew. That crucial list—one of my therapist's take-home assignments—had helped me realize my marital priorities were totally whacked.

"Divorce is always hard." Kevin tightened his grip on the wine glass. "Divorce is so much harder when a child is involved." He looked up at three coloring book pages taped to the wall above my head. I watched his eyes grow dark. "We're so close to it being over." Kevin proceeded to explain how his ex had been fighting for full custody and was using Kevin's dual-residence lifestyle against him. My chest ached with empathy.

"Why did it end?" I needed a clear picture of where their relationship stood and how it imploded. They were bound for life by their daughter.

"She wasn't the same person anymore." His hurt eyes connected with mine. He talked about how carefree and full of life she'd been when they'd met. In the last few years, her career in medical insurance had begun to consume her life. "All she wanted to do was make more money, talk about her salary, go to cocktail parties alone and rub elbows with executives." He took a long sip of the wine and refilled his glass. I nodded, feeling my humming heartbeat. *Sounds familiar.* Our parallel struggles to find happiness endeared him to me.

I stared deep into my glass of cab. "One of the hardest things about keeping a marriage together is that people change. Some people grow together, some people grow apart. When I was twenty-four, I just wanted someone to take care of me." A shaky sigh left my lips with the confession. "My priorities have changed. I want to be loved for who I am." I gazed into my wine glass again and pictured myself walking down the street. I was a proud workaholic with more moles, scars and baggage than I could count, and some man out there would love all of me—because I finally did.

Kevin nodded. "I know what you mean."

"When you're with the wrong person, your head will tell you." My eyes stayed fixed on my glass. "If you don't listen, your body will send you a message." I took a sip of cabernet, letting the silky tannins coat my tongue. "The subconscious is such a powerful force." A look of enlightenment flashed across his face; I soaked up his interest in my failed marriage and pressed on. "I was constantly sick when we were married." I leaned toward Kevin. I talked about my battle with chronic colds during the last years living with Paul, and skipped over the myriad infections my OBGYN could only chalk up to "your body chemistry just doesn't work with his." Even my body had rejected Paul! *Explain that, Dr. Ruth.*

"I haven't been sick in three months." My voice rang with pride. "I haven't felt this healthy in six years." I raised my wine glass in the air, toasting myself.

Kevin's eyebrows perked. He looked down at the glass in his hands. "She's really negative." His head cocked sideways. "That's interesting." He nosed the wine glass, lingering over its aromas. "How do you stay positive?"

My eyes moved from his face to the wine glass in my hand. "The doctors don't know what's wrong with me." I shrugged with a smirk. "It's some rare form of optimism." Our laughter lingered along with the wine's supple tannins—a hallmark of Alexander Valley cabernets.

"I've always been positive," Kevin said. "I haven't felt one-hundred percent healthy in so long. Maybe you're onto something." His dancing eyes were burning holes in the side of my head. I continued looking at my half-full wine glass.

"For years I threw myself into my work instead of addressing our problems, too." I pressed on, trying to relate to his wife's actions. "I was obsessed with making money and redecorating our houses. I thought it was just because I'm a workaholic and grew up poor, but that wasn't it." My free arm whipped around my upper body. Kevin sat intently across from me, his eyes locked onto mine. "But look at me now. I just left a wine tasting forty-five minutes after it started, and it didn't bother me one bit. I'm finally finding balance."

"You seem to be so at peace with all your decisions." He took another sip. "You're always smiling. I love that you're so full of life." His eyes roamed around my face again. I looked away, feeling my shadow of a doubt about his intentions curled up between us.

I shrugged my shoulders, smiling. "The only side is the bright side."

"Your upbringing must have had a real positive impact on your life."

"Ummm...yes and no." I squirmed on his couch cushion. "I'm a big believer in nature versus nurture. I believe we are who we are from the minute we're born. Our experiences in life shape us, but they don't change our destiny." I spoke slowly and clearly, emphasizing every word of my unexpected epiphany. I was born this way, and I didn't need Lady Gaga to hatch from an egg at the Grammys to teach me that. My decisions about who to date and what jobs to work had shaped my path in life. Sure, my "daddy issues" had made me a little needier and less confident than most girls for years, but I'd finally found my way on the long, bumpy road to happiness. Without a doubt, 2004 would be my greatest vintage.

I looked down at my crossed legs. "My marriage was not a mistake. I don't have any bad feelings toward him." I took a long, cleansing breath while Kevin refilled my glass. "Negativity sucks the energy out of people. It just wasn't meant to be. The right person is out there for both of us." I stared through the glass top on his coffee table, reflecting. "I wouldn't be the person I am today if I hadn't spent more than five years of my life with him." I sat on the edge of his couch with my shoulders back, feeling the pride ripple through my body. "The experience shaped me."

Kevin's eyes drifted toward a window. "I envy you." I watched his smile fade. I couldn't imagine dealing with all the paperwork and court hearings, and driving six hours from San Diego to Scottsdale every other week.

The sound of tiny footsteps pulled us from the deep conversation. I looked across the room to the oak staircase and watched Maya's ruffled nightgown appear before her face. Her piggy tails were lopsided. My thoughts drifted to summer days at the city pool near my grandmother's house.

"Hey, sugar bear," Kevin said. "Feeling better?" Maya stood on the bottom step and pressed her back against the wall. She looked down at her bare feet. "You remember Miss Lisa from the pool today." Kevin held out both hands to her. "Don't be shy. You're never shy." He stood up and walked over to the fridge. "Do you want some milk?"

She shuttled over and plopped down where her dad had been sitting. He returned to the couch with a sippy cup and cupped his hands around her ear. Maya's eyes widened as a smile spread across her face. It was the same cute look I'd seen at the pool, when Kevin had asked Maya to ask me if I wanted to eat lunch with them. I smiled as Maya scooted to my side of the couch. I stroked her messy hair.

"Will you color with me?" Maya asked, batting her long eyelashes at me.

We colored Cinderella drawings for about an hour while Kevin watched over us, sipping his wine. When he tucked Maya back into bed, I sat on the bottom step of their carpeted stairs and listened to him reading her a bedtime story. The man was playing my heartstrings faster than a Jimi Hendrix solo.

I moved back to the sectional sofa and grabbed a copy of *Golf Digest* from the bottom shelf of the coffee table. I thumbed through the pages, studying each golfer's form. Scoring less than ninety on a game of putt-putt would be like surviving the zombie apocalypse to me.

"You look so perfect sitting there all quiet." Kevin stood at the bottom of the stairs. "Why didn't you turn on the TV?" I looked up at him, grinding my teeth in shock. After years with a guy who showed his love by running the vacuum cleaner, Kevin's compliments made me feel as uneasy as a beach barista in July.

"I don't watch television anymore," I replied coolly. "The news is always bad news. Reality TV isn't real." Camping out every night in front of the television came to a halt as soon as I'd filed for divorce. There were too many Sonoma wine roads to explore. Russian River Valley, Dry Creek Valley and Alexander Valley were all within twenty-five minutes of my townhouse.

He dropped onto the couch next to me. "You are so amazing." My heart thumped. "I want to know everything about you." Kevin grabbed both my hands and gazed at my face like a long-lost friend who couldn't wait to catch up. I adjusted my weight, scooting away from him. "Okay. First, tell me what you love most about the wine business."

"What's not to love?" I laced my fingers around my knees, grinning. I've been asked some form of that question for fifteen-plus years, but most people just say, "I want your job." My eyes met Kevin's. "I work with a product that brings people pleasure. It's all about hospitality. I love making people happy, and when people go to a wine tasting or a restaurant and taste a wine they love, they're happy." My mind flew back to all those years working in restaurants, the perfect transition to a fulfilling career in wine.

"Your parents must be proud." Kevin looked into my eyes.

I glanced away, thinking of my father. *What did his death teach me?* Live the life you want, not the one that is expected of you. Only you have the power to change course. Girls without father figures can persevere. And most importantly, it was my destiny to dedicate my life to wine—to prove to all the naysayers that booze can be an integral part of a healthy, happy lifestyle.

Kevin grabbed my hands and squeezed. "It's been a great day. Should we open another bottle?" He hopped off the couch.

"Only if you have Champagne." After years of reserving sparkling wines for holidays and special occasions, I'd wanted to raise a toast to life every weekday.

Kevin turned back to me from the kitchen island. "Sorry. My wine stash is slim right now." I gazed at his cute face, fuzzy hair and tanned arms. Throbbing desire began clawing at my insides. I took the last sip of cab to fight it off.

My voice chirped from the couch. "I'll just have a glass of water. It's getting late."

"Keep going." Kevin strolled toward me with two waters. "I want to know everything about you."

I took the glass with both hands, feeling the lump in my throat. "Okay, fine. But it's the real me, unfiltered." I spoke proudly of my childhood in Kansas, my father's drinking, my move to South Florida and getting into the wine business. I felt strong and comfortable in my own skin, talking about all the milestones and potholes in my life. My pace quickened when I spoke about my connection with Fernando.

"So you believe we have more than one soulmate?" Kevin asked.

"For so many years, I thought Fernando was the only one." My eyes met his. "We weren't meant to be together in this lifetime. He entered my life to teach me what a soulmate was. I was supposed to feel that amazing connection so I'd never forget it." My tone dripped with conviction. "And I gave up hope for six years. Now I won't settle until I find that spark with the right person." My hands laced around my knees. I thought about my conversation with Roger at the bar in Cincinnati. Every man I'd dated, every drink we'd shared, had taught me something about life, about myself.

Kevin lifted his fingers and ran them slowly through my hair. My eyes closed as his lips barreled toward mine. His lips were spark plugs, recharging my heart and soul. Lights flashed in the darkness behind my closed eyelids. The connection rocked me from head to toe—just like Fernando's first kiss. I pulled away and gulped my water, rattled by the earth-moving magic of the energy between us.

He brushed my hair away from my face. "I've wanted to do that since this afternoon." He leaned into me, pressing his lips to mine again. A roller coaster of emotions looped through my body again. I pulled back, his lips chasing mine.

"I just want to look at you for a minute." Kevin's hazel eyes were like fiery flames. I looked away bashfully. His pursuit seemed as smooth as a First Growth Bordeaux, but I wasn't ready to reach for my corkscrew.

"What's wrong?"

I sat up and crossed my legs. "I'm just not used to someone making such a fuss over me." I scooted to the edge of the couch. "Especially someone I hardly know."

"I know this is crazy." Kevin turned his body toward me. "I know we just met. But there's just something about you. I feel that there's a connection between us. I haven't felt anything like this in a really long time. I'm following my instincts."

My heart buzzed in my chest. I glanced at his front door and shook my head. "I've heard that one before." My mind raced as the déjà vu punched me in the throat. I could see Fernando sitting at my bistro table, telling me he'd never felt anything like us before, and he didn't want to screw it up.

"We have all the time in the world." I reached for my near-empty water glass. "I should get going. Big meeting tomorrow." I hopped off the couch and grabbed my purse.

"When can I see you again?" Kevin asked, chasing after me.

I STROLLED INTO The Phoenician lobby at 7:05 p.m. My eyes scanned the pillared room dotted with clusters of lounge seating. I spotted Kevin standing at the concierge desk, chatting with a bellman. My heart bungee-jumped. He looked like a Tommy Bahama model, wearing light-colored slacks and a linen dress shirt. I wore a pink BCBG top, white capris and my favorite Via Spiga sandals. He grabbed my hands, and a big grin sprawled across his face. I tucked my hair behind my ears and waited for him to lean into me, his lips kissing mine softly. My pulse soared. I'd spent the entire day inside a conference room and had just finished pouring a string of new zinfandel vintages at a pre-dinner reception. Kevin laced his fingers in mine and guided me to the parking garage.

He opened the passenger door to a sparkling, white BMW sedan. I slipped into the leather seat, impressed but not surprised. When he turned the ignition key, The Black Eyed Peas blasted from his Bose CD player. My shoulders started bouncing to the beat. He leaned over and planted another long, soft kiss on my lips.

We spent the entire evening at The Capital Grille's bar, sipping Louis Roederer Brut Premier—my go-to non-vintage Champagne—and nibbling on crab cakes with corn relish. He grabbed my hand every few minutes. I kept pulling away to grip my flute. My romantic side was finally tethered to a practical one after a decade of failing at finding true love.

"I have so much fun when I'm with you." Kevin tipped his flute to mine. "I love just talking to you."

I rolled my eyes. "I need a shovel to dig out, you're laying it on so thick."

"Come on. I'm just being honest." Kevin collapsed into his fancy bar chair. I'd just spent ten minutes answering his questions about the difference between fumé and sauvignon blanc. Conversations with Kevin revolved around wine and my job—and his compliments. I could hardly even get in a question about Maya, golfing or surfing.

"Seriously," he said, grabbing my free hand. "I can't believe you have to leave soon. Can't you stay another day?" He pushed his knee against mine. I continued picking at the crab cakes.

I shook my head. "I've got to get home." Unpacked boxes still cluttered my new townhouse. Hearing Kevin's words continued to make every room in my head spin. From the beginning, he'd pursued me. *Were the stars aligning just 90 days after I'd filed for divorce?* I took a long sip of the Champagne, letting the zipping bubbles tickle my tongue. True Champagne from France had become my wine splurge of choice back home and on the road. It embodied the new me: lively, optimistic, polished, elegant and adaptable to any occasion.

Kevin turned his barstool to mine. "So how are we going to make this work?" His smile was bright and sincere. Champagne almost shot out my nose like a fire hydrant. I coughed and sat my glass on the marble bar.

My shoulders squared his. "What are you talking about? We just met. We're both still married." The words spilled from my mouth in disbelief. I wanted to turn into Superman and use x-ray vision to see his thoughts. Kevin had layers of mystery to offset his overt sweetness—like a jammy zinfandel.

"I haven't felt this alive in years," Kevin said, pulling his white napkin from his lap. "I know you feel it, too." He flashed his puppy-dog eyes.

I twisted my lips. "You're geographically undesirable."

"Come on!" Kevin leaned closer. "We live in the same state." Kevin proceeded to tell me he'd done some research on MapQuest and needed my home address to confirm the actual drive time.

"You realize there are countries smaller than California." I hid my face behind the wine glass. My mind was spinning faster than a grape hopper during harvest. *Stalker or sweetheart?*

I sat in silence, picking at the corn relish. Dating Kevin would fulfill my promise to myself and put a lethal fork in my pattern of dating people in my industry. My most sacred relationship had to be with someone who did not work in wine or food. But, for the first time in my life, I realized the most important part about dating was determining whether or not he deserved a girl like me. Kevin needed more decanting before I could make that call.

The bartender came over and refilled my water, buying me time to gather my thoughts. "This is all happening so fast." My fingertips slowly traced the rim of my Champagne flute. I cut a dainty piece of crab cake with my fork and reached for another sip.

The Champagne touched my lips again, covering my palate with layers of lemon curd, toasty bread and flint. It tasted creamy, satiny and fresh—so full of life, so refined.

I turned back to Kevin, hefting my flute. "Once upon a time, I was good at fast. Those days are behind me."

🍶🍺🍷🍸🍹

KEVIN NUDGED MY shoulder. "Aren't you going to invite me up for a drink?" I stood in the hotel lobby, looking down at my pink toenails peeking through my sandals. I felt like I'd just been thrown into a round of *Final Jeopardy!*, and I didn't know the answer.

I linked my hands behind my back. "I only have water."

Kevin's face lit up. "Perfect. I like water."

I slipped the plastic card into my door and slowly turned the handle. My hotel room looked like a Pottery Barn catalog spread with espresso furniture and earth-tone accents. Two olive green chairs with accent pillows bordered sliding glass doors to the patio. I marched right past the plush bed to the sitting area and motioned for Kevin to join me. I plucked two bottles of water from the mini bar, feeling the ball of nerves whirling in my stomach. As I set the waters on a tiny table between our two chairs, Kevin touched my bare shoulder. I winced.

"You're really burnt," he said softly.

"Thanks for the reminder." My voice snapped like a whip. My entire body was as red as a boiled lobster. My pink spaghetti-strapped top only accentuated my new skin color. I sat in the chair gingerly.

"Do you have any aloe vera?" His voice was kind and caring. I shook my head. "Lotion? There's got to be some lotion in here." Kevin scurried to the marble bathroom by the front door. My lips parted, but no words came out. My heel tapped nervously on the floor.

Kevin trotted back with a bottle of Bath & Body Works. "Turn around." He sounded like a parent talking to his child. I pouted with arms crossed then rolled my eyes and gave in. He stood above my chair, gently rubbing the cool lotion on my arms and shoulders. I grimaced with every touch.

"We should put some on your lower back, too," he said, kissing me softly on the ear. I felt the warmth of his lips against my hot flesh. Thoughts were spinning out of control in my head. I closed my eyes and took a deep breath. His hands glided over my shoulders and down my back. I jumped, frightened by the electricity of his touch. I grabbed the bottle of water and took a swig. He gripped my hands, pulling me up from the chair.

"We don't need to move." My voice barked. "You can do that here." I tugged at my top to reveal the small of my back. He continued to pull me slowly toward the bed, smiling. I looked at the fluffy king bed covered in pillows. My legs locked.

"I'm not going to do anything you don't want me to do," Kevin said sweetly. I shook my head and dug my heels into the carpet.

I crossed my arms over my chest. "Heard that one before, too."

"You need the lotion." He sounded sweet and orderly like a nurse. "I can't get it on all the burnt spots without removing your shirt. I mean it." He grabbed my arms. We stared at each other in silence, hands locked in the middle of the bedroom like two kids about to start a tug of war.

"Fine." I dropped my hands to my sides. My chest pulsed like a subwoofer in a low rider. I stood anxiously next to the bed like a customer in a massage parlor waiting for the masseuse to leave before getting undressed. The curtains were drawn. The bathroom light bathed the room in a low glow. I turned my body away from him and unlatched my strapless bra. I pulled my bra out of the bottom of my shirt and crawled onto the bed, pressing my face into a giant pillow.

Kevin pulled my top up to my shoulders. I kept my back to him, my chest glued to the comforter. He straddled my body, continuing to glide his cool, creamy hands across my bare back.

"I would give you a massage if you weren't in so much pain," he whispered. My heart did a flip and then a nosedive. I'd dreamed of dating a massaging man for years but didn't expect his offer to make me feel so uncomfortable.

Kevin kissed my shoulders then turned me over. His lips slid across my shoulder blades and onto my chest. I exhaled and shivered. He kissed me, deep and wet, and pulled my top over my head before I could give it a second thought. The electricity of his touch rocketed through me. My fingers instinctively flew to his chest. I could feel him unbuttoning his shirt. My mind felt paralyzed, lost in the heady moment of feeling his lips against mine, his fingers softly brushing across my body like feathers—that carnival ride of emotions I'd desperately missed since losing Fernando. His fingers moved to the zipper of my pants.

"Wait." I pushed my body weight against his like a barricade. I took a deep breath, my chest throbbing. "We need to stop." My voice sounded like a boot camp trainer's.

He kissed my nose. "I know, I know. I haven't wanted to stop since the first time I kissed you." His arms straddled me. I shook my head like a kid about to be fed a spoon of cough syrup. It was never too late to say "no."

I wiggled out from under him and looked into his eyes. "I really, really like you." I rubbed his arms. "You revived a passion inside me I thought was dead. I love how open you are about your feelings toward me." My hands caressed his bare chest. "But I made a promise to myself. I'm never having sex again with a man unless we're in love." I glanced down at his hands and touched his fingers. My voice remained steady. "I don't love you. You don't love me." I looked at my bare, quivering stomach. "I can't go through with this." I'd used sex as an icebreaker in many relationships—Robert, Marco, Raul, even Paul. I had so much more to offer than my body.

Kevin dropped to his elbow and lay down next to me. He pressed his lips against my shoulder. "Maybe it could be love," he said between kisses. "It just feels so right."

I pulled a pillow to cover my chest. "If it's meant to be, it will happen." My tone was sturdy and confident. "You're the one that said, 'Everything happens for a reason,' remember?"

🍸🍷🍸🍸🍸

"I'VE BEEN DOING some research," Kevin said on the phone. "There are several PGA golf courses near your place. I could drive all night and be there before dawn." I stood in my townhouse living room with my Black-Berry to my ear, grinning. My second long-distance love affair with a man from San Diego who liked to surf was in full swing. But now we had two game changers: cellphones and divorce papers. I remained cautiously optimistic about our future. "How far is Sonoma from you again?"

"Twenty-five minutes," I said in a purr, prancing past my lounge chairs. Kevin had been texting me at least three times a day since I'd left Arizona. His love notes ranged from "cant stop thinking about u" and "missing u like crazy" to "want 2 kiss u" and "want 2c ur blue eyes." My hopelessly romantic side drank it up.

"Sonoma Golf Club looks like a great property." He cooed the words. "I'm sure there's work for me there."

I gasped into my smartphone. "You're a nut job." The golf club was located near Chance's house, and I daydreamed about bumping into him with Kevin on my arm. "You can switch gears with your job, just like that?" My hand muffled a gasp of surprise as it left my lips. His words kept catapulting the relationship forward. My prudence continued putting on the brakes.

"Being self-employed is the best," he replied. "You should try it sometime." I let his suggestion sink into my psyche. I'd always eaten lunch at my desk and took calls on my chirping BlackBerry until seven o'clock at night. The winery had a meat-grinder work culture, which I'd fully embraced for two years. Meeting Kevin had helped me put the hectic pace in perspective. *Maybe I should start my own business someday.*

"Someday," I said.

"I could get some teaching gigs and spend weekends at your place." His tone was as giddy as an Auction Napa Valley winner. The idea of showing Kevin Sonoma County's best wineries and restaurants excited me more than the debut of Preston wine growlers. But I couldn't help but wonder how he'd have anytime for his daughter, bouncing between Southern and Northern California.

"Did you receive the packet from your mom yet?" he asked excitedly. In Scottsdale, we'd gotten into a conversation about zodiac signs, and I'd told him about my mom's hobby of writing astrology charts. "Cool! Can she do mine?" Kevin had asked. I'd quickly called in another astrological favor to Mom, wondering if Kevin had been possessed by Nostradamus.

"Yes." I pressed the cell phone closer to my ear. "And it's all here, all right." I collapsed into my cushy couch and propped my bare feet on the coffee table—something Paul never allowed. I looked down at the fat manila envelope, stuffed with Kevin's chart and a fifteen-page comparative report, overlapping Kevin's planets with mine.

"What does it say? What does it say?" Kevin chanted like a schoolboy who'd just snatched a secret note.

"It says I'm your good-luck charm." I grinned into the phone, looking out my giant, living room window. The findings blew my mind: Kevin was the best astrological match my mom had ever seen, and she'd run my boyfriends' charts at least twenty times.

"That's so freaking cool!" Kevin's voice cheered through the phone. "That is so right. I've been playing the best golf of my career since we met. Will you read a few pages to me?" I looked at the phone like he'd just asked me to lick his forehead.

"Ummm, okay," I replied, grabbing the envelope. A handsome pro golfer who loved to talk about life and spirituality, was an incredible kisser and was eager to learn more about astrology? Sounded too good to be true—just like Mr. STD, Michael. I could see the huge grin on Kevin's face as I recited the paragraphs summarizing our connection. *We could talk for hours. We could read each other's minds. We would have eternal luck while to-gether. We have a powerful physical connection.* The list went on and on.

"It's just the stars." I squeezed my BlackBerry, hearing my scoff. "It's just a guideline. You know, fun food for thought." I set the report back on my coffee table.

"Sounds spot on to me." Kevin's words tickled my heart. I looked up at my high ceilings, feeling my pulse ready to take flight. *Should I tell him about our grand trine? Not unless he collects crystal balls.* A special bond exists between two people whose natal charts form a grand trine. Grand trines involve three points (three or more planets) that form mutual trines to each other; when lines are drawn from each planet to the other person's chart, a triangle results. One of the most powerful indicators of special rela-tionships—like soulmates—occurs when a simple trine in one person's na-tal chart is effectively turned into a grand trine by another person's plan-ets in his/her chart. The planets said that Kevin was a better match for me than Fernando.

Still, I wasn't ready to give him my heart.

🍶🍷🍸🍹🍾

FOURTH OF JULY weekend seemed like a great time for a girlfriend get-away—some estrogen and chardonnay to distract me from Kevin. Melanie had a family friend who owned a cabin on the north shore of Lake Tahoe, so we drove to the mountains, cars loaded with beach chairs, bikinis and coolers of wine. Melanie invited two girls from Napa I'd never met, and I brought Kate, a wine marketing director who'd just relocated to wine coun-try from New York.

My fingers punched a text message to Kevin while the girls sipped their white wine on the chalet's deck.

"I just have a quick question about our trip," I said as they rolled their eyes. It had been ten days since Arizona, and my first trip to San Diego was less than a week away. Southwest Airlines was running a special on flights between Northern and Southern California, so I'd forwarded it to Kevin.

cool, i would luv 2 c u!!! he'd texted back. His calls and text messages were fueling the anticipation of our next rendezvous; he'd already had to cancel his first trip to Santa Rosa due to a golf clinic job in Palm Springs.

let's talk about my trip soon; can't wait! Xoxo. I hit the send button and returned to our girl party. I didn't know his address or what time he'd be picking me up at the airport. My event planner's brain was programmed to finalize trip logistics fourteen days prior to departure. We'd passed our deadline.

My BlackBerry didn't beep or ring for two full days. I checked it every hour, even turning it off and on to hopefully unlock a trapped message. The girls and I jogged the running trail along the lake's west shore, sunbathed on Commons Beach and danced at Altitudes nightclub in Harrah's Casino. But the familiar feeling of relationship limbo barreled through my veins again. Both of Melanie's friends were bitter divorcées and offered plenty of reasons for why Kevin had disappeared. I bit my nails and let my thoughts run in circles all weekend.

When I returned to Santa Rosa, I flipped on my laptop and Googled Kevin's full name. Nothing. I searched his name in quotes with the word "golf," then again with "Scottsdale," then with "San Diego." Zilch. I couldn't help but wonder: *Is San Diego the capital of men who live double lives and no one bothered to tell me?*

My chest began to twinge. I remembered how much it sucked to be on the dating circuit, waiting for a guy to call. Five days passed without a text from Kevin. After two weeks of his constant communication, I couldn't stop my mind from reeling with the woulda-coulda-shouldas. *I shouldn't have read him the astrology report. I should have never bought that airplane ticket. I should have never drove to his house.* Then my brain screeched to a halt.

Stop it, Lisa. Stop apologizing for being yourself.

I grabbed my BlackBerry and began thumbing a letter:

K, I'm not sure what happened, but I just want you to know that whatever it was, I would have understood. This is me. Remember? You know me. You can trust me. I would have been there for you, even if only as a friend. Scottsdale was a blast. I'm so glad we met. Everything happens for a reason. I wish you all the happiness in the world. Keep surfing, keep smiling, keep dreaming. And don't forget: be opti-mystic. L

A smile spread across my face as I hit "send." I pulled a bottle of Schramsberg—the closest thing to Champagne in America—from my fridge and grabbed a flute. My spirits may have needed a lift, but my conscience was clear. I'd gained so much from my brief relationship with Kevin:

1. Confidence. I'd stuck to my guns about sleeping with a man I'd just met.
2. Pride. I'd kept up my guard and didn't get emotionally attached too quickly.
3. Hope. I'd reaffirmed my belief that I could have an amazing connection with a man again.

I poured the bubbly into my glass, watching its golden hue erupt in celebration. I'd just begun the third decade of my life. My third trip to France would be in the works soon. I'd find a soulmate connection thrice in this lifetime. The best things come in threes. Just ask *The Lord of the Rings*.

My internal soldier in pursuit of the elusive Mr. Right regrouped and redeployed. *Being divorced isn't the scarlet letter of single life. Thirty is the new twenty.* I raised a toast to myself, letting the sparkling wine's layers of strawberries and cream dance on my tongue. *What a difference a decade makes.* I pictured myself in my white Cheesecake Factory uniform with my big hair, big dreams and a can of Keystone in my hand. *Look at me now.* The refreshing bubbles lingered on my palate, as I held my glass high with the Kung-Fu grip of confidence and perspective. I knew what kind of relationship would make me happy, and more importantly, when to say "no" to a man. I owned my own home, my SUV was paid off and my credit cards had zero balance. My heart belonged to Sonoma wine country, and my soul to a man whose path had yet to cross mine. My glass was more than half full. It didn't matter if it took five months or five years, my heart and soul were willing to wait for the right guy. The one who would respect me for the bumpy road I'd followed in life. The one who would run to me, not from me. The one who would unconditionally love the woman molded from all those experiences before him—because there will always be skeletons in my closet and bottles of Champagne in my cellar.

Until that moment arrived, I had plenty of bubbly on hand, and many reasons to celebrate.

Epilogue

The pilot anchored his seaplane to the white beach with ease, as if it were a canoe. I climbed out of the cabin and scurried onto the tiny island, excited to continue our little adventure. The Gulf of Mexico splashed at my feet, its clear, teal waters shimmering like emeralds in the summer sunshine. A day trip to the Dry Tortugas, seventy miles off the coast of Florida, seemed like the perfect way to introduce my man to my former life.

Devon descended from the co-pilot's seat. He was lean like a marathon runner with the kind of lanky legs most women would kill for—minus the hair. He always wore designer golf shirts and baggy cargo shorts to add a few pounds. I stood on the beach in my white shorts and tan halter top, admiring him from afar like usual. He stepped toward the pilot and extended his hand. Devon has always had this calming, gentle way of shaking a hand, making small talk or ordering a drink that immediately puts others at ease. He can be a part of a conversation without saying much; "I'm more of an observer," he'd told me on our blind date. That night at Tex Wasabi's bar in Santa Rosa, I'd kept looking at Devon's baby-blue eyes and button nose, waiting for his lips to move while he'd sipped a draft beer (strike one). The man took longer to open up than a bottle of Richebourg. I'd spent the next week trying to set him up with my assistant at Gallo, who was equally tall, thin and quiet.

I squeezed his hand. "Surprised?" For Devon's thirty-second birthday, we'd decided to spend a weekend in South Florida for the first time. I'd surprised him with a front-row seat to fly to Garden Key, the most famous in the island chain that strings from Key West into the Gulf of Mexico.

Devon popped his sunglasses atop his head of short, brown hair. "Very. I almost leaned over to the pilot and yelled, 'Da plane! Da plane!'" His full lips twisted with a smirk as his voice jumped an octave. I giggled at his imitation of Tattoo from *Fantasy Island*—nostalgia only children of the eighties can appreciate.

I looked up at him and cocked my head. "Aren't you glad I didn't take you to Disney World? A surprise visit to your old love nest?" My lips flashed a toothy grin. We'd met not long after Devon had moved to California to start a new life—about the same time Kevin had probably returned to the sand trap (i.e. his ex-wife). Devon had grown up in the Midwest and had just divorced his college sweetheart. They'd honeymooned at Disney's Blizzard Beach—a dream vacation for two kids from Michigan.

We both turned circles to take in the postcard views. Fort Jefferson's faded brick walls towered over us, its footprint covering most of the island. "I had no idea it would be like this." He plucked his Canon 60D off his shoulder and snapped a photo. Devon never left home without his camera and dreamed of leaving his day job in pharmaceutical research to become a full-time photographer.

We walked toward a moat surrounding the octagon fortress. The ocean breeze whipped my ponytail. "So, what would you like to do first?" Devon laced his long fingers with mine. My chest fluttered like it does whenever he says something sweet. *Always putting me first, even on his birthday.*

I threw our mesh bag of gear over my shoulder. "Snorkel."

We strolled past a cluster of mangrove bushes to a skinny, white beach that spilled into the ocean, stopping along the way to photograph the glistening water, the behemoth fort, the chattering seagulls. Devon is never in a hurry and never wears a wristwatch. Time has always been on his side. He grounded me. He slowed me down.

"Did you ever think you'd spend weekends doing something like this?" I looked up at Devon's baby face. The never-ending sky disappeared into the ocean behind him. Snorkeling together was another first for us. Three years had passed since we'd become adventure companions.

He brushed his thumb across the back of my hand, sending my pulse to its happy place. "All I wanted to do was get away from the cold. Move somewhere sunny." I'd told him I'd help him find a great wine gal if he'd help me find a great non-wine guy. We were two Midwest refugees with divorce parachutes, jumping head-first into every corner of Sonoma County I'd only dreamed of visiting while married: winery bocce ball courts, hiking trails, rocky beaches, tasting rooms with a view and Russian River Valley back roads.

I pulled his hand to my face and kissed it. "I'm glad you winked at me." Devon had found me on Match.com—my first and only posting of a public profile the week before my three-month membership expired.

We reached the beach and dropped our backpacks. "I'm glad you stopped trying to set me up with your coworkers," Devon said.

I emptied the bags of snorkeling gear onto a beach towel. "I'm glad you finally stopped being so shy." My tone was playful like it often is when we talk. This is how it's always been with us: joking, talking, exploring. The more time I'd spent hanging out in wine country with Devon, the more he'd opened up, and the more intrigued I'd become with the skinny guy behind the camera. Devon also loved running and hated couch potatoes. He spent every weekend hiking trails and driving winding roads, capturing the stunning California scenery with his camera. His favorite wine was Beringer sparkling white zinfandel, but hey—we all have to start somewhere.

Devon moved his sunglasses back to his nose. "It's all about the anticipation." We'd talked for hours every night—first on Yahoo! Instant Messenger, then on the phone and then in my living room. We'd dished about our failed marriages, our humble upbringings, our passions in life and our dreams of traveling the world. He knew what it felt like to scarf frozen pizza on the couch while watching *Dukes of Hazzard*. He knew what it felt like to do time in marriage prison. He'd learned from his journey, and all roads had led to Sonoma County wine country.

I gasped a laugh. "Where were you when I was twenty-two?" I pulled off my shorts and top then readjusted my bikini. For more than two weeks, we'd simply enjoyed each other's company. We'd focused on getting to know each other without the pressures of getting to first base. By the fourth date, Devon still hadn't tried to hold my hand or kiss me. If only someone had told me dating in my thirties would be so civilized and mature, maybe I would have gotten divorced sooner! The man had moved slower than a turtle. And I'd respected him for respecting me.

He took off his shirt and let me rub sunblock on his back. "Sometimes I wonder what would have happened if we'd met sooner. Would we have made it? Would we have been this happy?" My fingers spread the white lotion across his skin. I leaned in and tenderly kissed the big mole in the center of his back. During those late-night chats, I'd told Devon about my dream relationship—being with someone who adored and respected me. Someone who shared my hopes, ambitions and dreams because we'd traveled the same path, and met at a crossroads. Someone who gave me goose bumps every time he kissed me. I'd told him I'd never settle for less ever again. Divorce had made me more honest and direct—valuable traits for both personal and work relationships.

"I think we would have." Devon plucked the sunblock from my hand. "I'm glad we met when we did though." I turned and let him squirt the cold lotion on my shoulders, remembering our courtship. I'd never worried about whether Devon was going to call or if I was saying the right things to push his buttons. The relationship was relaxed and platonic. Once I'd finally stopped struggling to impress a guy—and focused on trying to determine if he was right for me, instead of trying to win his heart from day one—the guy pursued me. Devon called. He asked me out on dates. We hiked, we took long runs, we went wine tasting. Feelings blossomed. Desperation is the ultimate male repellent. Confidence is a stronger lure than any perfume. But, if I'd learned that pearl of wisdom at age twenty, I wouldn't have moved from Kansas to Florida to California. I wouldn't have gone into the wine business. I never would have met my Devon.

I grabbed my mask and spritzed it with no-fog spray then helped Devon with his gear. "After you get the no fog all over the inside of your mask, dunk it." I stepped into the clear, cool water and demonstrated. "Just breathe out your mouth, but if you do get a little condensation in your mask, this stuff keeps it from getting cloudy." *Now, I'm the teacher.*

With snorkel masks strapped on, we waded into the ocean and slipped on our blue flippers. "I can't believe it's taken me this long to bring you to Florida." I popped the snorkel into place.

Devon tightened his mask, chest bopping in the water. "None of your ex-boyfriends ever brought you here, huh? That sucks."

I spit out my snorkel mouthpiece. "They spent all their money on drugs." The turquoise water splashed around my chest as I sneered. *Well, most of them.* I'd told Devon about my mind-numbing string of ex-boyfriends when the time was right. Was I ashamed of my past? No. Embracing the beauty of my relationship baggage was not about confessing my dating history to a man, and worrying about him blowing away like a tumbleweed halfway through my Robert story. It was about me sticking my nose deep into the murky wine glass of my failed relationships, taking a long sniff and smelling only roses. No regrets. My experiences were assets, not liabilities.

Finding internal peace with my torrid love life had helped me shed that last layer of dating desperation. I was a great catch, and I would only be hooked on *my* terms. I can't help but laugh at the pessimism of my past. I thought I'd never find the perfect man. I never thought I'd get back down to my high school weight after age thirty. I'd never be able to afford a million-dollar home in wine country.

Our heads dropped into the water. We kicked toward Fort Jefferson's moat with the sun warming our backs. The cool, salty water tingled on my face and legs. I could see myself from the sky above, no longer floating on the surface of life, no longer a dating barnacle.

Purple and yellow coral rocks clung to the moat's underwater foundation. Rainbow-colored parrotfish pecked the coral with their bird-like beaks. My heart fluttered wildly, in awe of the moment: being in Florida with Devon, sharing our first snorkeling experience. I watched Devon's lean frame kicking ahead of me, bubbles streaming behind him. *Oh, how I love this man. I would canoe down the Amazon with wooden spoons for oars if he wanted to.* Devon is a mix of the best qualities of all my exes and none of the bad. He's got Chris's knack for constantly dreaming, Matthew's gift with words, John's love of dance music, Michael's endless affection, Raul's laid-back vibe, Fernando's intoxicating touch and stimulating conversations, Tyler's athleticism and shyness, Paul's stability and devotion, Chance's spontaneity, and Kevin's romantic openness and kind heart. Is he Mr. Clean? Only when he needs to be. He'd rather spend weekends in Las

Vegas clothes shopping. He knows who Franco Sarto is, but Franco Harris? Not a chance. He put the "m" in metrosexual. He'd rather drink sweet riesling than Côte-Rôtie, but I can live with that.

We kicked along the shallow edge of the moat, exploring the vibrant, underwater world that had opened a door in my life thirteen years before. We were like one person moving in the same direction. It felt so natural—so right and rewarding—to show a fellow Midwest transplant the world beyond the Great Plains: majestic mountains, fine wines, exotic foods, tranquil beaches.

My mind drifted to my BlackBerry, probably chirping in my backpack on the shore. I'd just started a new job as director of public relations for a boutique wine importer in Napa Valley, and one of our French winemakers had an interview at *Wine Enthusiast* magazine headquarters in three hours. I'd need to send some emails and take a couple calls before our day trip was over, but I no longer had to fear the wrath of my man. Devon has always admired my work ethic. He never gets mad when I work late, go on a business trip or ask him to have dinner with wine friends he's never met. He respects and loves me for the woman I am, and knows that my wine career will always be intertwined with our personal life. Devon realizes that I wouldn't be me without my past—the naïve, redneck beer guzzler who left home searching for true love and her calling in life—only to find both in wine country.

My breath quickened when a huge queen angelfish poked out from behind a brain coral. I shouted bubbles to Devon. That's the only kind of yelling we've ever done—simply trying to get each other's attention. From laundry and dishes to television and finances, not one thing in everyday life seems worth fighting over, especially when it took us a third of a lifetime to find each other. It's been a long road to happiness, and I will never forget the climb. We've had 4,986 days (and counting) of laughter, friendship, devotion, respect, discovery and timeless love. We kiss at least five times a day and double down on weekends. It's the kind of puppy love that makes most people gag. We never hold back our feelings, so there is nothing to hide. We give compliments, advice and hugs without expecting anything in return. That's how we nurture the awe-inspiring knack of keeping the thrill of our love alive and growing. Not having kids has also helped, allowing me to focus my energy on the two things that matter to me most—my man and my job. If there's a world record for the longest honeymoon, we plan to shred it. I light up for him every day. I do everything in my power to make him feel special and appreciated. This includes making him dinner from scratch, followed by back scratches, at least five nights a week. Our love is effortless, our relationship easy. The magic has never faded away.

We returned to the beach and lay down on our towels, side by side. I looked up at the cloudless sky through my rosé-colored glasses. "We're so lucky. I love our life." There will never be a family Christmas with cookie baking and matching pajamas, and that's fine by me. We prefer holiday travel that involves tiki drinks and bikinis—not parkas and snow drifts. Everyone has a different definition of happiness, and a life of new adventures and spontaneity is ours.

I turned and kissed him on the bicep. My lips stayed pressed to his skin. I closed my eyes and inhaled deeply. *I could live off his scent for days.* The deep attraction we share makes me work hard to stay sexy and keep the romance raging.

He kissed my forehead. "It's already time to start planning our next adventure."

I rested my chin on his shoulder. "Where to?"

"Wherever you want to go, beautiful." His tone was soft and tender. Devon is a go-with-the-flow kind of guy that loves keeping his woman happy. He likes it when I make decisions, but when I ask which shoes or earrings I should wear, he always gives honest opinions. More than once, he has said the magic words, "It's time to take you lingerie shopping."

I gazed up into his eyes. "More snorkeling?"

"How about Belize then?"

My face flushed with joy. "It's a date." Devon shares my wanderlust, always planning our next trip before the last one is over. Conversations revolve around new destinations, dreams and early retirement—not work. I love how this man can be spontaneous and organized, scientific and artistic, all at the same time. I'm as attracted to his brain as his body.

Devon rolled over and kissed me softly, yet deeply. My entire world went dark and bright white at the same time. His energy charged through me, shooting my heartbeat into orbit.

"You still give me goose bumps," I said, breathless. I nuzzled into the crook of his chest—my favorite destination on the planet. Every kiss is like the first. He adores me. He calls me beautiful. When Devon had finally kissed me one night in my townhouse, my entire body had melted. It was exhilaration of epic proportion from the anticipation of his touch and the thrill of a new love because we'd spent two weeks—yes, I said two whole weeks—discovering our parallel universes before our lips ever touched. And, the chemistry is megawatts above what I'd felt with Fernando. With that first kiss, I'd known Devon was The One, but I didn't start collecting wedding magazines. I didn't stalk him online or ask questions about where "this" was heading. I'd let him set the pace. A few weeks later, Devon had told me he loved me. He'd said it *first*, and we still hadn't slept together. I'd finally started a serious relationship slowly and respectfully. Love before sex: I'd kept my promise to myself. I'd felt stronger than a King of the Mountain jersey winner at La Tour de France.

Devon sat up and reached for his backpack. "I have something for you." My ears perked; Devon is always surprising me with gifts: diamond earrings, Tiffany bracelets, fancy dinners, designer dresses, airplane tickets. He still does. Did I mention we met on Match?

He pulled a chilled half-bottle of Billecart-Salmon Brut Rosé Champagne out of his backpack. "I hid it with my camera lenses."

My hands cradled the tiny bottle. "You're the best." I planted a firm, loving kiss on his full lips, letting the usual roller coaster of chemistry barrel through my body.

Devon lay back down on his beach towel. "We don't have any glasses though."

I pulled off the bottle's foil and twisted open its metal change. "I've got no problem drinking straight outta the bottle." My hands skillfully popped the mushroom-like cork. "I think I've earned that right."

Acknowledgments

This book would not have been possible without the support of my husband, Damon Mattson—the sweetest, smartest, funniest partner in crime a girl could ask for. In 2007, Damon took a job assignment in Ireland, which allowed me to take a sabbatical from the wine business to tackle writing this book. The project has taken about a decade to fully complete because I have a day job and an insatiable itch to keep adapting the book and making it better. Over the years, the wine world has witnessed the rise and fall of critter brands, rude labels and Two Buck Chuck. Souls were searched, the book changed from a memoir to a novel and back again, and scenes were revamped during winter vacations in Belize, Hawaii, Mexico, French Polynesia and the Maldives. As I neared the finish line on the final edit, our dream home took a brutal beating in the catastrophic wine country wildfires. Damon has remained totally supportive through every milestone, roadblock and setback in life, and I am so grateful and indebted to him.

Special thanks to my friends and wine colleagues who read manuscripts at various stages and provided invaluable feedback: Taylor Eason, Chad Arnold, Heather John, Patrick Comiskey, Jen Karetnick, Jim Conaway,

Erin Jimcosky, Katie Bower, Rachel Thralls and Rachel Nichols. Barbara Barrielle, Nicole Jacobs and Sarah Powers were also instrumental in helping flesh out titles and subtitles for *The Exes in My Glass*. I'm blessed to have talented friends like all of you in my life.

Big hugs to my Florida girlfriends, Danielle Girten, AnnMarie Spirk and Paula Geiger, who also read drafts. You were irreplaceable wing women during those late nights in Miami. As for Lon Gallagher—I will forever be grateful for that fateful pep talk, and I still owe you that bottle of Dewars. I also have to give a shout-out to my ex-pat friends, Gina Fierro and Heather Montague. Thanks for helping me sort out the themes and scenes over cups of tea on many rainy afternoons in Ireland. You'll always be my Galway girls.

Thank you to Jordan Rosenfeld, editor and prolific Facebook poster, who provided feedback on queries, book proposals, and manuscripts over three years, and a magnum of thanks to editors Gina Ardito and Jennifer Kaufman for catching the missed typos.

My career as a wine publicist and marketer has allowed me to meet and become friends with some wickedly talented women who write about wine, including, but not limited to, Alice Feiring, Andrea Immer Robinson, Elizabeth Kuehner Smith, Karen MacNeil, Leslie Sbrocco, Lettie Teague, Linda Murphy, Megan Krigbaum, Tina Caputo, Virginie Boone and Susan Kostrzewa. Reading your stories has made me a better writer. Thank you.

Without my day job, I wouldn't have the resources or skills to publish and promote a book like this, so I also have to give props to the coolest boss in the world, John Jordan of Jordan Vineyard & Winery. Thank you for letting me fly. And a jeroboam-sized thanks to the former management staff at Wilson Daniels Ltd. wine marketing, who supported my decision to move to Ireland to write the first draft.

I would also like to thank my true exes for inspiring this journey—especially those who have been supportive of this book—Lonnie Johnston and Charlie Cobb. Thanks for dumping me. You helped open some pretty awesome doors in my life.

About the Author

With a bachelor's degree in communications and a master's in heartache, Lisa Mattson's fate to author this book was sealed in elementary school when a snowball fight with her first boyfriend landed him in the hospital. He dumped her the following day.

Raised in rural Kansas, Mattson's childhood was filled with cheap beer and fried chicken—an ideal foundation for a career promoting prestige wineries. Many nights spent raccoon hunting also prepared Mattson for her first journalism job writing obituaries for a daily newspaper. She escaped to Florida during college, where she chased boys and caught rays while waiting tables. Not long after taking her first wine class at Florida International University, Mattson was sipping malbecs and editing stories for a wine magazine.

Twenty years and many ex-boyfriends later, Lisa Mattson is considered a thought leader in wine marketing, known for creating an award-winning winery blog, clever videos and compelling digital media content. Taking the not-so-straight-or-narrow road to finding her dream job and her dream guy was the most fulfilling—and humbling—journey of her life. *The Exes in My Glass: How I Refined My Taste in Men & Alcohol* is her memoir.

She resides in Sonoma County wine country with her husband, their Italian greyhound and a Champagne-centric wine collection.

Connect

Chat with Lisa online:

lisamattsonwine.com
facebook.com/exesinmyglass
twitter.com/lisamattsonwine
plus.google.com/+lisamattson
instagram.com/lisamattsonwine

Made in the USA
Columbia, SC
07 July 2018